Abraham Lincoln versus Jefferson Davis

Abraham Lincoln

VERSUS

Jefferson Davis

by Irving Werstein

THOMAS Y. CROWELL COMPANY

New York · Established 1834

This book is dedicated to the memory of my father,
Jacob Werstein (1890-1932)

Contents

Illustrations

Author's Note

THIS IS A BOOK about two men, two cities, and a time in history. The men are Abraham Lincoln and Jefferson Davis. The cities, Washington and Richmond. The time in history, the American Civil War. All are entwined and indivisible.

I have not examined the battles or explored all phases of the war, but, rather, have tried to reconstruct and recreate phases of those frightening days and to show how the War affected these men and these cities.

It would be impossible to divorce Lincoln and Davis from the men and events which engulfed them. I have given emphasis to some of these and ignored others as I felt their relationship with Lincoln and Davis warranted.

This is not a history of the Civil War. It is instead, a portrait of two important men and two important cities caught up in that war. I have tried to recapture them—sometimes in my own words and interpretations, sometimes in the words and interpretations of their contemporaries.

I have been fortunate to have received the encouragement and assistance of gracious people both in New York City and in Richmond. It would be impossible to thank adequately the distinguished Civil War historian and author, Mr. Clifford Dowdey, of Richmond, for the time he took from his own work to give me his views on Jefferson Davis and to show me around the historic spots of the city he knows and loves so well. Miss India Thomas of the Confederate Museum, also in Richmond, was both courteous and helpful.

Without the staff of the American History Room in the New York Public Library, I would have been completely lost and I herewith thank Mrs. Shirley Spranger, Mr. Leon Weidman, and Mr. Ralph Smith, for cooperation far beyond the line of duty.

Mr. Jay Williams, of Redding, Connecticut, helped me get to the core of numerous problems connected with this work.

The fine author and historian, Mr. Philip Van Doren Stern, gave me invaluable assistance from his fund of Civil War lore.

I want to thank Miss Candida Donadio, my agent, for kindness and loyalty. My editor, Mr. William Poole of the Thomas Y. Crowell Company, was unfailingly helpful. Many thanks are due John Blay for the use of pictures from his extensive collection. As always, to my wife who patiently and steadfastly never lost faith, I owe a debt that can never be repaid.

I. W.

New York City
April, 1959

ONE

Mr. Davis

"All we ask is to be let alone—"

JEFFERSON DAVIS, first message to
Confederate Congress, March, 1861

Yankee Doodle, fare you well
Rice and Cotton flout you,
Once we liked you very well
But now we'll do without you.

Secession song, 1861

THE PLANTATION called Brierfield spread its acres over a high bluff above the sluggish Mississippi and dominated the land for miles around. The soil in Warren County, Mississippi State, was rich and fertile. Brierfield was flourishing—its fields pregnant with burgeoning cotton. Tasseled cornstalks ripened in the sun and warm breezes riffled the growing barley.

One lost track of the seasons in that section of the South. The calendar gave the date as February 10, 1861—but the weather was summery. Cypress trees were green. Magnolias scented the air and in the flower garden that flanked the big house at Brierfield, roses were blooming.

On that seemingly peaceful day, the master of Brierfield was clipping roses in his beautiful flower garden. He was Jefferson Davis, a fifty-three-year-old gentleman planter. He was a West Point graduate, and had been a Mexican War hero, a Congressman, and a Senator.

With him was his second wife, young Varina Howell Davis. The couple seemed to have no care in the world except to fret over the length of the rose stems. As was his habit, Davis went about the work sternly, his deep-set gray eyes peering out from beneath heavy brows with a kind of unseeing intensity. He had the air of a surgeon performing a critical operation rather than a man in a period of relaxation.

Varina smiled as she handled the flowers and the smile softened her strong features. She moved stolidly from one bush to the next, her stocky, compact body bending ungracefully as she stooped to snip a low-growing rose.

Despite her sturdy build, Varina Davis was not an uncomely woman. Her face showed intelligence and her dark eyes shone with humor and warmth. She glowed with vitality and radiated good health.

Varina had been educated at the best schools in Philadelphia and her grandfather, Richard Howell, had served as a governor of New Jersey. But despite these Northern influences, she was a true Southerner. Her family owned a large plantation near Natchez. Varina believed wholeheartedly in all the Southern institutions and customs —including slavery.

She loved her introverted husband deeply and knew the genuine kindness and love that were hidden behind the cold, austere façade he presented to the world.

He was an impeccable gentleman in manners and dress—a rigid, self-conscious aristocrat. And although now he wore an old shirt, shapeless denim trousers, and a floppy straw hat, his usual attire was black broadcloth, a black silk handkerchief tied as a cravat around his neck, and a black satin waistcoat. His linen was of the best, his boots of the softest cordovan.

A strikingly handsome man who carried himself ramrod stiff, Davis had a demeanor of untouchable superiority. He exuded confidence—yet probably never really felt the assurance he displayed. For years he had suffered from chronic dyspepsia and neuralgic twinges which flared up whenever an important decision faced him.

But on that flawless morning, neither Varina nor her husband, whom she fondly called "Banny," had any inkling of the ordeal that was being readied for them. At about 10:00 A.M., a horseman galloped up the dirt road that led to Brierfield from the boat landing on the river. He had been riding hard and long. His horse was foam-lathered and dust powdered his own face and clothes.

As he reached the gravel carriage driveway that curved under an archway of stately cypress trees, the hoofbeats attracted Davis and his wife. They stood up and, shielding their eyes from the sun, watched the approaching rider. A Negro groom dashed out of the house and took the horse's bridle as the man reined in under the porte-cochere. The groom pointed towards the flower garden and led the sweating horse away.

The newcomer hurried towards the Davises, but Jefferson, who had dropped his shears, was already advancing to meet him, moving quickly with his long-legged stride. As Varina watched, an expression of concern crossed her face. She carefully set down the roses she had been gathering and slowly stripped off her gardening gloves, never taking her eyes from the two men, now standing and talking earnestly. The rider mopped his brow with a large bandana, reached into his pocket, and took out an envelope which he handed to Davis.

The tall, spare man tore open the envelope and read the telegram

Varina Howell Davis, wife of the Confederate President, shared with **her** husband all the trials and tribulations of the Southern attempt to gain independence. She was clever, intelligent, and perceptive. Few were her equal as wife, mother, and adviser.

it contained. He lowered the paper, his hands dropping to his sides and, turning to Varina, looked at her appealingly. She hurried to him and said, "What is it, Banny?"

He silently gave her the message. She read:

> Montgomery, Alabama
> February 9, 1861

Hon. Jefferson Davis
Jackson, Mississippi

Sir:

We are directed to inform you that you are this day unanimously elected President of the Provisional Government of the Confederate States of America and to request you to come to Montgomery immediately. We also send a special messenger. Do not wait for him.

> R. Toombs
> R. Barnwell Rhett
> Jackson Morton

Varina looked over at him with round, troubled eyes. "Oh, Banny! What is going to happen now?" she asked.

Davis shook his head somberly. "I don't know. I'll need all the strength God can give me."

· 2 ·

For nearly a week, the Confederate Constitutional Convention had been meeting in Montgomery, Alabama. Forty-four delegates from the six seceded states: South Carolina, Georgia, Alabama, Mississippi, Florida, and Louisiana—were attending the convention to draw up a constitution and to make a reality of the Confederate States of America which, as yet, existed only in the drastic action the cotton and rice states had taken—seceding from the Union.

Since February 4, quiet, sleepy Montgomery, Alabama, chosen as capital of the embryonic nation, had been the scene of exciting and momentous events. Delegates descended on the town bringing their wives and families and taxing the meager hotel facilities in Montgomery. A horde of office-seekers came, like camp followers. They were a motley crowd: United States Army and Navy officers who had resigned when their native states seceded; manufacturers and agents of manufacturers—mostly Yankees—looking for contracts from the new government; opportunists and careerists; crackpots and adventurers—each one clamoring to be heard, each trying to find a spot in the yet unformed government.

Prostitutes, thieves, and pickpockets came to Montgomery. Gamblers, confidence men and sharpers rubbed shoulders with statesmen and generals. Important men had to sleep in doorways because there were no accommodations for them in the overcrowded town.

Militia companies strutted pompously along the poorly paved main street. Bands tooted energetically. Hotheads argued in bars and taprooms, and dozens of fist-fights boiled up every night.

And, symbolically, not two blocks from the classic capitol building in which the delegates were hammering out the framework of a nation, slave auctions were held almost every forenoon. Unshaven overseers from back-country plantations ogled young Negro slave girls and made lewd jokes while bidding for human property.

No matter what high-sounding phrases about "democracy" and "freedom" were ringing out in the state capitol, the true face of the Confederacy was exposed in the slave market. Alexander Stephens, soon to be named Confederate Vice-President, declared "our nation is founded on the institution of slavery." Human bondage was the cornerstone of the Southern republic.

That week in Montgomery, a nation was being born and as in all births, there was scant dignity in the process. The pain was great, and the fear. Men gathered in gloomy groups to hold unhappy conferences. The baby was being born to trouble, for amidst solemn deliberations and constitutional discussions came the shrilling fifes and the thudding drums of the militia. Artillery caissons rattled over cobblestones. Harsh-voiced sergeants rasped commands, and cavalry troops dashed from one end of town to the other. This was true not only in Montgomery, but all through the South.

The very air smelled of war; and loud, boastful voices bragged that "one Southerner could whip ten Yankees." The barroom swashbucklers begged for a chance to fight. Young militia soldiers patted their old-fashioned muskets and pretended they were taking potshots at Yankees. They were a roistering crew, these young hotbloods, swaggering about the streets, twirling their mustaches and making martial flourishes. Their youthful voices echoed across the South in a rising defiant and belligerent shout, forming one ugly word: *War!*

The Confederate fathers sat in their council chambers and spoke of war as an abomination. They shuddered at the concept of "brother turning against brother"; but words were losing their values and the fire they had kindled over states' rights and the extension of slavery was turning into a holocaust. They claimed to want peace—but a peace "without compromise," a peace on their terms only. "Never," they cried righteously, "will we submit to abolitionist tyranny."

And while they talked peace, they committed acts of war: seizing Federal property, besieging garrisons, confiscating the mails, mustering troops, lowering the Stars and Stripes and raising the flag of disunion. All this because Lincoln, the Illinois rail-splitter, had been elected President against the wishes of the South.

They believed themselves the inheritors of the traditions of '76, of the men who had thrown off a despot's yoke. Yet, the way of life which they were promulgating was anachronistic, not progressive. It was feudal, not democratic—founded on slavery, not personal liberty. Their Cause was hollow and empty—but the experiment in rebellion went on and produced a four-year agony of waste and death and tears.

· 3 ·

Jefferson Davis had neither desired nor sought the presidency of the Confederacy. The helm of the newly launched ship of state had been thrust into his reluctant hands. He had envisioned another place for himself in the schemes of the young republic. Davis had fancied himself as the military leader—the field commander of the Confederate army.

He sincerely believed that his skill as a soldier bordered on genius. And as a matter of fact he had been hailed as one of the great heroes of the Mexican War and on the basis of that reputation had served a term as Secretary of War under Franklin Pierce.

Actually Davis graduated from West Point, in the Class of '28, twenty-third in a group of thirty-four, a record that was scarcely dazzling. Yet he brought away with him from the Academy an immense faith in what was known as "West Pointism"—the belief that only West Pointers could succeed in war. This was a common enough

Stern visaged and handsome, Jefferson Davis typified Southern gallantry and
determination as he took up the duties of his office in 1861, shortly before the
war began.

belief in that day and it persisted, although the blunders and inept-
ness of West Point officers had cropped up time after time. The
Mexican War had done much to restore the West Point professionals
to favor. Some, like Davis, had achieved national prominence.

The Confederate President's convictions about his superior military ability stemmed from the service he had seen on the frontier,
and in the Black Hawk War of 1831-1832 as well as in the Mexican
War.

He did particularly well in the Black Hawk War and his behavior
brought him to the attention of Colonel Zachary Taylor, who commanded Davis' regiment, the First United States Infantry. At the
end of the war, Taylor detailed the twenty-three-year-old lieutenant
as Black Hawk's chief escort to Jefferson Barracks where the Indian
was held for trial. It was a signal honor for the young, ambitious
officer.

The myth of Davis' military genius came to full bloom during
the Mexican War. In 1846, Davis resigned his seat in Congress
to take command of the First Mississippi Rifles, a volunteer
regiment from his native state. At the Battle of Buena Vista, February 23, 1847, the Rifles turned back a Mexican cavalry charge and
saved the day for the Americans. Colonel Davis was severely
wounded in the foot, but refused to leave the field until the victory
was won. He limped home and was acclaimed a hero—the toast of
Mississippi and the nation.

Davis was a determined soldier, but not a brilliant one. The army
units in which he served on the Wisconsin and Iowa frontiers were
small and had little to do except guard against desultory Indian
raids. No great command decisions had to be made and even at
Buena Vista, Davis had accomplished no military miracle with his
300-odd-man regiment. He had merely held his ground.

He had demonstrated that he was quick-witted, resourceful, and
brave—although not always dependable, because his peculiar nervous instability made him subject to debilitating dyspeptic attacks
which frequently kept him from duty.

As a result of his military record, Davis had come to be regarded
as the foremost soldier in the seceded states—a notion far from the
truth—and he did nothing to disenchant his admirers, for he believed
this shibboleth. Naturally when Mississippi seceded on January 9,
1861, Governor J. J. Pettus promptly commissioned her favorite

son, Jefferson Davis, Commander-in-Chief of the military forces of "the sovereign Republic of Mississippi," with the rank of Major General.

At that time Davis represented Mississippi in the U.S. Senate. He resigned to accept his martial assignment. And in leaving the Senate Davis reached his peak of eloquence—his valedictory was a beautiful and incisive oration which revealed an emotion and warmth that few suspected in the man.

The Senate chamber and galleries were filled to capacity on January 21, 1861, when it became known that Davis was to make his farewell speech. He cut an impressive and striking figure as he rose to address the Senate. Everyone leaned forward intently, eyes riveted on the stony-faced master of Brierfield.

He wore somber black, as usual. His compellingly handsome face was pale and drawn and lines of exhaustion were etched on the gaunt features. He had been ill for days—ever since Mississippi had announced her secession. Dyspepsia had laid him low; and a severe neuralgic attack had brought on a recurrence of an old eye ailment.

It was an agonizing affliction and the effects of his intense suffering showed clearly. But he stood precise and tall. Before speaking he swept the hall with his fierce eyes, noting both his friends and his enemies. Then he delivered his memorable address. His rich, mellow voice could be heard plainly in every part of the packed room.

The speech reviewed the reasons that had brought on the secession of his native state and the other states that had taken the same path. It was a concise and excellent survey of the South's grievances. His manner was neither defiant nor gloating; but rather, sorrowful and melancholic. The conclusion of his fifteen-minute discourse was most noteworthy:

> I feel no hostility towards you of the North. I wish you well and such is the feeling of my people. I express their desire when I say they hope for peaceable relations with you.
>
> I carry with me no hostile remembrances. Whatever offence I have given, Senators, in this hour of parting, I offer my apology for any pain which in the heat of discussion I have inflicted. I go hence unencumbered of the remembrance of any injury received and having dis-

charged the duty of making the only reparation in my power for any injury offered. Mr. President and Senators, having made the announcement which the occasion seemed to me to require, it only remains for me to bid you a final adieu.

At the very end, Davis lost his composure momentarily. Tears welled in his eyes. This was the most difficult step in his public career and his feelings proved strong enough to pierce his haughty front, if only for an instant.

A woman sobbed in the gallery. Some thought it might be Varina. Several Senators were seen to daub their eyes with handkerchiefs, but others sneered openly. Davis immediately regained his control and walked out of the chamber forever with great poise and dignity.

This was his third resignation from Congress. The first time, in 1846, he had given up his seat to fight in the Mexican War, which he had ardently espoused because he felt it would strengthen the position of slavery in the United States and spread the institution to the new territories which victory would surely bring.

In 1850, he had resigned again to become a gubernatorial candidate in Mississippi, running against Congressman Henry Foote, who beat him resoundingly.

After that loss, Davis retired from public life until March 7, 1853, when President Franklin Pierce appointed him Secretary of War.

In 1857, Davis was overwhelmingly elected as a Senator by his fellow Mississippians. He represented the Magnolia State in that capacity until 1861, when he once again tendered his resignation to lead the South in its vain struggle for independence.

Never a popular man in the Senate, even among some of his cohorts, Davis's cold manner and cutting remarks earned him many enemies, especially in the final months when the issues of secession and the extension of slavery brought bitter and acrimonious debate to the Senate floor.

Among his sharpest critics was Senator Andrew Johnson of Tennessee. Johnson said of Davis, "He is the most insufferable man in the Senate."

His dislike of Davis had grown because he felt the Senator from Mississippi scorned him for his plebeian background. Once, the two men had a vituperative exchange on the Senate floor. During a discussion about the merits of West Pointers and their achievements, a Senator had derided the Academy. Davis felt it was incumbent on him to defend his Alma Mater and demanded whether the scoffer believed that a blacksmith or a tailor could have done better in a particular situation than a gentleman soldier—a graduate of West Point.

This irked Andrew Johnson, who had been a tailor. He leaped up and accused Davis of arrant snobbery, of maligning the working class and defied him to prove that a "scrub aristocrat" was either more useful or more patriotic than a skilled worker.

Hot words passed between them, and for a while it seemed as though a challenge to a duel was imminent—in those days even Senators settled their quarrels with a bullet. But tempers calmed, at last—and to his credit, Davis apologized. His intention had not been to insult any member and certainly not any workingman. The apology was accepted, but Johnson still nursed his grudge and struck out at Davis whenever he could.

It was no accident that Davis admired so fervently the elite corps of West Point. He was a snob and lived along strict caste lines. Even as a boy he had regarded himself as too good for ordinary work.

Years before, he had decided he had gone to school long enough and his stern father, Samuel, set him to work in the fields picking cotton like a slave. After toiling all day, Davis decided school was not so bad after all. Those few hours marked the only time Jefferson Davis did manual labor in his entire life.

He later said that it was not the physical strain which he found objectionable—but "to have worked with my own hands in the field would have implied an equality with the laborers," he explained. Even at that early age, Davis had already deluded himself into thinking that he was superior to ordinary men.

· 4 ·

Outspoken Andy Johnson, the Tennessee tailor, had aptly described Davis by calling him a "scrub aristocrat." Davis did not stem from a patrician line. He did not have the background of the Tidewater planters or the South Carolinians, the true "Southern Bourbon" plantation owners.

Whether he liked it or not, Davis's ancestry went back to solid, everyday folks. There were no lace-cuffed gentlemen in the Davis clan—merely hard-working, tough farmers of Welsh-Scotch-Irish descent.

His father, Samuel Davis, was the offspring of Welshmen who had farmed in New Jersey and migrated to Georgia long before the Revolution. Sam was a sometime horse raiser, tavern keeper and unsuccessful dirt farmer. He was a rugged man and in the Revolution led a band of partisans who harassed the British in South Carolina and Georgia. While he never achieved the renown of Swamp Fox Marion, Sam Davis proved to be a skillful and valiant partisan fighter.

When the war ended, in 1783, the erstwhile hero returned to Todd County, Kentucky, where he married sturdy Jane Cook, a twenty-four-year-old South Carolina girl of Scotch-Irish lineage. At the time, Samuel was twenty-eight and had very few prospects of achieving financial success. He had no talent for business and a number of projects failed. His attempts at dirt farming ended in disaster—and as a horse raiser, he was far better planning ambushes of British columns.

After a series of crop failures, he opened a tavern in a border region which was still being ravaged by Indian raids. Since there was no other tavern for miles—and a steady stream of westbound settlers passing by, the Davis hostelry achieved a mild prosperity.

The Davises ran that tavern for twenty-eight years—and during that time Jane Cook bore Samuel ten children, between 1783 and 1808. The eldest, Joseph Emory Davis, was born early in their fruitful marriage. He was destined to be rich. The youngest was to become famous. Jefferson Davis was born June 3, 1808, in a log cabin, and "Little Jeff" soon became the family pet. By an odd quirk of history, a boy named Abraham Lincoln was born on February 12, 1809, not a hundred miles from "Little Jeff's" birthplace.

By 1811, Samuel Davis had tired of being an innkeeper because his real love was farming. So after nearly three decades as a tavern owner, the ex-partisan pulled up stakes and moved his brood to St. Mary's Parish, Louisiana, where he intended to take a whirl at raising crops—especially sugar cane and cotton. He located a fertile spread, but the unhealthy Louisiana climate proved too much for the Davis clan. Mosquitoes swarmed in from the marshes and bay-ous. Malaria was endemic and after a few bouts with the fever, Samuel fled with his family to more salubrious ground.

He settled in a less-infested region near Woodville, Mississippi, in the southwestern portion of the state. The soil was rich and crops could flourish there. In 1811, Mississippi was sparsely populated. It was still on the frontier. Land was cheap and a man only needed hard work and determination for success—two traits in which Samuel abounded.

Although he never became very wealthy, Samuel prospered, and, with the help of the whole family, soon acquired vast acreage and a score of slaves. All this he owned free and clear—no small triumph for a one-time farmer, tavern keeper, and horse raiser.

The Davises had come far up the economic ladder since the hand-to-mouth days of the Kentucky frontier. They no longer lived in a log cabin—and while their rambling, whitewashed frame house was no plantation mansion, it seemed like a palace to toilworn Jane Cook.

Samuel Davis, by no stretch of the imagination could be termed either a gentleman or a gentle man. He was cut in the mold of the frontiersman—rough, two-fisted, and iron-willed. He had the indestructible strength and hardiness to push back the wilderness and endure under any hardship. In other words, he was a typical American pioneer. But he was surprisingly devoted and gentle to his wife—and his love for her was touching.

He had another soft spot in his flinty makeup—his youngest child, "Little Jeff." By the time the future Confederate President appeared, the Davis children were almost full grown. The eldest, Joe, had already struck out on his own and in his mid-twenties was rapidly becoming Mississippi's outstanding planter. His plantation, The Hurricane, on the river below Vicksburg in Warren County was one of the finest in the state. In fact, the area where the river curved, near his land, was called Davis Bend. Canny Joe Davis was well on his way to garnering a vast fortune.

Samuel had not been overly concerned about the children who had preceded "Little Jeff"—he had provided for them as best he could, but given them no special consideration. He felt differently about this offspring of his middle age. He adored the clever and handsome little boy and was determined that "Little Jeff" should amount to something. Joe had succeeded without any formal education—but Samuel did not want his favorite to embark on life with such a handicap. He could now well afford to give the youngster the luxury of schooling.

When "Little Jeff" was seven—in 1815—he was enrolled at St. Thomas Aquinas Academy, a Catholic school in Springfield, Kentucky. While the Davises were not Roman Catholic, the best schools in that region were run by Dominicans who accepted everyone, regardless of religion; their main task was to combat illiteracy rather than to proselytize for the Church.

Young Jefferson stayed at St. Thomas Aquinas until 1817 and did not see his family during those entire two years. So he was eager for a reunion after that lapse of time. At nine, he was tall for his age and had changed considerably from the solemn-faced child who had ventured out of Mississippi in 1815.

He journeyed home by flatboat and on muleback, and when he reached his father's house, he stood on the threshold and peered into the parlor like a stranger. His mother was sitting in her favorite chair, darning clothes. She looked up at the handsome lad who was watching her.

"Ma'am, have you seen any stray horses wandering about?" the boy said, twinkling with mischievous humor.

Jane Cook rose, smiling. "No, but I've seen a stray boy," she said, clasping him to her bosom.

This time, Jeff balked at being sent off to school again—but after his exposure to hard work, he became convinced that schooling was far better than the backbreaking toil of the fields to which other children were subjected.

In September, 1817, he was at another school for a while and finally became a student at Transylvania University in Lexington, Kentucky, where he remained four years. It was at Transylvania that he developed a love for classics, learned Latin and Greek, and became a prolific reader. By the standards of his time, Davis was considered highly educated. He was only thirteen years old when he graduated from Transylvania—but even then he had evolved a cold, priggish, and formal manner which smothered the ebullience he had displayed as a small boy.

Samuel was growing old. He fell prey to a series of illnesses and the hardy frontiersman became an invalid. He retained his ambitions for the youth he still called "Little Jeff." He wanted his youngest son to achieve something more than mere economic success—he wanted the boy to have social prestige; to share the advantages enjoyed by the sons of the South's best families. But Samuel was no blue blood. His son had no chance of meeting the aristocratic young men of the region—unless he could somehow convince them he was their equal, even their superior.

In those years, West Point was the stronghold of aristocracy. Only the finest families sent their sons to the Academy. They were the only ones with the influence to obtain an appointment. Occasionally, some poor farmer's son or a workingman's son managed to make the grade—but that was depressingly seldom.

Having been himself a soldier, Samuel was greatly attracted to the military as a career for a gentleman. The sick old man decided that before he died he was going to see his son wearing cadet gray. His hope was never realized in his lifetime—but Jefferson Davis did later go to West Point. By 1824, Jeff's brother Joe had enough influence to swing almost anything in Mississippi—and he persuaded a Magnolia State Congressman to sponsor his younger brother for the Academy. Jefferson's papers were personally signed and approved by John Calhoun, President Monroe's Secretary of War.

Thus, Jefferson Davis became a cadet at the United States Military Academy—and a new and exciting way of life opened to him. The regimen met with his approval. It appealed to his sense of order and icy exactness. Still, there was in him a strange and perverse streak. He could not fully knuckle under to any discipline beyond that which he imposed on himself and as a result, he became a rebel of sorts against the stringent authority.

Shortly after his arrival at West Point, he had a letter from home informing him that his father had died. His answer to it reveals the inhibitions of this thin-lipped young man:

Dear Sister:

It is gratifying to hear from a friend, especially one whom I had not heard from so long as yourself; but the intelligence contained in yours was more than sufficient to mar the satisfaction of hearing from anyone. You must imagine, I cannot describe the shock my feelings sustained at the sad intelligence. In my father I lost a parent ever dear to me, but rendered more so (if possible) by the disasters that attended his declining years. When I saw him last he told me we would probably never see each other again. Yet I still hoped to meet him again; Heaven has refused my wish . . ."

Davis had few close friends among the cadets. Most he regarded as neither his social nor his intellectual equals. Yet among his classmates were such men as Albert Sidney Johnston, Joseph E. Johnston, Robert E. Lee, and Leander Polk, each of whom far outstripped him as a cadet and as a student.

It is hard to imagine this stiff-necked youth in the role of a carefree reveler—but that was exactly the form which his defiance of the West Point brass took. He generally kept out of trouble and was seldom punished—but he did break the regulations. His major offense was to pay frequent nocturnal visits to an off-campus pub, Benny Haven's, located a short distance from the Academy.

This place was off-limits to the cadets but heavily patronized by them. There, they drank ale from pewter tankards, generally raised the dickens and sang lustily. Their favorite tune was one written by a cadet and dedicated to the smoky tavern—it was a forerunner of Yale's famous "Whiffenpoof Song":

> To our comrades who have fallen,
> One cup before we go,
> They poured their life-blood freely
> out *pro bonum publico,*
> No marble points the stranger
> to where they rest below,
> They lie neglected far away from
> Benny Haven's, O!
> O, Benny Haven's, O! O, Benny
> Haven's, O!

But an occasional demerit for getting caught at Benny Haven's was not serious enough to warrant dismissal from the Academy and Davis stayed on; his grades enabled him to get by and he had some talent for soldiering.

He did get into one serious scrape, however, in 1826. It was nearly bad enough to nip his budding military career. Shortly before the Christmas holidays, most of the Southerners attending the Academy held an eggnog party at Benny Haven's for Yankee cadets, and Jefferson Davis was on the planning committee.

The party was successful—almost too successful—for by bed check, the festive cadets had not yet returned. The Cadet Duty Of-

ficer, an eager beaver named Hitchcock, headed for Benny Haven's
to round up the revelers and arrest them.

He should have considered that, by this time, the high-spirited
celebrants were beyond ordinary discipline. When he set foot in the
pub and announced his intentions, somebody knocked him down
and this was the signal for a Donnybrook, a sort of preview of the
sectional strife most of these young men would know in their life-
times. Northerners and Southerners sailed into each other. Fists and
bottles flew. Heads were broken and noses bloodied. Black eyes
were commonplace.

A frantic messenger brought the news to the Academy and the
Provost Guard came on the double, covering the distance in record
time. Their locust sticks thudded on heads and shoulders and finally the fractious cadets calmed down.

The rioters were marched back under guard and punishment came
swiftly. The insurgents were confined to quarters and sentenced to
long hours of extra duty. During all this, Davis displayed an unexpected talent as a free-for-all brawler. After the riot, he found himself genuinely popular with his fellow cadets. For the first time since
he had entered the Academy, he was regarded as a "regular fellow."

Interestingly enough, none of the future Confederate greats: A. S.
Johnston, Joe Johnston, Robert E. Lee, or Leander Polk had either
attended the party or been embroiled in the riot.

· 5 ·

After graduating from West Point in 1828, Jefferson Davis served
seven years in the Regular Army. A line officer, he did duty at Fort
Crawford, Wisconsin, and a dozen other border posts with the First
Infantry Regiment. The region was wild. Hostile Indians roamed
the area: Sac and Fox, Wyandotte, Menominee, Winnebago, and
Pottawatomie. At one time or another each of these tribes took to
the warpath.

Young Lieutenant Davis felt compelled to outshine every soldier
in his regiment. He rode further on patrols, went for longer periods
than anyone else without food and water; during clashes with hos-
tiles, the twenty-year-old officer was always up in the forefront
showing reckless courage in the face of bullets and arrows.

According to his brand of chivalry, Davis did not feel he was doing anything out of the ordinary. He acted as he believed a gentleman was required to act. He regarded himself as a knight errant of sorts, instilled as he was with ideas of high physical courage, deep personal honor, and fervent religious devoutness. It would have been strange if Davis had not displayed these qualities—they were the very cornerstones of the Southern aristocratic creed.

He proved himself a brave officer if not a particularly exceptional one. He was neither a good strategist nor an outstanding tactician. He had, however, two main talents as an officer—a fiendish eye for detail and an ability to make troops follow him. But he was never popular with his men. They respected him as a leader yet no warmth radiated from them to him or vice versa. He followed a rigid pattern of behavior which he once described: "Never be haughty to the humble or humble to the haughty." His men he treated justly but sternly, and strictly according to the book. He neither gave nor asked for more than regulations allowed.

Then, too, he was plagued during his military career by frequent illness. Some of it grew out of his nervous temperament and was manifested in violent dyspeptic and neuralgic onslaughts. At times, he writhed in agony from the pain that stabbed the left side of his face during the worst of a neuralgic seizure. He became afflicted with ameurosis, which endangered his sight and permanently impaired his left eye. For days at a time he had to remain in a darkened room. Once, at Fort Crawford, he suffered a siege of pneumonia and pulled through by sheer will power, long after the regimental surgeon had declared his case was hopeless and death only hours away.

During the brief fighting of the Black Hawk War, Davis displayed merit. It was in this campaign that an awkward young lawyer from Illinois—Abraham Lincoln—got his first taste of military life as a captain in a volunteer infantry company. But there was no meeting between them during the Black Hawk War—nor does any record exist that they ever had any personal contact during their entire lives.

After the war, the army settled down to routine again. Lieutenant Jefferson Davis was once more assigned to various frontier posts. He was stationed at Fort Crawford again in 1835. The garrison, located near Prairie du Chien, Wisconsin, was commanded by Colonel

Zachary "Rough-and-Ready" Taylor, who was yet to win fame in the Mexican War and become President of the United States. The brusque Colonel had ensconced his family on the post, including his three beautiful daughters, Anne, Sarah Knox, and Betty. They were young, lissome, and lovely. Of the trio, Sarah Knox was the most beautiful: a petite girl with wavy brown hair, a shapely figure and clear gray eyes. She captured the heart of every eligible officer in the regiment. A quick, high-spirited, mercurial girl, she fell wildly in love with somber Jefferson Davis—and he, the unlikeliest of men to have won her affections, found himself entranced with her. Soon, he proposed marriage to her and she accepted.

The match was a perfect one. The young people were in love. They were both attractive. Davis was extremely eligible. The fortune of his brother, Joseph, had reached the million dollar mark—a most unusual achievement for that time. He was surely one of the wealthiest men in the South—if not the entire country. He favored the marriage—and promised the couple their own plantation, adjoining his, for a wedding present. Apparently everything augured well for Davis and his prospective bride. Then, all at once, Sarah's father, the crusty Colonel, objected vehemently to his daughter's choice. The girl was amazed by her father's attitude—usually he agreed to anything she wanted. But this was one time Sarah could not wheedle her papa into a good and tractable mood.

The Colonel was adamant and positive. He did not care a whit for Jefferson Davis as a son-in-law. He gave no rational reasons for his disapproval of the impending wedding. At one time he shrilled, "I don't want my daughter married to an army officer, to lead the life her mother led, to face hardships and uncertainty."

But his daughter Anne had married an army officer—to whom Taylor had never objected. His daughter Betty was planning to wed another army man with the Colonel's blessings. Obviously the Colonel was not giving his real reasons. He simply did not like Jefferson Davis, but he never explained why he had such an antipathy toward the young officer.

In an attempt to remove his prospective father-in-law's objections to the marriage, Davis resigned from the Army. Still Taylor would not give his approval. Then, despite his objections, the wedding plans went on apace. Since her father would not consent to holding the ceremony at Fort Crawford, Sarah arranged for it to be held at her aunt's home in Louisville, Kentucky. She pleaded with her father to attend but that tough old soldier refused to budge from the fort. Even after she had boarded the steamer that was to carry her down-river to Louisville, Sarah made a final tearful bid to soften her stern parent. He had come to her cabin for a last farewell, and she begged him on her knees to change his mind. But like the father in a melo-drama, Taylor walked out and left his daughter sobbing on the floor.

Jefferson Davis and Sarah Knox Taylor were married on June 17, 1835, by the Reverend Ashe of Christ Church, Louisville. The reception garden party was attended by the elite of Louisville society. A society reporter of a local journal wrote:

> Miss Taylor is very beautiful, slight and not very tall and seems a young woman of decided spirit. She was dressed in a dark traveling suit with a small hat to match.

> Lt. Davis was dressed in a long-tail cutaway coat, brocaded waist-coat, breeches tight-fitting and held under the instep with a strap. He wore a high stovepipe hat. He is of slender build, has polished manners and is of a quiet, intellectual countenance.

The pretty bride and her grave husband spent their honeymoon at Brierfield, the fine home standing on the plantation Joseph Emory had given them. In addition to the house and the land, he gave his younger brother twenty slaves. The stars seemed to bode well for the newlyweds—aside from the intransigence of Colonel Taylor, nothing marred the smooth path of their marriage. They had youth, money, and love. The world was spinning for them . . .

· 6 ·

In September Jefferson took his bride to visit his sister who had a plantation in Bayou Teche, Louisiana. Malaria came early that year—and the strain was deadly. All through the lowlands, people were dying from the fever—white and black, master and slave. There was weeping in the big houses with tall columns, and the sound of sobbing was heard in flimsy slave quarters. Death observed no color line.

A few days after the Davises arrived in Bayou Teche, both were stricken by malaria. They burned with fever and as Davis tossed in delirium, his young wife succumbed to the illness. Her last hours were agonized and she died babbling and incoherent with pain.

The bereaved husband made a slow and dispirited recovery. He showed no interest in anything around him, after he went to live with Joseph, at The Hurricane. The beautiful house at Brierfield was closed down, the windows shuttered, the rooms silent and dark.

For nearly a decade, Jefferson Davis lived almost as a recluse, seldom venturing off the plantation grounds. He busied himself with the minutiae of running the enterprise. Although the house at Brierfield had been closed, the fields were still being cultivated—and between The Hurricane and Brierfield, Jefferson found himself immersed in paper work, bookkeeping, and administration. He had to deal with overseers and straw bosses and the problems involved in maintaining almost one thousand slaves.

Joseph shrewdly left the clerical details to his brother—while he attended to the business end of the operation. He found buyers who were willing to pay the highest prices for the Davis brothers' cotton. Under his guidance, Brierfield prospered and Jefferson became a rich man—through Joseph's efforts, for he himself was so deeply engrossed in shuffling papers that he knew little about running a plantation and making it pay.

It was Joseph, too, who rekindled his intellectual curiosity. The elder brother provided him with books reflecting the great thinking of that day and of former times. Joseph discussed politics with his star-crossed brother. He artfully prodded Jefferson's thinking along political lines and subtly groomed him for a career in politics.

Jefferson nibbled at the bait. He became interested in the constitutional niceties of states' rights and the knotty question of slavery expansion. Gradually, he developed into an ardent advocate of Southern expansionism and became convinced that slavery was not a wrongful practise. He fervently believed that the "peculiar institution" was the cornerstone of Southern economy and that the South's growth depended on the growth of slavery.

He emerged, at last, from his self-imposed exile and spoke with other planters about his beliefs. The more aggressive ones were in full agreement with his ideas, with his ambitious plans to increase Southern holdings—Mexico should be absorbed; all of Central America to the Isthmus of Panama was to be annexed; Cuba taken over and the slave trade reopened so that these lands could be stocked with an adequate number of slaves.

He envisioned a Southern empire far greater than the North could ever hope to be and saw the control of the North American continent resting in Southern hands. Once he climbed the wall of seclusion, Jefferson Davis made up for the lost years and soon was known as one of the most articulate slavery spokesmen in Mississippi.

Joseph was highly satisfied with his brother's progress—but not yet through with his role as Pygmalion. He felt there was more he had to do. Jefferson was now thirty-seven years old and still unwed. He had not so much as looked at another woman since Sarah Knox's untimely death. Joseph's next step was to find a suitable wife for his protégé.

He had a most likely prospect in mind. She was Varina Howell, a daughter of his best friend, a wealthy planter. Although the girl was only seventeen, she was, as Joseph knew, unusually mature for her age. He had always held her in high esteem—and she, in turn, admired Joe Davis. She thought of him as one of the family and always called him "Uncle Joe."

Varina had never met Jefferson, but wily "Uncle Joe" soon fixed that. He invited her to a gala party which he was giving at The Hurricane. The best people in the state received bids and Varina eagerly accepted.

Joseph introduced her to Jefferson and sat back to watch developments. Although some twenty years older than the girl, Jefferson took to her at once. He appreciated her quick ways and sharp wit. For a female, she had an amazing knowledge of public affairs and he was amused by her burning attacks on many of his political theories. She was a Whig, while he was a Democrat—a party she had always regarded as solely for the "uncouth rabble."

She summed up her earliest impression of him in a letter to her mother:

... I don't know whether Mr. Jefferson Davis is young or old. From what I hear, he is only two years younger than you are.

He impressed me as a remarkable kind of man, but of uncertain temper; and has a way of taking for granted that everybody agrees with him when he expresses an opinion, which offends me; yet, he is most agreeable and has a peculiarly sweet voice and a winning manner of asserting himself.

The fact is, he is the kind of person I should expect to rescue one from a mad dog at any risk but to insist upon a stoical indifference to the fright afterward. I don't think I shall ever like him as I do his brother Joe. But, would you believe it—he is refined and cultured, yet a Democrat!

Varina's analysis of the master of Brierfield was keen and penetrating. But she did not realize that she would soon fall in love with him. Despite the difference in their ages, Davis was irresistibly drawn to this remarkable girl. For years, he had asserted that he would never marry again; he was convinced that his one true love had died during the terrible days at Bayou Teche. But he found love again with Varina.

On February 26, 1845, they were married—and their marriage was to become one of beauty and strength, an enriching relationship that survived crushing tribulation and personal tragedy. It was an alliance of love and respect far stronger than the awful events which engulfed it.

After so many years of unhappiness and loneliness, Jefferson Davis seemed to have found himself. Varina had restored his will and his ambition. He was ready, now, to embark on a career for which he enjoyed peculiar qualifications. He actively entered politics; his rich voice helped him capture crowds; his icily intellectual mind enabled him to dissect issues and draw conclusions which, though frequently narrow-minded, reflected the thinking of his people and his region.

Shortly after his marriage, Davis was elected to Congress as Representative-at-Large from Wilkinson County. He journeyed to Washington with his bride and prepared to enter the Congressional arena. He brought many advantages to this new field—intelligence, sincerity, and physical attractiveness.

He had one outstanding flaw, which almost negated his strong points. Davis possessed little understanding of practical affairs. He had spent too many years in his ivory tower untouched by the mundane problems of day-to-day living. At no time in his life had he ever been forced to eke out a livelihood through his own efforts.

Someone else had always cleared the way and he had secured all his advantages without struggle.

His father had provided his education. The property he owned, the very house in which he lived came from his brother. His prosperity, achieved from cotton planting, was a result of Joseph's manipulation. He had accomplished nothing on his own. As a result of his sheltered existence, Davis developed a warped picture of the world. Even in the army, which had been his major career, he had led an existence divorced from the realities of everyday living. This hothouse environment resulted in an emotional immaturity which led him to feel that anyone who disagreed with him was insincere.

This was a grievous fault, indeed. None of his own ideas had evolved from competition and insecurity. Work and suffering had nothing to do with formulating his concepts. Locked away in the pleasant surroundings of the splendid plantation, Davis pored over the writings of other men. He absorbed their thoughts and used only those which strengthened his own opinions of the aristocratic society which he upheld—a sort of gentleman's club for those who had never made a compromise with the sordid commercial world peopled by money-grubbers and venal materialists.

Davis's world had little connection with reality. He saw things as he desired them to be, yet, paradoxically, he was a stringently truthful man—and one of high principles. Unfortunately, his idea of truth was far from actual conditions. His social outlook was primarily feudal. Once he said: "Some are fit only for the hard toil of the field, others are plainly designed for the easier task of managing and directing the labor of others. Thus, the planters prosper, the 'mudsills' are contented, and the slaves are the happiest of living men." Oddly enough, this anachronistic philosophy had many subscribers, especially in the Deep South where slavery thrived and poor white dirt farmers struggled under the benevolent despotism of the big plantation owners.

Great events were already in the making when Jefferson Davis took his seat in Congress. War was brewing with Mexico and Davis was one of those who helped stir the cauldron. He was in favor of the war and many Southerners gave him vociferous backing.

Only the dauntless, sickly Georgian, Alexander Stephens, dared speak against his fellow Southerners and the impending conflict. The dwarf with the body of a fourteen-year-old and the courage of a giant insisted that a war with Mexico was evil, that it was blatant aggression and oppression.

No one heeded his words nor suffered even a moment of guilt in supporting the war. Some time later, a freshman Congressman from Illinois spoke against the "infamy" of warring on the unfortunate country to the south—but to no avail. Very few people paid attention to what Abe Lincoln was saying in those days.

The Southerners who supported the war, especially those from the cotton states, were hard-boiled businessmen who saw dollars sprouting on every boll of cotton. They might describe themselves as aristocrats with no basely commercial thoughts—but in actuality Cotton was King and the sovereign crop spelled money.

Without slaves, these planters could not exist. Slaves provided their labor. Slaves ran their plantations—and if the owners were to flourish, slavery had to flourish too. The war was a golden chance to spread slavery and they did not intend to let it slip by.

True, Northern merchants did not oppose the war—but their motives were as base as those of the Southerners. Both groups were out for gain and it mattered little if blood sprinkled their harvest of dollars. So the firebrands and warhawks had their way and the armies marched off to attack Mexico.

Davis resigned from Congress in 1846 and sped back to Mississippi where he rose to command of the First Mississippi Rifles. At Buena Vista, he reached the peak of his military glory. And, on that murderous field, he won still another victory as he lay wounded on a stretcher. General Zachary Taylor, his former father-in-law, commanded the American forces. "Old Rough-and-Ready" rode to where the wounded man was lying, dismounted and knelt by his side. "My daughter was a better judge of men than I am," the General rasped. "I'm sorry, my boy. Truly sorry." He patted Davis on the shoulder, mounted his horse and trotted away.

· 7 ·

The hectic years rolled by. In 1847, largely on his war record, Davis was returned to the Senate by his admiring fellow Mississippians. He spoke vibrantly on the Senate floor, always a champion of Southern rights. He was a brilliant spokesman for slavery. In

1850, he became an ardent advocate of the right of secession, urging that slavery be extended to the Pacific Coast and California on the pain of disunion.

His co-workers in this cause were the fieriest Southern nationalists. Davis even suggested a secession convention of the Cotton States to be held in Memphis, Tennessee. That call came ten years too soon. Few Southerners seriously considered breaking away from the Union over the question of slavery in California. Only the most fanatical rallied around Davis—and his proposal was soundly rejected. For another decade at least, the fabric of unity was to remain intact.

Unrealistically, Davis believed his cause could still triumph. A gubernatorial election was under way in Mississippi, and the Whig candidate, Congressman Henry Foote, was an outspoken foe of slavery extension into California. Davis decided to fight the battle on home soil. He declared himself a candidate for the office and took to the hustings. Despite his vigorous campaign, which degenerated into personal vituperation, Davis was whipped.

He had raised the slogans of "states' rights" and "Southern destiny"; he had declaimed against "abolitionist tyranny"—the very battle cries of a decade later. Only the owners of the large plantations gave him their support. Small farmers and tradespeople repudiated him. The time had not yet come to lower the Stars and Stripes.

The defeat wounded Davis. He felt the people had rejected him. Because they had disagreed with him, he turned away from them and retired to Brierfield where, for the next three years, he busied himself with the plantation.

His holdings expanded. The acres under cultivation mounted. The number of slaves he owned increased steeply. Towards them, Davis was scrupulously honest and fair. He was a considerate and humane master who saw that his slaves were well housed and well fed. He treated them with consideration and kindness and was never rude or harsh. To a large extent, his slaves were self-governing; any infractions were punished by a court composed of the slaves themselves. Davis was justly proud of the conditions among his people. Whenever anyone criticized the institution of slavery, he always pointed to his own plantation as proof that the evils in the system could be eradicated.

Davis and Varina lived a pleasant but secluded life during the three years he had withdrawn from public service. But in 1853 this interlude ended. The New Hampshire conservative, Franklin Pierce, had been elected President. He remembered the firebrand Mississippian who had turned the tide at Buena Vista, and made him his Secretary of War.

This appointment was complete vindication for Davis. He had been recognized for his merits and selected for high office—and had achieved his newly won success without compromising his principles. With Varina at his side, he made the tedious journey to Washington, and assumed his place in the Cabinet.

He ran the War Department well, if not smoothly. Davis behaved liked the head of a small business who had not the slightest confidence in any of his employees. He smothered himself in paper work that a clerk might handle. Every account, every requisition on even the most trivial matter received his attention. No function of the Department was carried out unless he had given it approval. The last button on the overcoat of the last private in the most remote outpost became his personal concern.

In those days, of course, the War Department did not have to deal with any vast organization. The regular army—officers and men—numbered only 15,000, about the size of a modern division. Most of the work was routine, and the war office was not a training ground for a great administrator.

But despite his involvement with trivia, Davis did carry through much-needed reform in the military establishment. He vigorously campaigned for a raise in soldiers' pay—and got it. He won appropriations for the repair and maintenance of army posts and coastal forts. It was largely at his insistence that outmoded muskets were altered with rifling and percussion caps.

Davis had ability. But his efficiency was marred by a streak of pettiness which constantly cropped up, like a running defect in a magnificent tapestry. The most notable example of his picayune behavior involved the senior soldier of the army, General Winfield Scott. Once "Old Fuss and Feathers" presented the government with a bill for travel allowance at the rate of 16 cents per mile. Davis cavalierly disallowed this claim and permitted the doughty soldier only 8 cents per mile. A lasting ill-will rose between the men and was never mended through the years.

During his tenure in the War Office, Varina bore her first child—Samuel Emory Davis—but the infant died at the age of two, in

1855. This was the first of a series of similar tragedies which haunted the couple. In all, they had six children, four boys and two girls. Each of the sons was to predecease his parents.

But these losses were merely personal sorrows. The greatest tribulations were yet to come. In 1857, when Davis left Pierce's cabinet and was re-elected to the Senate, the day of wrath was drawing nearer.

· 8 ·

The rift between North and South widened every hour and in the deepening crisis the shadow of slavery and States' Rights loomed menacingly. Events hurtled toward a showdown. Bloody, senseless fighting broke out in Kansas between the pro- and anti-slavers. The fanatic, John Brown, swept out of the west to enact his tortured drama at Harper's Ferry.

If, in 1850, secession had been the cry of only the most radical, the tide was shifting now. Many still hesitated to dismember the Union but strong sentiment was rising to do something drastic about "abolitionist oppression."

The voices grew angrier and more strident. All that was needed to tip the scales was an extra push. That came in 1860 with the election of Lincoln, who had been anathema to the South. South Carolina led the protests. If the Republican was elected, the Carolinians had vowed, the Palmetto State would secede from the Union. On December 20, 1860, a little more than a month after Lincoln had been voted into office, that threat was carried out. The impending crisis had become a reality. The floodgates were open and the torrent swirled across the unhappy nation.

Davis was in the forefront of the secessionists. He was among the stalwart figures around whom the movement rallied, although he did not shine as the most violent or the most outspoken. Men like Robert Toombs, Robert Barnwell Rhett and William Lowndes Yancey became the spokesmen for the cause of disunion. Davis was counted among those who still hoped for a peaceable solution, a bloodless parting of the ways between the cotton states and the North.

Meanwhile, the flood tide of secession rolled on. Senators representing Mississippi, Texas, Arkansas, Louisiana, Alabama, Florida, and Georgia held a caucus in the Capitol at Washington on January

5, 1861. They agreed that their respective states should withdraw from the Union and form a Southern Confederacy. It was the most momentous decision made on the North American continent since the Continental Congress had declared independence from England on July 4, 1776.

The senators further recommended that no later than February 15 a convention be convoked in Montgomery, Alabama, the most centrally located of the Cotton States. The purpose of this assemblage would be to draft a constitution and consolidate the self-styled Confederacy. The committee to expedite this meeting and draw up an agenda was composed of Jefferson Davis, Mississippi; John Slidell, Louisiana; and Stephen R. Mallory, Florida.

The pace began to quicken. South Carolina confiscated all Federal property within its borders—storehouses, arsenals, post offices, customs houses, and courts. Forces carrying the Palmetto Flag, under General Pierre Beauregard, laid siege to Fort Moultrie in Charleston harbor. The old stronghold was manned by a small force of regulars commanded by Major Robert Anderson. Recognizing that his position in Moultrie was untenable, Anderson moved his tiny garrison to Fort Sumter and the fateful game was in full swing.

The cotton states seceded in rapid order; the bad news broke over the bewildered country like overlapping thunderclaps in a severe electrical storm. On January 9, Mississippi seceded; Florida, January 10; Alabama, January 11; Georgia, January 19.

The Peach Tree State did not depart without a struggle. Union sentiment was high there and three prominent Georgians—Alexander Stephens, his half-brother, Linton, and Herschel V. Johnson—voted against secession in the state legislature but these protests were drowned in the exultant shouts of the secessionists.

The dismal roll call continued—on January 26 Louisiana joined, and Texas came in February 1. What no foreign despot had been able to achieve, the Southern planters had accomplished—namely, the dismemberment of the United States of America.

In each of the seceded states, the same procedure was followed. United States property was taken over by state authority. Rifles and ammunition from the arsenals and forts went to arm the state troops. Everywhere fifes shrilled and drums thudded and troops marched.

The lower South was having a huge carnival, as though no one realized the deadliness of the steps that had been taken. Here and there were islands of Unionism, men who looked askance at the mushrooming secession drive. Even in Charleston, South Carolina, there was such a man—Judge James Louis Petigru, the state's outstanding lawyer. The old man, who had a delicious sense of humor, described the secession of South Carolina in these words: "South Carolina," he said, "is too small for a republic and too large for a lunatic asylum."

With the entry of Texas into the secession camp, the movement came to a halt. In a way, the trend had been disappointing to the secessionist leaders. The border states—Kentucky, North Carolina, Tennessee, Missouri, and Arkansas—had not come over in the first onrush; neither had Virginia, Delaware, and Maryland. They served as a buffer between the Union and the seceded states. Although they were slaveholding states, these border regions had a more balanced economy than the seceded group and depended less on the slave-operated system. They fully accepted the right to secession, and did not believe in coercing the seceded states back into the Union—but the moment had not yet come for them to act. The border states waited to see what was going to happen, and the divided nation waited with them.

Probably the worst blow to the Confederacy was the fact that the most influential of all Southern states had not declared herself for the Cause. Virginia, the Old Dominion State, stood majestically on the side, like a great lion disdaining to join the snarling pack that was dismembering the Union.

Roger Pryor, a Virginian, made a speech in Charleston, South Carolina, discussing the attitude of his native state in the present crisis: "Give the old lady time," he said—"she is a little slow and rheumatic . . . but if you would bring in Virginia in an hour . . . strike a blow! Spill some blood in her face!"

The blood spilling was yet some months away and Virginia remained impassive amidst the stirrings and the rumblings of the upheaval.

The Montgomery Convention convened on February 4. The constitution it drew up was little better than a carbon copy of the one that had been scrapped. The Confederate constitution did have one significant change—it provided a six-year term of office for the President and forbade him to succeed himself.

The forty-four delegates from the six states that sent delegates chose an oddly assorted pair to share the burdens of the Executive of the Confederate States of America. Two more disparate men than Jefferson Davis—frustrated soldier, idealist, nationalist, and gracious gentleman—and gnomelike, brilliant, pain-racked, legalistic, constitutionalist Alexander Stephens could not be found. There were worlds between the President and the Vice-President.

Seldom were two more incompatible men placed into positions of joint responsibility. Stephens was no admirer of Davis and grew to hate him. "Little Ellick" was a necessary evil to Davis; the constitution called for a Vice-President so there had to be one. Actually Davis had no special antipathy towards Stephens. Anyone else would have received the same sort of treatment from him—almost total indifference. Davis simply ignored the man in the same way he had the clerks who had served him in the War Office. But in Alexander Stephens, he faced a formidable foe. The Georgian was no mere clerk and did not intend to be treated like one.

The lines were drawn; the passions were aroused. Everyone watched Washington City and Montgomery for a clue to what was coming next. It was like an exciting play and even had about it an air of unreality, as though all this was only a melodrama that would turn out well in the end.

But it was not a contrived drama written by a hack playwright. It was life and only too real. The reality caught up with Jefferson Davis on that bright and sunny morning when the roses were blooming in the flower garden at Brierfield and the weather mocked the calendar.

He turned from his dream of being the South's leading soldier and prepared to face the strange destiny that was awaiting him in Montgomery, Alabama . . .

TWO

Mr. Davis

"The time to compromise has passed and those who oppose us shall smell powder and feel **Southern steel** . . . **No** compromise, no reconstruction, no reconciliation can now be entertained . . ."—

JEFFERSON DAVIS, Montgomery, Alabama,
February, 1861

Now I'm a good old Rebel,
And that's just what I am,
For this fair land of freedom,
I would not give a damn.

Secession song, 1861

THE OLDEST living resident of Montgomery, Alabama, could not remember a time when there had been more excitement in the drowsy city than on February 18, 1861. It was a combination of Mardi Gras and the Fourth of July. Flags bedecked every building on Main Street.

There were all sorts of banners and buntings including the brand new Stars and Bars of the Confederacy. In some places, overenthusiastic decorators had raised the old flag—but nobody seemed to give a hoot that the Stars and Stripes was fluttering in the sunshine.

Montgomery was scrubbed and shining for the big event and even the shabby and dilapidated houses in the Negro quarter sported freshly painted shutters, whitewashed fences, and gleaming windows.

The occasion for the celebration was the inauguration of Jefferson Davis and Alexander Stephens as President and Vice-President of the Provisional Government, Confederate States of America.

At a later date, an election would be held to allow the qualified voters a chance to endorse their provisional leaders. If the electorate backed them, Davis and Stephens would be reinaugurated, this time for a six-year term as the legal and constituted heads of the Confederate government.

Early in the morning of the big day, bands began playing in every part of the town. Grogshops and taprooms were crowded, and, hours before noon, drunken men were staggering about the streets, whooping and shouting and waving whiskey bottles. Everyone was in high spirits and good humor prevailed.

Lanky farmboys wearing clean denims cavorted in the dusty roadways, pummeling each other and wrestling, carrying on vigorous horseplay. Crowds thronged around the capitol, spilling across the broad lawns and eating picnic lunches on the grass while waiting for the swearing-in ceremonies to begin.

Carriages, hansoms, buggies, and surreys were parked hub-to-hub along the carriage drive of the capitol. Busy little Negro boys, white teeth flashing, grabbed the bridles and cried, "Watch yo' rig, massah! Only five cents!"

Well-fed men glowing with early-morning whiskey flipped coins to the boys and trudged on foot to the western side of the building where the oath-taking was to be held at 1:00 P.M.

Brightly gowned women mingled among the somberly dressed men, and their garments made vivid splashes of color against the green lawn and the dazzling white marble of the building. It was all pleasant and gala with no hint of future ordeals.

The ladies carried gay bouquets and twirled parasols. The young and pretty ones flirted with youths in stiff new militia uniforms of every shade and hue and style. There were baggy-trousered Zouaves, trimly uniformed West Point officers, and even a general or two to add distinction.

The young soldiers tried hard to act fiercely martial—but succeeded only in looking like what they were—smooth-cheeked youngsters playing soldier. Their uniforms were either too large or too small. They handled their weapons with gingerly awkwardness and in essaying company maneuvers wound up in hopeless confusion. These military tyros often sauntered blithely out of rank to chat with friends or to pick up a girl.

But all this added to the fun. No one really took the soldier boys seriously. Let them have their lark. Nobody was going to shoot at anybody, and the muskets and the cannon were only for show. The Yankees weren't stupid enough to make trouble. In the first place they didn't even know how to fight. Everybody knew one Southerner could whip ten damyankees.

But all that aside—the best Confederate brains were saying that once the government was established it would be immediately recognized by England, France, and Russia. England was ready to ship mountains of war matériel to the South. The canny Britons knew they had to help the Confederacy—or else there would be no cotton for the mills of Lancashire and Yorkshire, the textile workers of Manchester and Leeds would have no work, and millions of souls would be going hungry in the British Isles. No, no—neither Lord Russell, nor Lord Palmerston would risk unemployment and starvation at home when the simple solution was to recognize the Confederacy and ensure a flow of cotton.

The new nation was sitting pretty. What could the United States do? Was Abe Lincoln going to risk war with England and France—maybe even Russia—to force the seceded states back into a Union they did not want? Not even the backwoods clod the Yankees had

Crowds flock to the grounds of the state Capitol in Montgomery, Alabama, for the inaugural ceremonies installing Jefferson Davis as Provisional President of the Confederacy on February 18, 1861.

elected President could be that thick-headed. Abe Lincoln was supposed to have horse sense, at any rate. He'd better use it to good purpose. The best course he could take was to let the Southern states go without any interference. Perhaps, in a decade or so when tempers cooled down, there might be good will between the United States and the Confederacy. After all, the people had a common heritage. They had lived for a long time under the same flag and the same government. There was no reason the two nations couldn't exist and thrive side by side.

That, of course, depended on the Yankees and Abe Lincoln. If he tried to push the proud Southerners, he was going to be sorrier than the man who kicked a hornets' nest thinking it was a football. Peace or war. Let the chips fall either way. The Confederates could hold out either the hand of friendship or a fist.

Still not everyone was certain that war was not in the offing. Some, in fact, felt it to be inevitable. In his farewell speech to the Senate on January 20, 1861, the flamboyant Georgian, Robert Toombs, had given a martial tone to his address:

> The Union, sir, is dissolved . . . You see the glittering bayonet and you hear the tramp of armed men from yon capitol to the Rio Grande. It is a sight that gladdens the eye and cheers the hearts of other men ready to second them . . .

On the very day of his arrival in Montgomery, President-Designate Davis had sounded bellicose in a speech to the crowd that had greeted him at the railroad station.

> The time to compromise has passed and those who oppose us shall smell powder and feel Southern steel. No compromise, no reconstruction, no reconciliation can now be entertained . . .

These were warlike words. Yet, none of the Confederate leaders actually wanted war. It was all right to rattle sabers, sound trumpets, and teeter on the brink—none of this was actual warfare. But those with the clearest vision understood that the war clouds, once gathered, could not be easily dispelled.

War had, in fact, been narrowly averted on January 8, 1861, up in Charleston harbor when a youthful Citadel cadet tugged on a lanyard and sent a shell screaming towards a merchant ship flying the

Stars and Stripes. The vessel, the *Star of the West*, was carrying supplies and reinforcements for Fort Sumter. Fortunately, Confederate zeal was better than Confederate aim and nobody got hurt.

The cadet, George E. Haynsworth, of Sumter, South Carolina, won the dubious distinction of firing the initial shot in the ghastly conflict that was soon to come.

Had it not been for the forbearance of Major Robert Anderson commanding Fort Sumter, war would have broken out on that very day. Instead of answering the Southern batteries, he held his fire and the blood bath was thus delayed for a few months.

It was ridiculous to suppose that the stiff-necked Yankees would keep swallowing these provocations indefinitely. They could not go on accepting with passivity the seizure of forts, arsenals, and property and hostile acts against the flag. Sooner or later, there was bound to be retaliation—and with it would come war.

Even more to the point, was it feasible for Yankee business men to allow the South complete freedom to build up its industry on a competitive basis? Surely, at some future time, the Confederacy would develop into an industrial as well as agricultural nation.

And what about the abolitionists? Would they sit back and placidly watch an unbridled slave empire flourish on their very doorstep?

Although the guns were now silent, the war had actually begun. The silence was only a counterfeit of peace. How many of the eager, clumsy young men in ill-fitting, gaudy uniforms would be alive a week, a month, a year from now? They would be corpses moldering in thickets—uniforms tattered, young faces turned into grinning skulls.

However, on that merry February morning all the grimness and desolation still lay ahead, and the day was a gala one. It was a carefree birthday party for the Confederacy which was becoming a physical entity, with all the machinery of a stable government.

To Jefferson Davis, the day brought fruition for all the years he had carried the banner of slavedom. It had not brought him everything of which he had dreamed. He was not fated to lead men in battle; but as President he was commander-in-chief of all the Confederate forces—the armies being formed and the nonexistent navy. He was filling a role more far-reaching than a mere military one. It was for him to mold his country, to make it strong and enduring. What he did would control its destinies for centuries.

When future generations would read about these stirring times, Jefferson Davis would be noted as the "Father of his Country." His name would be a household word. No village green would be without his statue. Like the great man of Mount Vernon, Jefferson Davis would be immemorially etched in the minds of his countrymen. This was a glory which made him feel humble.

He thought of this land whose chief executive he was about to become: a beautiful country, rich and fertile, which stretched across rivers and mountains, with a thousand miles of seacoast from the Atlantic to the Rio Grande. Nine million people, black and white, lived within its boundaries. Its potential was limitless; its wealth abounding. King Cotton flourished in its productive soil. Tobacco, corn, wheat, and rice were plentiful. Cattle, sleek and fat, grazed in its pasture lands. The economy of the nation was based on cotton, a firm and strong foundation.

The people were virile and determined; they were a proud, liberty-loving race whose united will was unconquerable. Within its borders, the Confederacy held the seats of culture and refinement. Its people were welded together in the righteousness of their Cause; the noblest of all causes—liberty and independence. They were the inheritors of the traditions of '76, the descendants of the men who had followed Marion in the swamps and had shivered in the snow at Valley Forge. Their forefathers had heard the doleful British bandsmen playing "The World Turned Upside Down" on that distant day when Cornwallis had surrendered at Yorktown, Virginia.

Such opportunity for immortality came to few men and Davis was grateful he had been chosen. If he had doubts and misgivings, his peculiar temperament aided him in stifling them. Since he believed in the success of the Confederacy, he felt it had already been achieved. He proceeded to act as though his was the established nation, not the United States.

He summarily rejected the view that secession was rebellion against the Federal government. Nothing the Confederacy was doing even vaguely smacked of revolution. Because he held these convictions, the rest of the world must surely see he was right, and recognition by the leading European powers, he believed, was only a matter of course.

Promptly at 1:00 P.M., Davis stepped out on the west portico of the capitol and the people cheered wildly. He was dressed, as always, in good taste and impeccably. He looked like a leader with his tall, spare frame, hollow-cheeked countenance, and those intense, burning eyes.

William Lowndes Yancey introduced him in a grandiloquent speech, saying:

> How fortunate is our country . . . She has found in the distinguished gentleman she has called to preside over her public affairs the states- man, the soldier, and the patriot . . . The man and the hour have met.

Davis then made a milk-and-water inaugural address which dis- played a disappointing paucity of ideas and contained nothing either new or noteworthy. But if anyone in the audience was disappointed, he did not show it. Cannon boomed a salute. The Columbus Guard, from Columbus, Georgia, a crack militia outfit attired in sky-blue pants and red coats, led the parade that filed past the capitol. Bands blared martial music. Vendors hawked sweets and hot yams. Ladies tossed bouquets at their President. School children serenaded him. A fireworks display evoked admiration. It was a big day for Mont- gomery.

The proceedings were glowingly reported by a local journalist with a pen dipped in purple ink:

> Ten thousand hearts beat high with joy, admiration and hope for the new president. No man, not even George Washington was ever called on to preside over a people with more acclamation and confidence than General Davis . . .

· **2** ·

President Davis wasted little time in going about the business of government. He set up his office in the Exchange Hotel, while other governmental departments found space wherever it was available in the overcrowded city. Some functions were carried out in an abandoned factory; some took over various rooms of the state capitol.

The first practical task facing the President was the selection of a cabinet. He went about this delicate chore in a most unpractical manner. Davis operated under the assumption that it was necessary for each of the original seceded states to have a post in his cabinet. In another era, this sort of political mummery would be called "pork barreling"—but according to Davis it was the only "honorable" way to act. Those who founded the nation must be rewarded.

He tried to please everyone with the men he selected—and, as a result, succeeded in pleasing almost no one. His first cabinet was a patchwork. The wrong men were in the wrong jobs—and many who were better qualified than those selected were left outside the chambers of government.

The ill-starred first cabinet was composed of the following:

Secretary of State	Robert Toombs, Georgia
Secretary of Treasury	Christopher Memminger, South Carolina
Secretary of War	Leroy Pope Walker, Alabama
Attorney General	Judah P. Benjamin, Louisiana
Secretary of Navy	Stephen R. Mallory, Florida
Postmaster General	John H. Reagan, Texas

A great many eyebrows were raised when the cabinet appointments were announced. People wondered why such outstanding Confederates as William Lowndes Yancey, Lewis Wigfall, Howell Cobb, and Robert Barnwell Rhett had not been picked. A lot of grumbling was heard about the general lack of ability shown in the cabinet. Critics argued that this appointee or that did not qualify for the post in which he had been placed. But, for better or worse, Davis had married the Confederacy to his cabinet and that was the way it was going to be.

The Secretary of State, Robert Toombs, was a brilliant, portly man with black, flashing eyes. He had the bulk of a bear and was slovenly in his dress and manners. His chin whiskers and shirt front were often stained with tobacco juice, his clothing wrinkled and unkempt. In addition, he was vain, hot-tempered, and ambitious.

There was almost immediate friction between Toombs and Davis. At the outset, the Georgian made it clear that he had no intention of allowing himself to become chief clerk to the President.

Davis, following the pattern he had set as Pierce's Secretary of War, promptly tried to reduce his cabinet members to the status of rubber stamps. But in Robert Toombs, he had latched onto a wild

President Jefferson Davis poses with his first cabinet in Montgomery, Alabama. (L to R) Benjamin, Mallory, Memminger, Stephens, Walker, Davis, Reagan, and Toombs.

The original Lincoln cabinet lines up for a group portrait in the presidential study. (L to R) Blair, Smith, Chase, Lincoln, Seward, Cameron, Bates, and Welles.

bull. Toombs had his own ideas about the way he wanted to run his office. Clashes with the President and annoyances soon grew into animosities.

Instead of keeping his dissatisfaction within the presidential family, Toombs turned into a frustrated blowhard who went around spreading dissension everywhere and harming the Cause he dearly loved. In "Little Ellick" Stephens, his old friend, Toombs found an ardent and effective anti-Davis supporter.

They were an oddly assorted combination, these two Georgians— massive Toombs and scrawny Stephens. The talented, tormented, sickly Confederate Vice-President had had only two loves in his melancholy life. They were the United States Constitution and the sovereign state of Georgia. He had fought bitterly against secession until the final moment—and when he could no longer prevent it, he reluctantly turned his back on the Constitution and went along with the Peach Tree State in its decision.

Elevated to high position in the Confederate government, Stephens was no ardent advocate of all its aims. He firmly believed in States' Rights and was no enemy of slavery. But his ties with the Union were strong. At his insistence, the Confederate Constitution was closely modeled after that of the United States—so closely, indeed, that it was an almost perfect replica.

Nor did Stephens abandon hope for a *modus vivendi* between the two sections of the dismembered Republic. Unlike other Southern leaders, he felt Lincoln was no menace to the welfare of the South. Stephens, more than any of his colleagues, had firsthand knowledge of the man from Illinois. He had known Lincoln back in 1847 when the two men were serving as Congressional representatives. Lincoln and Stephens had both voiced opposition to the Mexican War. As a result, each respected the other, and amicable feelings were often openly expressed between them.

Two days after South Carolina's act of secession, President-Elect Abraham Lincoln wrote to his ex-colleague:

I fully appreciate the present peril the country is in and the weight of responsibility on me. Do the people of the South really entertain fears that the Republican Administration would, directly or indirectly, interfere with the slaves or with them about the slaves?

If they do, I wish to assure you, as once a friend, and still I hope, not an enemy, that there is no cause for such fear. The South would be in no more danger in this respect than it was in the days of Washington.

I suppose, however, this does not meet the case. You think slavery is right and ought to be extended while we think it is wrong and ought to be restricted. That I suppose is the rub. It certainly is the only substantial difference between us.

The difference was great enough to bring on a dreadful calamity to the nation, and to send Alexander Stephens along the road that led to Appomattox.

Where states' rights were concerned, Stephens was a zealot. Any action by Davis and the central government which, in his opinion, even slightly impinged on these cherished rights, was at once bitterly denounced by the diminutive Vice-President.

Stephens might have been an able lieutenant to Jefferson Davis. Instead, he was pushed further into the background by the President who failed to confer with him on important issues and, frequently, patently ignored him. Instead of utilizing the Georgian's fertile brain for the benefit of the Confederacy, Davis's attitude turned Stephens into a bitter and cynical enemy. It was no wonder that "Little Ellick" joined with Robert Toombs to help undermine the President in the minds and the hearts of the people.

Stephens was a proud man who had stoically born suffering and misery from birth. His frail body encased a lion's heart. This fiery-eyed dwarf was a fighter, and by snubbing him, Davis had touched the pride that had carried him through a life that would have shattered another man.

Stephens and Toombs were the keystones in the opposition that sprang up against Davis even before the Confederacy had taken its first faltering steps. It was odd that Stephens, the friend of Lincoln, should also be a friend and associate of Toombs who had shouted from the floor of the United States Senate: "Abraham Lincoln is an enemy of the human race and deserves the execration of all mankind!"

The cabinet situation was muddled. If Davis felt he could not depend on Stephens and Toombs, he surely must have had little confidence in the man he had named his Secretary of War. Leroy Pope

Walker was almost a caricature of the typical Southern gentleman. Slow-moving, he was a stickler for etiquette and gracious manners—but had no other apparent virtue to recommend him for the office he held.

Walker's appointment was the perfect example of Davis-style "pork barreling." He happened to be an Alabaman and a man from that state was needed in the cabinet, so Walker was the choice. He was certainly not the most outstanding secessionist in Alabama. Those honors went to William Lowndes Yancey—but Davis knew that in Yancey he would have a man who could neither be easily led nor be handled.

Therefore, Walker, a competent lawyer with no experience or talent for the military, sat in the War Department and Yancey was shipped off to England as an envoy to the government of Her Britannic Majesty, Queen Victoria. In England, Yancey cooled his heels in the antechamber of the Foreign Secretary, Lord John Russell, and wasted his talents in espousing the almost hopeless task of winning British recognition.

Davis, the self-styled military genius, had never intended to put a strong man in the War Department. He was the constitutional commander-in-chief—a part he played to the hilt. Every commission for every second lieutenancy had to bear his approval. His initials had to go on every requisition for shoes, blankets, cartridge boxes, rifles, knapsacks, and socks.

With nothing much to offer except a sturdy loyalty to the Cause, Walker made an excellent foil for Davis in the War Office. He agreed with everything the President said or did. As an administrator, he spent his time writing long-winded letters to every petty petitioner. He faced every circumstance with a polite smile and in an impossibly well-mannered fashion. His one foible was a mildly boastful attitude towards the potential conflict. He was firmly convinced that "one Confederate could whip ten Yankees." A cynical listener on hearing him repeat this stale boast said, "Damn it, we ain't going to be fightin' with our fists—and even a Yankee can kill a man with a bullet."

Christopher Memminger, the Secretary of Treasury, was a German-born, South Carolina–raised orphan boy. He had at least a solid foundation in banking as a qualification for assuming his job. But

the Treasurer of the Confederacy had to be more than a banker—
he needed the skills of a magician to fill the empty coffers of the
Republic.

The tactics and techniques of ordinary banking were thoroughly
understood by Memminger—but he had neither the breadth of vision
nor the imagination to carry out the difficult job he had undertaken.
A stolid, heavy-handed Teuton, oppressively earnest, Memminger
stood on his upright character—a scant distinction in a region where
honor was an expected virtue. When the times called for brilliance
and inventiveness, solidity and uprightness were poor substitutes.
Memminger plodded along trying this tack and that—but never
really achieving financial soundness for his bankrupt country.

Everyone joked about Stephen Mallory and the Confederate
Navy. Music hall comedians compared it to the Swiss Navy. But
tough Steve Mallory was no laughingstock, as he was soon to show
his critics. He went about the overwhelming task of creating a navy
—and while he never did produce a full-fledged fleet, he helped bring
on some innovations which changed the course of naval history. Not
the least of his achievements was the ironclad. Mallory also conceived the deadly commerce raiders—and even came out with the
first naval use of a submarine and an electrical torpedo.

He created the ironclads and the raiders and a fleet of river gun
boats to fight on the inland waterways. While the Rebels never came
close to matching the Union Navy, Mallory tried hard and gave the
enemy a difficult time. He ran his department well and accomplished
much. However, he suffered the least presidential interference. Fortunately for Mallory, Davis had no desire to prove he was a great
admiral as well as a great general.

Bluff John Reagan, the Postmaster General, managed to set up a
fairly efficient postal system in the face of huge odds and discourag-
ing obstacles. He held his post for the duration of the war, as did
Mallory. In a cabinet which during four years had contained three
Secretaries of State, three Attorney Generals, two Secretaries of
Treasury and six Secretaries of War, this was no small achievement.
One of the prime reasons for this feat was that Davis showed little
interest in those two departments. In his favorite, the War Office, the
most changes were effected.

The man in whom Davis placed his full confidence was Judah P.

Benjamin, nicknamed "The Brains of the Confederacy." A Barbados-born Jew whose father had owned a smoked-fish store in Charleston, South Carolina, Benjamin, the Confederate Attorney General, was brilliant, suave, and cosmopolitan.

In his youth, he had migrated to New Orleans from Charleston. He made a name for himself as a young attorney, married into a Creole family and eventually became the leading lawyer of the state, earning between $40,000 and $50,000 a year from his profession.

The son of the poverty-stricken Jewish shopkeeper also had an eminently successful political career under the guidance of John Slidell, a crafty New Yorker turned Louisianan. Slidell was a model politician, a master of every political trick. He knew he had a winner in Benjamin, and led the lawyer through the political maze so successfully that Benjamin was elected to the United States Senate.

In all the years he stood for political office, Benjamin was never once defeated for an elective post. He had a talent for winning over the voters. Not only was he a brilliant speaker, but also he had a personality charming enough to overcome the prejudices against his Jewish birth. He had a way of smiling under all circumstances which either won him admirers or earned him bitter foes.

His enemies labelled his perpetual smile "the Benjamin smirk." It has also been said of him that "if Lee was the symbol of the Confederacy, Benjamin was its antithesis . . . all his skill and erudition, all his wiliness and shrewdness were mobilized not for the good of the nation—but for Benjamin's well-being . . .".

Despite all the criticism he faced, Benjamin remained steadfast and loyal to the end. He expressed the heart of Confederate defiance in his Senate valedictory on the day Louisiana seceded:

> You may carry desolation into our peaceful land and with torch and fire you may set our cities in flames but you can never subjugate us . . . Never! Never!

It was this same spirit which carried him through the terrible days of defeat, enabled him to make his way to England, ruined and penniless, and raised him to the heights as one of that country's most noted members of the bar.

Northern decriers sneeringly referred to him as "the Jew with the heart of an Egyptian" because he so ardently espoused slavery. However, Benjamin was a product of Southern and not Jewish culture. He favored slavery as a Deep South plantation owner, because it was an economic necessity and not because he enjoyed seeing people in bondage. Like every other planter, he could not have maintained his position without slavery.

Throughout his tenure in public office, he was often the target of anti-Semitism, although he had strayed far from the faith of his fathers. He was married to a Catholic and years later was buried in a Roman Catholic cemetery in Paris.

Marvelously capable, Benjamin was wasted as Attorney General. The office had a title but no functions since no governmental court apparatus had been established. From the first, Davis relied heavily on Benjamin. Here was the man of superior mind and judgment to whom the President could turn for advice and assistance. Most important, Benjamin understood the choleric nature of his Chief; the failings of his temper and physical condition.

Davis needed a tactful man who could differ with him and yet not rasp his nerves. It was a relationship that lasted throughout the war years and into the agonizing hours of darkest failure. If Davis had a tendency to surround himself with the wrong people, Benjamin was an outstanding exception. Another was Robert E. Lee.

But, at the moment, in February, 1861, only weeks before the outbreak of war, Davis sat in his office at the Exchange Hotel, surrounded by his ill-assorted cabinet and set himself to the work of hewing out a nation.

It was ironic that this man of aristocratic pretensions should have in his cabinet so many of humble origin and background: a fishmonger's son, an immigrant orphan, a bluff Texas countryman. None of them were Southerners molded in the Davis concept of a Southerner; not one stemmed from distinguished lineage, not one was a full-fledged "gentleman."

The founders of the Confederacy had taken their stand. The next steps were to be made a thousand miles away in Washington City where each day brought closer the moment when Abraham Lincoln would place his hand on a Bible and be sworn in as the sixteenth President of the United States of America.

Twenty millions of Americans awaited that moment—and while they waited in tense expectancy, all through the South came the cadenced tread of marching men shouldering rifles that bore the stamp "U.S.A." and had lately been stored in Federal arsenals. Everywhere in the South the Old Flag was being hauled down. Men who had recently been singing "The Star Spangled Banner" were humming a new song with a lilting, catchy refrain—a song called "Dixie."

THREE

Mr. Lincoln

"In your hands, my dissatisfied fellow countrymen, and not in mine, is the momentous issue of civil war . . ."

ABRAHAM LINCOLN,
First Inaugural Address, March 4, 1861

Weeping sad and lonely,
Hopes and fears how vain!
Yet praying,
When this cruel war is over,
Praying that we meet again.

Union war song, 1861-1865

IN MARCH, 1861, Washington was a city of dark rumors carried on every breeze from the Southland. There came whispers that foretold dire events not in harmony with the budding trees and blossoming flowers. Spring arrived early that year—and the capital had been basking in vernal mildness since the last fortnight in February.

The delightful weather plus the anticipation of a presidential inauguration should have thrown the city into a festive mood. But the rumors which crept into homes and restaurants, taverns and hotels, dampened the fun.

The rumors harped constantly on the same themes: Abe Lincoln would never live to be President. Men with purpose and courage had sworn to stop the inauguration in one way or another. Wait until March 4. Just wait until Monday morning. They'd burn Washington and only ashes would be left. Black Republicans would dangle from the lampposts. Fifty, a hundred, a thousand well-armed, well-mounted, fanatical secessionists were waiting to sweep in from Maryland and Virginia to murder Lincoln, General Scott, and every other damned government official. The revolution was coming . . .

Anxiety blighted the capital city of the torn nation that pleasant spring night of Sunday, March 3. Yet, the city showed no outward signs of fear and panic. In public places, men glanced with suspicion at strangers whose pockets bulged in a shape that could be formed only by a revolver; possibly these outsiders were conspirators, assassins, or detectives—no one was sure about them; no one even dared ask questions. Still, no one appeared overly concerned or worried. That was all under the surface.

Yet that same night, Washington stirred with unaccustomed movement. Cavalry squads of the regular army clattered busily up and down Pennsylvania Avenue. Infantry patrols toured the tough slums: Negro Hill, English Hill, and Swampdoodle. The military activity had one beneficial effect: that night there were no muggings, no assaults by criminals, and only a few fist fights. This was an astonishing record for the capital, where the police were notoriously inefficient and corrupt. Crime was rampant. A man who ventured out alone in the streets after dark was either very brave or very drunk.

Everything about Washington smacked of newness and ebullience, lustiness and crudeness. It was a rough and sprawling city. Even physically, it was unfinished. In 1861, Washington was still in the process of construction. The Capitol itself swarmed with workmen. Its original dome had been declared unsafe when it developed a crack and had to be removed. The new one, of cast iron, had only its base in place and the roof of the Capitol resembled an open wide-mouthed chimney. Above the dome's base were crisscrossed scaffolds, a network of ropes, and a jutting crane that poked skyward out of the unsightly jumble.

The original sandstone building was being enlarged by the addition of two marble wings, and that project had not yet been finished. The overall effect of the Capitol jarred one. Beams, planks, marble pillars, keystones, iron plates, tools, and scraps lay scattered about haphazardly. The disorder was overwhelming. Workmen's shacks and jerry-built tool sheds dotted the grounds with their splintery ugliness. The Capitol symbolized Washington as it was—in the process of being shaped and molded.

The city planners had been ambitious; but their elaborate ideas had not yet been fulfilled. Streets, laid out so neatly by the cartographer, suddenly turned into country lanes and winding forest trails leading nowhere, even within city limits.

Washington had developed into a loosely connected series of settlements, some more densely populated than others. It had little in common with the great cities of the North—and while Southern in character, it held only the worst qualities to be found in a Southern metropolis. There was confusion, disorder, laziness, slovenliness, and a total lack of sanitation. Scores of Negroes lounged on the streets— and, if you were a Yankee, you realized with a shock that slavery existed in the District of Columbia and was sanctioned by the government.

Despite the cosmopolitan nature of its function as the governmental seat of the United States, Washington was an uncouth city lacking both dignity and charm. Only a block or two from the Capitol, hucksters peddled oysters and fish. Ducks waddled in the mudholes of the streets. People heedlessly tossed slops and garbage into gutters and canals. A constant stench poisoned the air—it came from rotting garbage and poorly disposed sewage. Pigs wallowed and rooted in the roadways, even on the grounds of Capitol Hill. Dingy boardinghouses, cheap, greasy restaurants, dismal rows of frame buildings, mean grocery shops, and scores of saloons and groggeries made up the business sections.

Pennsylvania Avenue, envisioned as an imposing boulevard on which the Capitol would confront the White House, never quite achieved the dream. The avenue was wide, but instead of providing a fine prospect, it had turned into a muddy, unsightly eyesore. No prepossessing buildings gave it elegance. It was a poorly paved, dimly lighted, ugly gash across the city from the Eastern Branch to Rock Creek; and it grew proportionately more miserable along its entire length. A contemporary observer described it as a "broad, muddy stretch of ugliness."

The thin layer of cobblestone laid down as pavement soon crumbled under the heavy traffic which plied the thoroughfare from the Capitol to Georgetown. The iron-rimmed wheels of lumbering wagons and omnibuses pulverized the stones. Faulty drainage caused the roadbed to sink in many places and the road was pockmarked with deep holes that were usually filled with stinking, stagnant water. In dry weather, the dust was choking; rain turned the Avenue into a treacherous bog with a particularly obnoxious brand of clinging yellowish mud.

On the north side of the street, in the vicinity of the Capitol, were the better restaurants, shops, and hotels. Here, the sidewalk was made of brick and served as the main promenade. On the south side, the focal point was the Central Market, a grubby bazaar; an array of sheds, shacks and hovels, which backed on the canal into which a noisome flood of sewage poured constantly.

The several hotels—the National, the Metropolitan, the Kirkwood, and Willard's—were huge, ungainly buildings devoid of any attractiveness. The National, at one time, had enjoyed a reputation as the most popular hostelry. But shortly after Buchanan was inaugurated, an epidemic of intestinal illness struck its patrons. Buchanan himself had been one of the victims, and his nephew died as a result of the food poisoning suffered there.

Since the National was a favorite rendezvous for Southern Congressmen, a wild story had circulated that the mass poisoning resulted from a Republican plot to kill off the leaders of the Democratic party. Investigation revealed that the trouble had emanated from a more mundane cause; sewage gas had seeped into the kitchen and tainted the food. Consequently, the National suffered a decline in business and popularity even after repairs had eliminated the sewage gas.

Willard's, the largest and most patronized caravansary, was located at 14th Street and Pennsylvania Avenue. Washington social life centered around the hotel. Politicians and lobbyists came there to see and be seen; careerists hung around its bars and public rooms; deals were made at the dinner table in its enormous dining saloon. Cynics swore that the seat of the United States government was not the Capitol, but the saloon in Willard's.

The hostelry was noted for its astounding menu which displayed an assortment of items that could ruin one's digestive system. For breakfast alone, one could order fried oysters, thick beefsteaks, clams, *pâté de foie gras*, *blanc mange*, turkey, duck, chicken, and roast beef. The midday meals and dinners were no less impressive; and it was not uncommon for determined office seekers to consume three such improbable meals daily while entertaining politicos who might help them in their ambitions.

To those without vision, Washington would always remain as it was in 1861—a mudhole surrounded by half-completed pillars, columns and porticoes. Although work had begun on the capital at the turn of the century, it still gave the impression that the first foundations had barely been dug.

According to Henry Adams who spent much time in Washington: "As in 1800 and 1850, so in 1860, it was the same rude colony camped in the same forest, with the same unfinished Greek temples for workrooms, and sloughs for roads." Another contemporary observer pointedly remarked: "In sixty years, men may build a small city—but not Rome."

Wherever one looked about the capital he saw the pretentious efforts to duplicate the Eternal City. Classical structures had to house the government; Corinthian columns; splendid, heroic statues; an obelisk to commemorate the Father of the Country, which stood only one-third completed on a mud flat; and a half dozen magnificent buildings, frescoed, muraled, and extravagantly decorated— these were the only results of more than a half century's efforts.

· 2 ·

Despite its physical crudity, Washington boasted a social set. This aristocracy lived graciously on the outskirts of the city in suburban Georgetown and in the better sections of town. They lived in excellently furnished houses of red brick, surrounded by walled gardens blooming with a profusion of flowers. In the more distant environs of the city were fine estates and wooded areas, ideal spots for picnicking in good weather.

The hub of the social elite was the so-called Southern "chivalry": Virginians from the Tidewater, Bourbon politicians, cotton planters, and slaveowners. Abolitionists and Republicans were rarely admitted to the most select circles. Only gallant Southerners and their sympathizers were freely accepted. Foreign diplomats with elegant manners were always welcome. They jibed with the behavior standards imposed by Washington blue bloods.

A correspondent of the New York *Herald* once sarcastically described Washington in these terms: "It is the abode of a very slow and respectable people who cool themselves during the hot weather by the delightful remembrance that they are of gentle blood."

In 1861, Washington's social arbiters had shown in words and deeds where they stood on the grim questions of the hour. Almost unanimously, they supported "brave" South Carolina and her secessionist sister states. The capital city's society clique deplored the election of the "clod from Illinois." They bemoaned the fate of the nation now in the hands of "abolitionist fanatics." But worst of all, worse even than the antislavery "oppressors," was the new President. How could such a western bumpkin fit in with people like themselves—persons of refinement and culture? This election was a certain indication of the level to which the United States had sunk. Small wonder South Carolina had resorted to secession and that the cotton states had followed her glorious example.

In another day, Abraham Lincoln was scheduled to become the sixteenth President of the United States. The consequences that would follow were certain to have a bearing on the destinies of thousands—and, the Washington smart set believed, would mark the end of the nation that had been born eighty-five years before. A wag pointed out how easy it was to transpose a letter and turn the name of the country into the "Untied States."

The uneasy Sabbath passed. As darkness fell on Washington a battery of artillery rolled into place near the Treasury Building. Two more batteries clattered over the cobblestones and swung into positions at the Capitol. Troops came marching up and deployed around the partially repaired structure.

These maneuvers were skillfully conducted. Blue-uniformed Regular Army artillerists readied their pieces for action in minutes. No matter how muddied the political scene, the army was still the army. Under any conditions, discipline and training showed. The Regular Army establishment was small—but its components were professionals and every man knew his job.

The supreme military commander, Lieutenant General Winfield Scott, was fifteen years older than the national capital. At seventy-five, he no longer could heave his unseemly bulk into the saddle. He tottered painfully on swollen, dropsical legs. His thoughts usually ran along gustatory, not military lines. Scott was a sagging ruin, a quivering heap of flesh. He grunted and wheezed like a blue-ribbon hog and was a caricature of the glorious days when he had been the country's golden warrior.

Yet despite his infirmities and the bloated ugliness of his body, the General was still a soldier, and a good one. That fateful Sunday night, he sat ponderously at his desk, staring with rheumy eyes at a map of the city. His pudgy finger pointed to this place or that, and he whispered hoarsely to his military secretary, Lieutenant Colonel Erasmus D. Keyes; notes were jotted down and the necessary orders given in the General's name.

The old man was aware of the calamitous effects that might take place if he overlooked even the smallest detail of security precaution. Scott moved his few men to cover potential danger spots like a master chess player. The blue protective line was stretched thin. District Militia Companies were riddled through with secession sympathizers and it was not a happy time for the old soldier.

But somehow, Scott's very presence in Washington seemed to bring an air of comfort to the Unionists. To them it mattered little that he was decrepit and enfeebled. The mere knowledge that the venerable hero had taken charge of the city's defences was sufficient. He symbolized past prowess and glory. Many found security in the

Once Lieutenant General Winfield Scott had been a golden warrior. But in April, 1861, he was seventy-five years old, a sagging, tired hulk. The North looked to this weary soldier as its leader in the struggle for the Union.

greatness of his past. The General was an old, weary man. But, to the frightened North, he was the strong father who would shelter them from the dangers lurking in the dark.

Although Scott was a Virginian, his fealty belonged to the Federal government. He was commander of the Army and for over a score of years, the military destinies of the country had been guided by him. A grateful government and an adoring people had not been reluctant to shower him with honors. Only one man before him had worn the three stars of a Lieutenant General—George Washington.

During the years of Scott's tenure as top man of the Army, nearly every important military position had been filled by Southerners. They had a practical monopoly on the Army.

Of the six military departments into which the country was subdivided, only one, the Department of the East, was headed by a Northerner—aged General John E. Wool, a hero of the Mexican War. Nobody saw anything odd in this state of affairs. The Southern officers were invariably high-spirited men with the habit of command. Scott liked them personally. They were crack soldiers and stemmed from his own cultural background.

This Southern grip on the Regular Army had an interesting side effect. Many Northerners who had forged distinguished records at West Point and were eager for an army career, soon found the upper echelons of the military establishment were in reality a private club that worked along discriminatory policies. Promotions above field grade were seldom given Northerners. This tacit pro-Southern favoritism drove a lot of Northerners from the army. Outstanding cadets like Henry W. Halleck, George B. McClellan, Joe Hooker, Ambrose E. Burnside, William T. Sherman, William S. Rosecrans and numerous others—all ambitious men, frustrated by the lack of opportunity for personal advancement in the army—resigned and entered civil life.

When war broke out, dozens of excellent Union officers who would soon prove their merit on the battlefield returned to the service from private careers. Had these staunch Unionists not been limited by Southern domination of the military in the prewar years, the complexion of the Civil War, especially in its early days, would surely have been altered. Among the officers who remained loyal to the Old Flag, only the two ancients—Scott and Wool—had ever commanded units larger than a brigade. This was not the case with the Confederate army.

But, on this inauguration eve, which some people gloomily predicted would be the last ever held under the Stars and Stripes, those soldiers still true to the Union did their duty unflinchingly. Despite personal feelings, Southern officers from states which had not yet seceded, remained at their posts.

The Regular Army enlisted men were hardened professionals. Like policemen, they took no political stand and simply obeyed orders. If the command were given to send grapeshot into a secessionist gang attempting to storm the Capitol, the lanyard would be pulled, even if the gunner recognized his own father in the assaulting crowd.

Troops filed off into the night. Lonely sentries leaned on their bayonetted rifles and peered into the shadows. From somewhere on the untidy Capitol grounds came the aroma of boiling coffee being prepared over a tiny, twinkling campfire. Not even the prospect of national crisis could dim the soldiers' taste for the brew. And somehow the sight of men gathered around a fire sipping coffee from their mess cups was a reassuring one. It was familiar and homely and recognizable—and pointed up the fact that everything had not been turned topsy-turvy.

By daybreak, the military preparations were completed. Scott had assigned the six hundred-odd regulars under his immediate command to the most vital points. When the President-elect proceeded from Willard's, where he was staying, to the Capitol, crack troops were already detailed to guard his carriage. En route, carefully selected marksmen were to be stationed on rooftops and in windows with orders to "shoot to kill anyone attempting to use a weapon or to interfere in any way with orderly procedure."

Underneath the temporary speakers' platform that had been erected in front of the Capitol steps, fifty sharpshooters were posted to cover the crowd from every direction. The old general had tried to plug every gap; where bayonets and bullets could protect the new President, Scott had placed his men. Whatever was to happen now, would happen.

Fifty years of soldiering had taught him to prepare for the expected and to anticipate the unexpected. At last, he folded his hands on his huge stomach and sat nodding at his desk. His bulk sagged even more as he slept; the man carried too many responsibilities and too many burdens—not the least of which were his years. But people still saw him as an heroic figure endowed with a capacity for superhuman achievement. To the adulating public he was still the stern, hard-eyed soldier of Chapultepec, strong and fearless, a dashing hero. Now, the whole North was taking its own strength from him—but the old man had gone beyond endurance. He had no more strength to give . . .

· 3 ·

In the midst of the inaugural preparations, the troop movements, the parade planning, and the busy rapping of carpenters' hammers making last-minute additions to the platform on the Capitol grounds, Washington was deluged by an invasion of outsiders. For days, every stagecoach, river boat, and train had been disgorging hordes of triumphant Republicans at depots and landings. The visitors had come for the inaugural ceremonies. They not only swelled the population and taxed every facility in the city, but also complicated the security problem.

Thousands of gawking tourists converged on Pennsylvania Avenue, gaping and staring at the partly finished buildings and the uncompleted magnificence of their capital. Even the dingiest and filthiest rooming house had no bed for rent. The hotels were crammed, with cots being set up in alcoves and lobbies. Fantastic rates were being paid for a mattress on the floor of a hallway or a parlor. Queues that ran for a block stretched before every restaurant and the prices for the most inferior food soared to incredible levels.

Among the throngs of visitors to Washington were many dignitaries: congressmen, ex-congressmen; senators and ex-senators; twenty-seven governors and former governors. In the main, the crowds were types familiar to the capital. Everyone had already seen tippling Baltimore plugs, New York ward heelers, and twangy-voiced New Englanders. Prominent personages were no novelty to the sanguine Washingtonians. But the taciturn, tobacco-chewing Westerners who had thronged in by every possible means of conveyance added something new to Pennsylvania Avenue.

Although obviously unused to city ways, they were canny, and steered clear of sharpers, bunco artists, streetwalkers, and gyps.

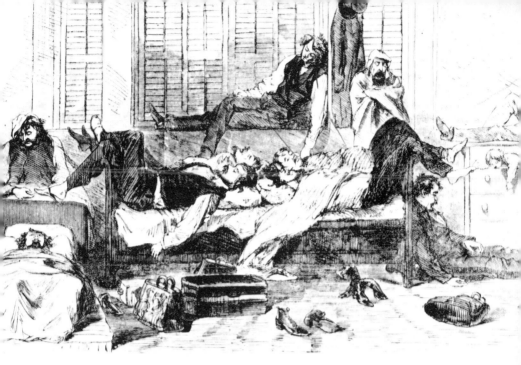

Overflow crowds poured into Washington for the Lincoln inauguration. Hotels were jammed beyond capacity and scenes like this were common.

Chief Justice Roger Taney administers the oath of office to Abraham Lincoln at the Capitol, on March 4, 1861. Among the onlookers are ex-President James Buchanan and, standing beside him, the "Little Giant," Stephen A. Douglas.

Deft-fingered pickpockets were thwarted because these wily prairie and mountain men had secured their wallet pockets by pinning them.

These lean, windburned, and sunburned men and their calico-clad women had traveled many miles to see Abe Lincoln installed as President. He was one of them—and they spoke of him as a member of the family. There was no need to put on a splash for Abe. No sense throwing greenbacks around foolishly, drinking hogwash whisky and raising a fuss. In the first place, the Westerners were loath to part with hard-earned dollars; and, despite the shortage of sleeping accommodations, a Westerner would rather walk out of a lodging-house where space was available than pay the exorbitant profiteering price demanded. Sleeping in a hallway or under a tree represented small discomfort to them—men and women alike.

The spate of visitors brought a bonanza to Washington's numerous whores and gamblers. But if that influx had been mainly from the West, the trollops and card sharps would have entertained few customers. They had no experience in dealing with people who gladly walked a mile rather than take a hack and who cheerfully lugged heavy valises for blocks in preference to paying a porter his two-bit fee. They were austere, hard-working, and diligent folks—the men and women who had broken the plains and turned arid reaches into fertile fields. They were not without humor, but their fun was earthy and crude—a rough-and-tumble people filled with gusty laughter and unshakable loyalties. Still sparked by the ardor of the pioneers, they were fiercely devoted to the Union in a manner only hard-scrabble farmers like New England's down-Easters could understand.

A hope of the Confederacy was that the West would secede from the Union and either join forces with the South or form its own independent confederation of states. It was a baseless hope, for while there were elements in the Western states which might be susceptible to Southern cajolery, the bulk of the population was scornful of the slavocracy—and ready to prove it by sending the young men off to bleed and die for the federal government and the Old Flag.

Now, these people had journeyed to Washington to see Old Abe stand before them, place his hand on the Good Book, and swear to uphold the Constitution of the United States. The inauguration, they felt, was a solemn business, coming as it did at a time when the "secesh" were tearing down the Stars and Stripes. Abe Lincoln needed men with knobby fists and clear heads behind him—not whisky-swilling bums and roisterers . . .

One of Washington's main attractions proved to be Willard's. Thousands milled about in the streets surrounding the hotel, hoping to catch a glimpse of its most distinguished guest, Abraham Lincoln. The lanky Springfield lawyer was comfortably ensconced in the hostelry's most luxurious suite, Parlor No. 6, an impressive corner apartment on the second floor with a good view of Pennsylvania Avenue and the grounds of the White House.

The secession crisis beclouded Lincoln's greatest triumph, the apogee of a difficult life. His climb from the obscurity and poverty of a frontier boyhood to the Executive Mansion had been a glorious accomplishment. Quite unlike Jefferson Davis, Lincoln had had no big brother Joe to pave his way. Nor had his keen knowledge of people been attained from books—although he was an avid reader—but through the arduous struggles of everyday existence.

A streak of historical irony pitted Lincoln against Davis. The Southerner was the epitome of a social class diametrically opposite to all that Lincoln represented. The man from Illinois knew nothing of plantation life. He had none of the qualities by which slave-owning Southerners judged a man. He dressed badly, his movements were awkward, he told jokes which roiled Southern sensibilities, he smacked of the rough, unpolished frontier. Yet despite his ungainly deportment, shrill Western speech, gauche manners, and careless dress, even those who were not his followers were quick to concede that the man had a winning personality. And only his most ardent enemies denied that Abe Lincoln possessed a high order of integrity, human decency and courage.

What Lincoln lacked in polish, he made up in sound common sense, mother wit and inborn sagacity. Compared to his Confederate opposite number, Lincoln was an uncouth yokel. Davis, on the other hand, was blessed with all the appearances of leadership, with his grave mien, gracious dignity, and burning eyes. But his clinical manner divorced him from the masses—and it was a serious personality defect.

The Confederate's weakness was Lincoln's greatest strength. The masses loved him. He was their spokesman and inspiration—tangible proof of the American dream that someone of humble origins could make his way to the top. Labor knew Lincoln was its friend.

As far back as 1847, at the inception of his political career, he had written:

> Inasmuch as most good things are produced by labor, it follows that all such things of right belong to those whose labor has produced them. But it has so happened, in all ages of the world, that some have labored and others have without labor enjoyed a large proportion of the fruits. This is wrong and should not continue. To secure to each laborer the whole product of his labor, or as nearly as possible, is a worthy object of any good government.

A wide gulf of class and concept separated Lincoln and Davis. The latter held himself superior to the working class. Lincoln, who had, himself, been a workingman, tendered to the working class both respect and friendship.

Abraham Lincoln was born February 12, 1809, on a miserable backwoods Kentucky farm. Sam Davis, father of the Confederate President, and Abe's father, Tom Lincoln, were men with much in common. Restless, sturdy pioneer types who could swing an axe and walk behind a plow, they were hardy products of their frontier environment.

If Sam Davis had visions of middle-class respectability, similar ambitions never touched Tom Lincoln. He was satisfied to struggle on one small patch of dirt or another—and showed no interest in obtaining an education for his son. Such nonsense, Tom Lincoln believed, wasn't for the likes of him or his kin.

Young Abe differed from his father's views. This typical frontier youth who grew to manhood in the still untracked country of Indiana had a burning need to read and write and study. He had much more to him than was apparent on the surface. To the casual observer, there was nothing exceptional about Abe Lincoln. He was merely another strong, gangling country lad who enjoyed lazing in the sun, telling rollicking stories, and playing foolish pranks. He could outwrestle and outrun most of his friends. He was exactly like any other youth of his time and place.

Even as a young man, Abe Lincoln knew popularity. The loungers at the crossroads store were tickled by his rib-splitting yarns and always delighted to be in his company. However, nobody really thought Tom Lincoln's boy would ever amount to anything. Some regarded him as a clown and a buffoon; but he was not the outgoing jester he seemed. Underneath, he was a lonely, introspective youth, uneasy with himself, and terribly shy with women.

Abraham Lincoln migrated to New Salem, Illinois, from Indiana. It was a pioneer village of log cabins. Cows roamed the single, dusty main street. Pigs snuffled around the cabins. Produce-laden farm wagons rolled through New Salem. Barefooted children played noisily around the village pump. Loungers squirted tobacco juice under the noontime sun. New Salem was only a settlement, but compared to the isolated backwoods, Abe Lincoln found it a teeming metropolis.

He liked the village and flourished there during his adolescent years. People began hearing about the lanky young fellow who expressed some pretty smart ideas on political questions. Because he was brash and ambitious, New Salem became too confining for Lincoln. He moved to Springfield, the bustling state capital—and there he spent the major part of his life, building a law career and developing a growing importance in the state's political arena.

Lincoln's political rise was swift. He gained the approbation of the electorate. The voters knew and respected him for his honesty and frankness. They tagged him with the nickname "Honest Abe." It was not a misnomer, although Lincoln was no naive, open-faced bumpkin. He was capable of shrewdness, subterfuge and sharp tactics masked by a carefully nurtured, highly disarming awkwardness and shuffling diffidence. Many a courtroom opponent had been drawn in by Lincoln's apparent fumbling—only to be trapped when he grew careless.

Affiliation with the Whig party brought Lincoln his first elective post—the voters selected him for the state legislature. After several terms in that office, he stood for Congress and was successful. Lincoln was emerging as a real power in Illinois politics. But his high road to political success ended in the Mexican War. The Whig party policy was to embarrass the Polk administration by objecting to the war, but not opposing it to the point of hamstringing the war effort. The Whigs slapped at the administration whenever the opportunity presented. Lincoln was one of the most outspoken of the Whig bloc in Congress. He spoke out, not only because of party discipline, but also because he had strong convictions that this war was wrongful.

In 1849, when his congressional term ran out, Lincoln found that his Mexican War stand had effectively damaged his chances for re-election. The Whig party bosses felt he was no longer of use to them, and, worse than that, the voters did not seem to care about the rightness or wrongness of the recent conflict.

All they knew was that the army had won a great victory; the Stars and Stripes waved over vast new territory; the conquerors had come marching home flushed and glowing with their valorous deeds over a weak and disorganized enemy. The army had wiped out its shameful performance in the War of 1812. The American citizen-soldier had demonstrated, in Mexico, that the volunteers could fight; on another level they had also clearly shown that they drank to excess, pillaged with zeal, maltreated women, and generally carried on brutally and boorishly. But nobody gave their wrong-doings a second thought; nobody recalled the filth and the blood and the misery. War was fun—especially when you were on the victorious side.

So Lincoln returned to Springfield and found that his erstwhile supporters had turned from him and that the party bosses were giv-ing him the cold shoulder. Sure, they said, Abe Lincoln was smart and honest, but he had been smeared with antiwar paint. The Whigs were in enough hot water over the party's war stand and it just didn't make sense to back a man who had been too outspoken. As a result, Lincoln was dead, politically. Now forty years old, the back-woods lawyer regarded himself as a complete and dismal failure. He found small comfort in his law work and his home life offered no solace to his melancholy moods.

In 1842, he had married Mary Todd, a high-spirited, stormy, and socially prominent Kentucky belle, after a turbulent courtship. Mary was a self-willed, tyrannical woman accustomed to having her own way in everything. Because of her background, she felt herself socially far superior to Lincoln. Emotionally unstable, she bedeviled her husband by her peculiar antics; but there was never any doubt of his love for her. In her own fashion, she returned his love. Lincoln treated her with unfailing kindness and understanding even in her worst tantrums. From the depths of mutual weaknesses, Abe Lincoln and his wife drew from each other deep and abiding strength.

Mary Todd was no timid woman—when it came time to fight, she could battle fiercely. In those dark days after the Whig leaders and the voters deserted Lincoln, Mary buttressed him against his desire to leave Springfield forever. She instilled in him her will to fight and made him stand his ground. He was tempted to accept an offer as governor of Oregon Territory but Mary remained firm. She made him see that instead of sulking on the far frontier, his place was in Springfield where he could devote himself to building up his law practise. He accepted her decision and, as a result, soon restored all the prestige he had lost during that disastrous term in Congress.

· 4 ·

For some years, Lincoln dedicated himself to the law. He made frequent trips around the Eighth Judicial Circuit which he served as a traveling lawyer. This brought him into many quarters of the state and he became both a familiar and popular figure all over Illinois.

An excellent lawyer, Lincoln was able, quick-witted, and scrupulous. He once quit a case at its most critical phase when he discovered his client had not been truthful. Lincoln strode out of the court, went to his hotel room and sent the judge a message: "My hands are dirty and I came here to clean them."

He became in time one of the state's leading attorneys. Railroads, corporations, banks, and prominent individuals sought his services. Despite certain deficiencies in his legal education, he was a tremendously successful jury pleader. "If I can get it past the technicalities and into the hands of the jury, I'll win it," he often said in pretrial discussions of a case.

As Lincoln's skill and reputation increased during the ensuing five years, he developed new confidence and a feeling of importance which he had previously lacked. He was now a man of means, well-regarded not only in Springfield, but also throughout the state. The very politicians who had spurned him back in '49 began eying him with interest and started dangling visions of elective office before him as an incentive to re-enter the political scene.

It was, finally, neither the blandishments of the politicians nor his own ambition which impelled Lincoln to take up political cudgels again. He returned to fight the Kansas-Nebraska Act of 1854, a measure introduced by Senator A. C. Dodge of Iowa and supported by the "Little Giant" from Illinois, bombastic Stephen Douglas.

The Act, which was designed to supersede the Missouri Compromise of 1850, provided that settlers of all new territories, no matter where located, might decide their own status—slave or free. The law.invoked a principle known as "squatter sovereignty," which simply meant that the side having the most people in a given place at voting time would control that territory; it was this concept which opened the sluice gates of hatred that was soon to engulf the country in the bloody tide of civil war.

Kansas was turned into a recruiting ground for proslavery and freestate quasimilitary bands. Abolitionists led by Henry Ward Beecher sent packing cases marked "Bibles" to their supporters in Kansas. When opened, the cases contained Sharps rifles and forty rounds of ammunition for each gun—not the Good Book. These weapons became known as "Beecher's Bibles." Secret organizations were formed all over the territory. Men identified each other with mysterious handclasps and strange passwords. In some parts of the region if a man was not "sound on the goose"—that is, a proslaver— he would be shot on the spot as an abolitionist. Slavery sympathizers were treated with no more regard by the other side. Kansas seethed. Raiders galloped through the darkness leaving a trail of burning houses and barns, poisoned herds, ruined crops, and, too frequently, weeping women, suddenly widowed. Both sides perpetrated such outrages. They were an outgrowth of the Kansas-Nebraska Act.

Lincoln, aroused as he never had been before, threw himself energetically into the struggle against the bill. In five years he had changed drastically. Intellectually, he had matured; the disappointments of the past, the torments of his personal life had taught him forbearance and had added a soberness to his demeanor. He was no longer brash and headstrong; his thought processes had become disciplined and he had developed the art of managing men. And, although his wife still looked askance at his social manners, he had developed a pleasant polish without losing the charming insouciance of the past.

If Lincoln had changed since the days of his enforced political retirement, the country had also undergone startling metamorphoses during the same half decade. The slavery controversy, briefly quiescent, now raged with disturbing fury. The states were torn asunder.

Fratricidal guerrilla warfare flared in Kansas. Sectional animosities rose daily.

Beneficial changes had taken place as well. The very nature of the country, most specially Lincoln's own beloved Northwest, had been altered. It was drifting from an agricultural toward an industrial economy. Canals and waterways, highways and railroads, were bringing great wealth and power into the section from the east. The importance of north-south river traffic was diminishing; faster and less cumbersome connections were growing along the east-west routes.

New alignments doomed the moribund Whigs and developed a fresh, vital organization formed on an almost completely sectional basis. Lincoln rose quickly in the ranks of the new Republican Party. He staked his political future around the slavery issue. No longer was Lincoln merely imbued with aspirations for public office; his ambitions were now strengthened by deep principles regarding slavery. He was firmly and indelibly against further extension of the "peculiar institution." He believed slavery was not only anachronistic and feudal, but also polluted the morals of the nation.

In numerous speeches he urged the country to rally solidly and to placate the South no more by further compromise. This was a time for determined political resistance and not equivocation, he declared. He felt that if slavery was not allowed to spread and kept within the areas where it presently flourished, it would wither away of its own accord.

Lincoln understood how deeply rooted the institution was in Southern tradition; unlike the abolitionists, he did not demand slavery must be wiped out at once. No matter how disagreeable the thought of human bondage might be, slaveowners enjoyed constitutional protection; any move to separate them suddenly from their property would certainly have evil consequences.

Although he proposed some gradual form of eventual emancipation, with proper compensation for slaveowners, Lincoln rejected the use of force and did not subscribe to the mournful prophets who gloomily predicted war between the states over the question.

Lincoln had forged a credo for himself on the matter of slavery— and now he attempted to set a course which would not violate these principles . . .

· 5 ·

National interest concerning Lincoln began to grow in the years between 1854–1860 as he gradually emerged from his former obscurity, especially during his famed series of debates with the fiery advocate of "squatter sovereignty"—Stephen Douglas. During those historic arguments, Lincoln's stand on slavery earned him the hatred of the South and a large following in the North. As a result of his increasing repute, Lincoln was chosen as the Republican candidate for Senate in 1856 and again in 1858—both times being defeated by his nemesis, Douglas.

In June, 1858, Lincoln made a momentous speech when he accepted the Republican senatorial nomination. His words electrified the nation:

A house divided against itself cannot stand. I believe that this government cannot endure permanently half-slave and half-free. I do not expect the house to fall . . . but I do expect it will cease to be divided . . . it will become all one thing or another.

Enraged howls rose in the South. "Warmonger!" the Southerners shouted at Lincoln. "Provocation!" they cried.

All through the Northern states, political bosses turned for a closer look at the Republican from Illinois. The President-makers, the back-room boys, puffed on their cigars and began thinking seriously about Lincoln, whose words crackled with wisdom and understanding, as the potential Republican candidate for the elections of '60.

Although he was not yet the man of the hour, Lincoln had piled up impressive returns during his two unsuccessful attempts to unseat Senator Douglas. Despite the tarnish of defeat, he loomed larger than ever on the Illinois political scene and his gawky shadow began to spread across the Northern tier of states.

Lincoln, personally, did not even hope for the nomination in '60. He felt he could play a useful role in the campaign and if a victory was forthcoming for the Republicans, might even be rewarded for his endeavors with a cabinet post.

But the choice of a Republican candidate was still wide open, and became even more of a scramble as the national crisis continued to deepen. In October, 1859, the bearded fanatic of the plains, John

Brown, with the blood of the Pottawatomie massacre still staining his hands, made his futile raid on Harper's Ferry and the nation quivered in dread.

The atmosphere grew increasingly frenzied and early in 1860, Lincoln visited New York City where he delivered an address before several thousand people in the great hall of Cooper Union. The speech outlined the Republican position on slavery, masterfully tracing the history of the institution from its inception in the colonies.

The brilliant Cooper Union address brought Lincoln sharply to the attention of Eastern Republican leaders. They began to see him as a potential standard bearer with an appealing quality which could rally the masses of voters. And while he was still only a possibility to Easterners, energetic men in his home state began working enthusiastically to win him the Republican nomination when the party held its convention in Chicago on May 14.

Lincoln's self-appointed managers included Jesse W. Fell, Leonard Swett, Ward Hill Lamon, David Davis, Joseph Medill, Norman Judd, and others. The group was headed by David Davis, a mountain of shrewdness, who tipped the scales at more than 300 pounds. He was influential, wealthy, and fearless—a sagacious and crafty political brawler who knew his way around smoke-filled rooms. Davis had been a judge in the Eighth Judicial Circuit and was a long-time intimate of Lincoln. He admired Lincoln's humor, his superior mind and integrity as a human being. The other Lincoln drum beaters were as enthusiastic about their candidate, and each of the men on the Lincoln strategy board was a power both in Illinois and on the national scene as well.

But if others saw him as presidential timber, Abe was less certain of himself than were his sponsors. He wrote Jesse Fell:

What's the use of talking of me for President, when we have such men as Seward, Chase, and others who are much better known and whose names are so intimately associated with the principles of the Republican Party? Everybody knows them. No one, scarcely, outside of Illinois knows me. Besides, is it not a matter of justice, due to such men, who have carried this movement forward to its present status in spite of fearful opposition, personal abuse, and bad names. I think so.

Even this self-deprecation could not stop the appreciable ground swell building up in favor of Lincoln. By the time the Republican convention opened in May a large bloc of Lincoln supporters existed among the delegates who had converged on Chicago, although smart money was being placed on Senator William H. Seward to be chosen as the candidate.

Seward, the Mr. Republican of his day, had a long and distinguished career of public service. He had been elected to the governorship of New York State at the age of thirty-seven, the youngest man ever to hold that post. A brilliant speaker, Seward was still active and vigorous despite his sixty years. His ardent espousal of unpopular causes had earned him many enemies. As an antislavery spokesman, Seward was despised in the South. His battles on behalf of the foreign-born won him the gratitude and friendship of immigrant Americans and the hatred of supernationalists, Know-Nothings, Barn-Burners, and the like. From the time of his governorship to the day of his death, New York's foreign-born citizens worshiped Seward as their hero and protector.

The wily New York Republican boss, Thurlow Weed, had long regarded Seward as his protégé. Weed was determined to make his man the first Republican President. He went to the convention exuding confidence. None of the potential nominees came close to Seward's fine public record. He was the leading light in the Republican party—a man eminently qualified for the presidency although he had many political enemies, far inferior men who, while unable to further their own presidential aspirations, were determined to balk Seward's.

Among others, this group included handsome, arrogant Senator Salmon P. Chase of Ohio, whose public life was as successful as his personal life had been filled with heartbreak and tragedy. In seventeen years, he had endured the deaths of three wives and four children. These ordeals, enough to crush a weaker man, instilled Chase with a burning drive for power and fame. His ambitions were fanned by his daughter, Kate, one of the most beautiful women of her day. She was proud, selfish, and ruthless in promoting her father's aspirations.

Like Seward, Chase thought he was entitled to the nomination. In his vanity, he believed the Chicago convention would bring his dreams of the presidency to fruition. But he, too, had made enemies on his upward climb—and some of them were members of the Ohio delegation. Not even in his native state could Chase be assured of unanimity.

Simon Cameron was another aspirant for the candidacy. The scheming Pennsylvanian, called the "Political Czar of the Keystone State," was said to "reek with the stench of a thousand shady deals." Only in one area of his political life was Cameron honest and forthright. He was sincerely and wholeheartedly against slavery. But that was not enough; Cameron was disliked by most Republican leaders. He could not even count on the Pennsylvania delegation where the anti-Cameron forces were led by an ardent Lincoln supporter, John Curtin, the gubernatorial candidate.

There were other likely choices for the Republican nomination— but for one reason or another there was a lack of enthusiasm for any one of them.

The convention appeared hopelessly split over the leading contenders, and as a result, the name of Lincoln was heard more frequently in the caucus rooms and among the knots of whispering delegates. He seemed to be the logical dark horse. He was not yet prominent enough to have created strong enmities. Both the radical and conservative wings of the party found something to like in him. He had assets which wily political bosses appreciated: his public record was clean and required neither excuses nor defence; his humble background and hard-won success made him popular with the masses. Lincoln became increasingly attractive as a potential candidate.

He dropped his reluctance when his friends proved to him that he had an outside chance to gain the nomination. The presidency was a goal to which he had never aspired—but once the possibility of achieving it had whetted his ambition, Lincoln showed as much avidity as any man in pursuing the post. He began taking an active interest in the efforts being put forward to promote him, and shortly before the convention, he wrote to an Ohio supporter:

My name is new in the field and I suppose I am not the first choice of a very great many. Our policy then, is to give no offence to others— leave them in a mood to come to us, if they shall be impelled to give up their first love.

The convention was held in a huge plank structure erected for the purpose by the city of Chicago. It held an audience of ten thousand delegates and spectators. The rambling, jerry-built building was called the Wigwam. And, there, in that rickety, splintery pile, the Republicans met to choose a candidate in an atmosphere of treachery, mistrust and ill will. Hulking David Davis ran Lincoln's floor campaign with a fine display of flimflammery, connivance, and shrewdness. He used every trick to influence delegates, and by the time the nominating session of the convention was called to order on Friday, May 18, 1860, Davis had gained considerable support.

Senators Seward, Chase, and Cameron were placed in nomination, as were Edward Bates of Missouri and the favorite sons of various states. Nominating speeches evoked the usual hoopla that still persists in present-day political conventions—cheering, parading, stamping, whistling—all the outward manifestations of alleged enthusiasm. Mainly, the hallooing gave the bored delegates a chance to let off steam, although much significance was placed on the fervidness of the ovation on behalf of each candidate. Campaign managers carefully staged "spontaneous" acclamations for their hopefuls. Some put on pretty good shows.

But when Norman Judd nominated Abraham Lincoln, the outburst that greeted his name overshadowed all the rest. An eyewitness later described the Lincoln demonstration in these terms:

> The wild yell that went up made soft vesper breathings of all that had preceded. No language can describe it. A thousand steam whistles, ten acres of hotel gongs, a tribe of Comanches headed by a choice vanguard from pandemonium, might have mingled in the scene unnoticed . . .

The level of enthusiasm for Lincoln was a good example of management by David Davis. Keenly aware of the need for an ardent Lincoln demonstration after Judd's speech, Davis huddled with Ward Hill Lamon and Jesse Fell; a strategy was evolved. Lamon and Fell found a printer who was willing to counterfeit the gallery admission tickets to the Wigwam. These were handed out to Lincoln sympathizers by the hundreds. By the time Judd spoke, the hall was jammed with vociferous Lincolnites. Arguments and fights flared up outside the Wigwam when bonafide ticket holders arrived to find the place filled to capacity. Lamon ignored the confusion and calmly posted claques at strategic spots. When Lincoln was officially nominated, the shills broke out in the wildest and most frenzied display of the convention.

Delegates were impressed by the unexpected enthusiasm for Lincoln. The ruse had worked; unpledged delegations turned to Lincoln, while others, backing weaker candidates, scuttled their men to get behind the dark horse from Illinois.

The first two ballots were indecisive, with no candidate gaining enough votes to be awarded the nomination. Between roll calls, Davis and his aides were busy. They buttonholed delegation chairmen and begged, blustered, and bought votes. Davis pledged the Indiana group that its chief political hack, Caleb B. Smith, would be made Secretary of the Interior and that William P. Dole, another Hoosier ward heeler, could have the Commissionership of Indian Affairs if the delegation cast its solid vote for Lincoln on the upcoming ballot. He bargained with crafty Simon Cameron and convinced the Keystone State boss to throw his weight on Lincoln's side and against Seward. The price Davis had to pay was the promise that Cameron would be chosen for a cabinet post if Lincoln won the November election.

Judge Davis and his colleagues engaged in this skulduggery in the teeth of explicit orders from Lincoln who had sent a telegram from Springfield where he was awaiting the convention results: "I authorize no bargains and will be bound by none."

His managers were cynical enough to believe that Lincoln had issued this guileless statement to catch the public eye; he was not so naive in political matters, they reasoned, as to hobble his promoters by taking from them the most potent weapon in a politician's arsenal—the power to make deals. But even if Lincoln's motives were the purest, his board of strategy decided to ignore the telegram.

"He ain't here and we are," Davis said, mopping his sweaty brow. "He don't know what we're up against."

Despite frantic efforts by Thurlow Weed on Seward's behalf, the third ballot of the convention gave the nomination to Abraham Lincoln of Illinois and picked Senator Hannibal Hamlin of Maine as his running mate.

The Republican slate swept into office in November against a hopelessly split opposition. The Democrats had held their convention in Charleston, South Carolina, during April. There, in the cradle of secession, the delegates had been unable to agree on a candidate. Southerners walked out—and the Democratic Party was splintered.

Obviously, the loyal remnants of the party could not allow the Republicans to win by default. A second convention was held in Baltimore during June. The results were disastrous for any hopes the Democrats might still have entertained. No unity was reached and two Democratic candidates appeared on the election ballots: the secessionist wing backed John C. Breckenridge, the Kentuckian, who was Vice-President in the Buchanan administration; the Regular Democrats called on dynamic Stephen Douglas. A splinter party known as the Constitutional Unionists entered yet another candidate, John Bell of Tennessee.

Such diffusion practically ensured a Republican victory, but the leaders of the new party did not allow themselves to become overconfident. The Republicans conducted an energetic and persuasive campaign with a platform that was founded on a policy of no new slave territories and no more slave states.

Various groups gave support to the Republicans: old-line Whigs, old-line Democrats, abolitionists, free-soilers, and even disgruntled Know-Nothings blessed the party's cause. All these assorted organizations had in common was a general opposition to slavery. The word "Republican" was avoided, frequently because of its abolitionist connotation, and in different parts of the country, the party appeared on the ballot under many names, among them: People's Party, Popular Party, Union Party, Anti-Nebraska Party, Anti-Slavery Party, Free-Soil Party and National Union Party. Any label was good enough so long as it removed the stigma of abolitionism from the Republican candidates.

In November, the voters voiced their approval of Abe Lincoln. The final tabulations showed Lincoln with 1,860,000 votes. Douglas the runner-up, was able to record 1,375,000 ballots. Breckenridge and Bell had polled enough votes to defeat the "Little Giant."

Although their methods differed, both Lincoln and Douglas were against future expansion of slavery. The President-elect believed in congressional action to contain the practise within its current boundaries while Douglas maintained that it should be settled by "squatter sovereignty." Either way, the "peculiar institution" was bound to lose—and Southerners rankled under this additional evidence of Northern "oppression." The long era of Southern domination on slavery was forever broken.

· 6 ·

The lights were burning late in Parlor No. 6, at Willard's Hotel, on Sunday, March 3, 1861. Many details still had to be ironed out during the waning hours before the inauguration. Lincoln sat at his desk frowning over the final draft of his address. The lamplight emphasized the gauntness of his bony face. He looked up wearily from his work. The speech was the most important of his career. Outside his room, the suite was bustling with politicians, office seekers, military personnel, presidential aides and hangers-on.

But, in all that hectic atmosphere, he maintained a façade of calmness. His serenity elicited confidence from everyone he met, with few exceptions. One of these was a visitor who kept a meticulous diary, and recorded in it a most unfavorable impression of the incoming Chief Executive. The entry read, in part:

> He is not a great man certainly, and, but for something almost woman-like in the look of his eyes, I should say the most ill-favored son of Adam I ever saw . . . He owned to me that he was more troubled by the outlook than he thought it discreet to show . . . Half an hour with Lincoln confirmed my worst fears. I should say he is at his wit's end if he did not seem to me to be so thoroughly aware that some other people are also in that condition . . .

If Lincoln was worried, he had good cause to be. No man since Washington had faced problems such as those plaguing the incoming administration. Seven states had already seceded. The South was arming for revolution. Forts Sumter and Pickens were besieged. Secessionists were stirring in Virginia and the Border States. Treason and disunion was rife. A single error of judgment, a wrong move, might set off a war. Besides all this, Lincoln had the vexing task of choosing a proper cabinet.

He had given this irksome duty much thought from the moment he had been advised of his nomination. The seven men who would be his advisers had to be the best he could find. But two cabinet posts had been bespoken by his managers at Chicago. Lincoln no more cared to have Caleb Smith and Simon Cameron in his cabinet than he desired a place in it for Jefferson Davis. But the deal had to be honored in the interests of party unity. Both Smith and Cameron had the power to make trouble for him—and Lincoln already had all the troubles he could handle.

An amusing story arose from Lincoln's reservations about accepting Cameron. He is supposed to have discussed the merits of the Pennsylvanian with Congressman Thaddeus Stevens, who also hailed from the Keystone State. Stevens had little regard for Cameron and seldom missed an opportunity to deride him.

"Is Cameron honest?" Lincoln allegedly asked.

"Mr. President—I assure you he would not steal a red-hot stove," Stevens replied.

The story spread swiftly around Washington and Cameron was incensed. He demanded an apology from Stevens. The sharp-tongued legislator said, "I apologize. I am quoted as saying that Simon Cameron would not steal a red-hot stove. I now withdraw that statement."

If any single point can underscore the basic difference between Jefferson Davis and Abe Lincoln, it was the way in which each man selected his cabinet. Davis chose only men whom he could dominate. Lincoln on the other hand, with the exception of Smith and Cameron, selected the strongest and most influential men he could find. Four of his cabinet choices had been his rivals for the presidential nomination, and probably each of the seven in his cabinet believed himself superior to Lincoln in experience, intellect, and leadership. As it was finally constituted, the cabinet lined up as follows:

Secretary of State	William Seward, New York
Secretary of Treasury	Salmon P. Chase, Ohio
Secretary of War	Simon Cameron, Pennsylvania
Secretary of Navy	Gideon Welles, Connecticut
Attorney General	Edward Bates, Missouri
Secretary of Interior	Caleb B. Smith, Indiana
Postmaster General	Montgomery Blair, Maryland

The four who had been potential presidential nominees at Chicago—Seward, Chase, Cameron, and Bates—harbored neither respect, friendship nor admiration for their Chief. Seward, in fact, regarded himself as the real leader of the nation; rumors arose that Lincoln had agreed to act as a rubber stamp, a figurehead, while Seward actually ran the country.

Lincoln smiled at these reports and when a friend warned him against the cabinet, saying, "They'll eat you up," the President replied, "They're just as likely to eat up each other."

Lincoln had no fear of surrounding himself with strong men; he possessed a singleness of purpose that carried him above personal likes and dislikes. To him, the central task was the preservation of the Union. He knew that eventually this would mean the dissolution or destruction of the Confederate States—no small undertaking. He was neither so vain nor self-deceiving as to believe such a titanic mission could be accomplished without the aid of the top brains and experience in the country. So he gathered such men into his cabinet. It mattered little to him that his subordinates reluctantly accorded him the homage which his office demanded, or that they held themselves above him. The odd assortment of people and principles assembled in the Republican party was the only instrument available to deal with the Confederate menace. Lincoln resolved to use the people and the principles for the salvation of his beloved Union . . .

· 7 ·

The long night, beset by martial stirrings, finally passed and the morning of the eventful Fourth of March was at hand. At first light, the weather was bright and cheerful, but the sky soon became cloudy and a raw chill rose with Marchlike inconstancy. Washington awoke early. By daybreak, the Avenue was crowded. Thousands who had spent an uncomfortable night in the open, or in poor accommodations, lined up at public fountains to splash cold water on their sleep-puffed faces. Restaurants and eating establishments did a rush business. Grog shops and saloons were packed, even at the earliest hour. Streams of noisy celebrants headed up Pennsylvania Avenue towards the Capitol, long before the ceremonies were scheduled to start.

Military preparations were quickened. Tough regulars patrolled rooftops, and spectators who had gloated over their vantage points were irate at being ordered away from windows and roofs. Rifles poked out of upper-story windows. Squads of cavalry with drawn sabers were deployed in the side streets ready for swift action in the event of a disturbance. Lines of Metropolitan Police cordoned the sidewalks. Burly plainclothes detectives imported from New York and Philadelphia mingled with the crowds. Alert men were on guard everywhere with weapons primed and cocked. Up on Capitol

Hill snub-nosed cannon were shotted and blue-clad snipers peered from behind the Corinthian columns of the templelike building.

The doubts of the past hectic months were now behind Lincoln. The man who had sneaked into Washington under a cloak of secrecy and surrounded by armed guards, was about to assume his role under the eyes of a vast assemblage. His words would be weighed, his every gesture reported. The agitated nation was scrutinizing him as no man before him had ever been examined. Any hesitation by him would be amplified. It was a time for courage, strength, and dignity—qualities which Lincoln possessed in plenty.

Anxiety spread as the inaugural hour approached. Increasing tension brought a spirit of depression to the people. The good humor of the morning disappeared. The spectators showed little festiveness. Hostile eyes peered through the slats of shuttered windows. Some houses along the route were boarded up and apparently deserted. Many did not display the national colors, although no one was bold enough to flaunt a Confederate flag. The cutting March wind tore at the bunting that decorated some buildings, and the gaily colored ribbon fluttered in ragged shreds. The auguries were ominous. A rumor persisted that a thousand Virginia daredevils were going to sweep across the Long Bridge that very night and kidnap Lincoln at the Union Ball which was to be held in a giant structure called the "Palace of Muslin." The building had been especially erected behind the City Hall for the inaugural celebration.

But the temper of the crowds and the gloominess of the day could not turn back the clock. A few minutes past noon, a leather-lunged sergeant bawled "Present Arms!" The cavalrymen on 14th Street and the infantry arrayed along the Avenue outside Willard's snapped to attention. A military band blared "Hail to the Chief." Mr. Lincoln and Mr. Buchanan, arm in arm, stepped out of the hotel's side entrance and climbed into an open carriage flanked by trustworthy troopers.

A hundred marshals riding garishly festooned horses led' the parade. Thirty-four pretty girls, representing each of the states, rode in an open vehicle, forming a picturesque and comely tableau—but the spectators watched the spectacle in glum silence.

Bands played marching tunes. Soldiers stepped out smartly, regimental banners crackling in the raw wind. Lincoln and Buchanan sat beside one another in the open carriage. The outgoing President stared moodily with tired eyes. His withered cheeks were pale and he was pleased to be relieved of the awful problems which had been hounding him. Lincoln seemed ill at ease. He clutched a gold-headed cane and kept his eyes fixed straight ahead, apparently unmindful of the snorting, prancing horses, the gleaming cavalry sabers, and the loaded carbines hanging loosely in saddle scabbards.

The inaugural parade moved on towards the Capitol, more like a military expedition passing through hostile territory than a triumphant procession. When the bands stopped playing, a disturbing silence cloaked the Avenue; it was broken only by the tread of marching feet, the stamping horses, and an occasional faint cheer or half-hearted handclapping. From time to time along the route, someone jeered at the presidential carriage. But the onlookers barely caught a glimpse of Lincoln and Buchanan, the view being blocked by the curtain of cavalrymen. If the parade was supposed to whip up popular enthusiasm, it fell far short of its purpose.

The progress of the cavalcade brought a few minor disturbances. At one point, some drunken rowdies lurched off the sidewalk through the police lines, cursing the soldiers. One of them grabbed at an infantryman's rifle and a blow from the gun butt dropped him to the pavement. A man shouted oaths at a group of Republicans marching in the parade and was clubbed by a policeman. In the Capitol grounds, a small man with red whiskers climbed up into a tree and addressed the crowd in bellowing tones and with wild, oratorical gestures. His unintelligible harangue ended abruptly when a policeman grabbed his ankle and yanked him from his perch.

After a series of delays, the ceremonies got under way. Handsome, silver-haired Senator Edward Baker of Oregon stepped to the speaker's rostrum and eloquently introduced the President. Amid scant cheers, Lincoln rose from his seat and went to the small table that had been provided for his address, but could find no place for either his stovepipe hat or the gold-headed cane. He paused in bewilderment and was obviously embarrassed. His erstwhile rival, Stephen Douglas, who was sitting close by, solved his dilemma. The "Little Giant" reached out and took the hat. The men smiled warmly at each other. Douglas nodded reassuringly and Lincoln turned to face the audience, adjusting his silver-rimmed spectacles and shuffling the pages of his momentous speech.

In his strong, high-pitched voice, Lincoln began to speak. The

Although tension gripped Washington on March 4, 1861, and heavily armed soldiers patrolled the grounds, great crowds turned out to see Abraham Lincoln

take the oath of office on the steps of the national Capitol.

crowd strained forward to listen. Interest rose as he continued with candor and passion in an earnest appeal to the dissident South:

> . . . in your hands, my dissatisfied fellow countrymen and not in mine, is the momentous issue of civil war. The government will not assail you. You can have no conflict without yourselves being the aggressors. You can have no oath registered in Heaven to destroy the government, while I shall have the most solemn one to preserve, protect and defend it . . .

The crowd was pleased with what it was hearing. Lincoln's words were conciliatory, yet with no hint of surrender. The high spot of his speech came in its closing passages, which were tender and brilliant. They caused reluctant men to cheer him and marked Lincoln as a real leader in whom the people could place their faith:

> I am loath to close. We are not enemies but friends. We must not be enemies. Though passion may have strained, it must not break our bonds of affection. The mystic chords of memory stretching from every battlefield and patriot grave, to every living heart and hearthstone, all over this broad land, will yet swell to the chorus of the Union, when again touched, as surely they will be, by the better angels of our nature.

As the speech ended, a great sigh went up from the crowd followed by a prolonged outburst of applause and cheering. When the ovation petered out, Chief Justice Roger Taney tottered forward, like an animated cadaver enshrouded in black robes. He held out the thick Bible before Lincoln. The President placed his hand on the Book, Taney gasped out the oath, and in a firm voice, Lincoln swore to uphold and defend the Constitution of the United States. He was officially the nation's sixteenth President.

Bands struck up "Yankee Doodle" and other patriotic airs. Parade cannon fired salutes. The President and his party went inside the Capitol and the large crowd started drifting away. Soldiers formed into ranks and were marched off. The artillerists on Capitol Hill hitched up limbers and caissons and rocked away in a cloud of dust. The inauguration was over and contrary to all the wild talk, nothing had happened, thanks to General Scott's careful measures. That grand, decaying hulk still knew his business when it came to grapeshot and bayonets. . . .

FOUR

Mr. Lincoln

"Must a government, of necessity, be too strong for the liberties of its own people, or too weak to maintain its own existence?"

ABRAHAM LINCOLN, April, 1861

The Union forever,
Hurrah, boys, hurrah!
Down with the traitor, up with the star!
While we rally round the flag, boys, rally once again
Shouting the battle cry of freedom!—

Union war song

LINCOLN HAD an immediate taste of the pressures he could expect during his tenure in the White House. He scarcely had settled down at his desk when swarms of office seekers clamored to be heard. This horde of ward heelers and hack politicians hovered like buzzards over carrion. Nothing discouraged them; they were thick-skinned, impervious to rebuffs and harsh treatment. Lincoln, the first Republican President, had patronage to dispense, and they were in the capital to receive it. Their undignified conduct bordered on riot. At first, Lincoln regarded the job-hungry men with tolerant amusement. He understood their situation—twelve years before, in the Taylor administration, he, too, had been an office seeker, rushing to Washington in quest of a sinecure as Commissioner of the Land Office. His trip had been in vain. Someone with more influence got the job.

However, after a few days the President lost patience with the persistent men besieging his office. When one of them rushed up in the street and thrust credentials at him, Lincoln cried, "No, blast it! No! I won't open shop in the street!"

All the hotels were crowded with patronage seekers, Willard's especially. Never had the hostel been so filled. Men stood four and five deep at the bar clamoring for whisky. A clerk told a New York newspaper correspondent:

> A few days ago, two thousand and five hundred dined here, sir. I guess you could not well equal that. Everyone wants a place and it must be found or he'll know the reason he's not in Abraham's bosom.

The throngs of job hunters interfered badly with the organization of the government. Even cabinet members found it hard to reach the President. In a letter to his wife, Secretary Seward described the uncomfortable situation:

> Solicitants for office besiege the President and he finds his hands full for the present. My duties call me to the White House one, two and three times a day. The grounds, halls, stairways, closets are filled with applicants who render ingress and egress difficult.

The condition became almost unmanageable as more and more

of the party faithful flocked into Washington hoping to land on the public payroll. Senator James W. Nesmith of Oregon unleashed a bitter denunciation of these "political leeches." He said in part:

> The Administration is very much embarrassed. A throng of countless spoilsmen desire place. I have found every avenue to the office of every Secretary and every head of a bureau of this government crowded with hungry office-seekers—old men and young men; long, gaunt, lean young men; old, limping, bald-headed gentlemen—choking up the avenues. Here are forty thousand office-seekers fiddling around the Administration for loaves and fishes, while the government is being destroyed. A great many have been disappointed. It would take a miracle such as that performed by our Saviour when he fed five thousand people with five loaves and two little fishes, to satisfy all these greedy camp-followers. If I were in the place of Mr. Lincoln, considering that the Union is dissolving and disintegrating under our feet, I would turn the Federal bayonets against the office-seekers. I would drive them from this city, and I would not leave a man to tell the tale. I would determine first whether we had a government or not.

The Senator's advice went unheeded although many agreed that it would be a good idea to clean out the office-seekers by spitting them on bayonets. Lincoln continued to face the clamoring job-hunters. When the behavior of these men disgusted him so much that he could no longer keep silent, he said gravely to his old friend William Herndon: "If our American society and the United States government are demoralized and overthrown, it will come from the voracious desire for office, this wriggle to live without toil, work, and labor . . ."

One of Lincoln's favorite authors, the humorist, Robert C. Newell, who used the pseudonym Orpheus C. Kerr (Office-Seeker) saw the funny side of the situation and wrote:

> . . . if Abe pays a post-office for every story of his childhood that's told by job hunters who claim to have known him, the mail department of this glorious nation will be so large that a letter smaller than a two-story house would get lost in it . . .

This chaotic and unpleasant condition was not unique to the Lincoln administration. Just as many Southerners were trying to find themselves a soft berth in the Davis government. The situation grew so bad in Montgomery that two leading Southern papers, the Augusta *Chronicle* and the Macon *Chronicle* ran joint editorials which said: "Let President Davis swear by the horns of the altar that no man who asks for office shall get it, and the evil would abate."

Mary Boykin Chesnut, an ardent Confederate, whose husband was an important aide to Davis made this entry in her remarkable diary:

> Everywhere political intrigue is as rife as in Washington. Everybody who comes here wants an office, and the many who, of course, are disappointed, raise a cry of corruption against the few who are successful. I thought we had left all that in Washington. Nobody is willing to be out of sight, and all will take office.

On both sides, the scramble to get aboard the gravy train almost derailed governmental procedures. In Washington, Lincoln had more serious problems than dispensing crumbs from the victory table. His foremost task was to hit upon a method of dealing with the unpleasant reality presented by the Confederate States of America.

Various pressure groups were working on him to accept their way. In Congress, extremists favored a war of extermination. On the other hand, such prominent capitalists as William B. Astor, William H. Aspinwall, Cornelius Vanderbilt, William C. Dodge, and A. T. Stewart urged him to make a compromise that would ensure peace.

Only eight days prior to the inauguration, Dodge, the multimillionaire who had vacated Parlor No. 6 at Willard's in favor of the President, came to Lincoln as the chairman of a delegation of twenty-five New York business men who opposed any hostile action towards the South.

"It is for you to say, sir, whether the whole nation will be plunged into bankruptcy, whether the grass shall grow in the streets of our commercial cities," Dodge intoned pompously.

"Then I say it shall not. If it depends on me, the grass shall not grow anywhere except in the fields and the meadows," Lincoln replied, his eyes twinkling.

"Then you will yield to the just demands of the South? You will not go to war on account of slavery!" Dodge cried.

"I do not know that I understand your meaning, Mr. Dodge . . . the Constitution will not be preserved and defended without being enforced and obeyed in every one of the United States. It must be so respected in every part of every one of the United States. It must be respected, obeyed, enforced, and defended, let the grass grow where it may," Lincoln said.

When someone asked him about the admission of new slave territories, Lincoln said, "It will be time to consider that question when it arises. Now we have other questions which we must decide. In a choice of evils, war may not always be the worst . . ."

· 2 ·

The war danger was real; it had many faces and assumed many shapes. The harried President had to decide which shadows were the more menacing. He was surrounded by hostility on every side, not the least of which came from the haughty men he had placed in his cabinet. They still did not realize that in Lincoln they faced a leader —not a frightened and bumbling politician.

Seward still fancied himself at the head of the government; Chase, Cameron, Blair and Bates regarded Lincoln with mild disdain, believing him ill-equipped to overcome the trials ahead. Of the cabinet members, only Gideon Welles, the Secretary of the Navy, seemed to grasp the importance of the man in the White House.

Welles kept a diary in which he wrote his frank opinions of his colleagues—and did not exclude himself from his devastating probing. He knew himself, his strength and his weakness, and in a candid word portrait describing Gideon Welles, he wrote: "I am a man with feelings easily given to irritation and one that is often lost in gloomy melancholy."

Bewhiskered "Uncle Gideon," the son of a Connecticut shipbuilder, was the butt of many jokes bandied around Washington because of his quick temper and prim ways. Admittedly a curmudgeon who was plunged into the deepest of black moods by even the smallest setback, Welles was also a shrewd and observant man with a talent for detail and executive work. Early in his cabinet days, he penned the following impression of Lincoln in his diary:

William H. Seward, Secretary of State.

Simon Cameron, the first Secretary of War
in the Lincoln cabinet.

He is not Apollo, but he is not Caliban. He was made where the material for strong men is plentiful; and his loose, tall frame is loosely thrown together. He is in every way large—brain included, but his countenance shows intellect, generosity, great good nature and keen discrimination. He is an effective speaker because he is earnest, strong, honest, simple in style and clear as crystal in his logic.

When he wrote that entry into his diary, Welles was the only cabinet member with a high opinion of Lincoln. But later, one by one, each grudgingly admitted that the former rail-splitter and prairie lawyer was his equal and even his superior.

The cabinet, the Congress, the whole nation was gradually made aware of Lincoln's most positive trait: he had an unbending resolve and an unyielding firmness once he decided what course to take. He arrived at his conclusions after much pondering and long reflection— Lincoln had a quick mind, but rejected snap judgments. While in the process of arriving at a decision, he seemed hesitant and unsure. But once he fixed on a specific action no obstacle could swerve him from his purpose.

The first cabinet member to discover this trait in Lincoln was Secretary of State Seward, who quickly learned that the Chief Executive had no intentions of abandoning the presidential powers to his "Prime Minister"—as Seward was jocularly known.

Seward urged the evacuation of Fort Sumter, believing this action would "take the wind out of South Carolina's sails." Lincoln did not agree with the New Yorker about Sumter. He also took issue with Seward's feelings on the dangers of secession. The Secretary of State minimized the perils. He had strong faith in the innate loyalty of South Carolina and the other "wayward sisters." He had expressed his sentiments at a political dinner in New York City on Christmas Eve, 1860, just four days after South Carolina had separated from the Union. Speaking before a select audience in the Astor House, Seward declared:

> The seceded states do not humbug me with their secession. I do not believe they will humbug you and I do not believe if they do not humbug you or me, they will succeed in humbugging themselves . . . Let no one doubt the loyalty of South Carolina to their [sic] beloved Union! That state would rise as one man if New York were attacked

by a foreign foe . . . if South Carolina were similarly attacked, every state in the North would spring to its defense!

This belief in the loyalty of the cotton states carried Seward to conclusions which seemed surprisingly naive for a man with his political experience and intellectual capacities.

Seward proposed a string of conciliatory measures to placate the Confederates. Besides surrendering Fort Sumter, these peace moves included concessions and compromises on slavery, perhaps limited extension of the institution into new territories along a line to be negotiated, and mediation of all Southern grievances.

And once all this was done, Seward still had an ace to play—a maneuver he was certain would make every seceded state rush home to the fold. He proposed to declare war against a foreign power! The potential foe was not hard to determine; both France and Spain were conducting imperialistic adventures in the Western Hemisphere —the former in Mexico, the latter in the Caribbean area. According to Seward they were violating the Monroe Doctrine, which was ample cause for war.

Once the United States was involved in a conflict with either or both of these powers, Seward believed, the South would flock to defend the Old Flag and reconciliation would take place to the accompaniment of thudding drums and screeching fifes as Yank and Secesh marched together under the Stars and Stripes!

Lincoln politely told Seward he thought all this was nonsense. In the first place, the President did not go along with the theory of Southern loyalty to the Old Flag. He believed the Confederacy was an outgrowth of a long-range plan conceived by crafty men determined to gain their ends at any cost. Concessions and compromises would do no good; and rather than entice the departed states back into the Union, Lincoln argued, the secessionists would regard such actions as weakness and fear.

Once the Confederates felt they had cowed the Federal government, further demands would be forthcoming, until the Stars and Bars would be flying from the Capitol. The day of appeasement was over. If the Republic was to survive it had to take a stand—and a strong one.

Involvement in a foreign war as a solution for the nation's crisis would also be playing into Secessionist hands, the President thought.

If the Confederacy wanted assurance of success, its best hope lay in the United States expending strength in a fruitless war which would benefit no one but the Davis government. Lincoln did not believe that hard-core Secessionists had any intention of rallying to the succor of the North.

Seward's idealistic plans were dumped into the wastebasket and Lincoln turned to wrestle with the problem in a realistic fashion. His major dilemma was to ascertain exactly how far the masses of the North were willing to go to save the nation. He knew that a majority favored preserving the Union, but an active minority preferred to let the Southern states depart "in peace." A mere desire to keep the Union was not enough—the use of force might become necessary.

Were the prosperous farmers and busy workmen of the North ready to die for the Union? Were they prepared to face the ordeals of cruel civil war? These were the unknown factors and nobody could rightly gauge the true temper of the North.

Lincoln had to take action and could not afford to make a mistake. He had no margin for error; the wrong move could be catastrophic.

The President sat alone in his study, his brow furrowed, his eyes troubled, and pondered the decision that was his alone to make. His precise legal mind neatly weighed the alternatives. If he ordered Federal troops to recapture Federal property by force, he was likely to incite immediate war; a war in which he would be branded the aggressor.

He knew this was a gamble, for he risked alienating the thousands in the North who backed the Union but eschewed war and would not fight unless an enemy struck the first blow. He reasoned, too, that if the first shot should come from Northern guns, not only his own people, but the rest of the world would consider him the instigator and his government would lose all sympathy abroad.

If war came, Lincoln concluded, it must be Jefferson Davis and not he who gave the fatal order. Then the Confederates would have the burden of guilt; they would be making a revolution against the established government; they would stand before the world as rebels without the moral excuse of self-defence. More than that, a military assault by Davis would, Lincoln shrewdly guessed, awaken the dormant patriotism of the Northern states and unite the nation for crushing retaliation against the rebellion.

Seldom before in history had there been such a time. Hostilities might break out in any of a dozen spots. Provocations were great and tempers growing short.

Not every Union officer was willing to surrender his command without a fight. Men with guns in their hands glared at each other angrily and suspiciously. The climate was becoming unbearable. A word, a gesture, could bring on the ultimate moment which would send brothers into a death struggle and hurl the estranged nation over the brink of civil war . . .

· 3 ·

Washington reflected the nightmare of the political and military stalemate. Government clerks, Southerners from states which had not yet seceded, especially Virginians, did not resign their jobs. They continued their accustomed routines, often handling confidential matters. Many who sympathized with the Confederacy did not hide their loyalties. Secession cockades were flaunted openly. Some officials even smuggled copies of governmental orders to Confederate agents.

Handsome Major John B. Magruder, a Southerner, who commanded a strategic artillery post, strutted about elegantly, like a matinee idol, dramatically avowing loyalty to the President. Actually the flamboyant officer was in constant touch with Confederate emissaries.

Commodore Franklin Buchanan, trusted commandant of the Washington Navy Yard, after swearing fealty to the administration, decamped suddenly with almost his entire staff; to everyone's dismay, he left ample proof of his treason. Hundreds of shells and bombs in the naval arsenal were found filled with sand instead of gunpowder.

And all the while, various Confederate Peace Commissions were in Washington, trying to find some means of settling the impasse. Delegates from Virginia were closeted with the President arguing the pros and cons of secession; the prosecessionists threatened the withdrawal of Virginia from the Union in order to make Lincoln accede to all their demands. The President refused to be intimidated. He knew that strong Union sentiment existed in the "Old Dominion," especially in the western part of the state. Several previous votes in the Virginia House of Burgesses had rejected secession. So the leaders argued back and forth; emissaries from both sides met in whispered conferences; mysterious agents from the South entered and left Washington on devious business. The muddied situation grew even more confused and even more muddied.

And through the gathering clouds loomed the weather-beaten gray-stone walls of Fort Sumter in the Charleston Harbor. The massive bulk gained importance with each passing hour; the fate of the obsolete fortification had become inextricably linked with the fate of the nation.

The Stars and Stripes fluttering from the flagpole of Fort Sumter irked the Carolinians. The young hotbloods of the Palmetto State forces gazed across the narrow stretch of water from the mainland and cursed. While the Old Flag still flew, they were constantly reminded, the United States and not the Confederacy was supreme.

Although he was plagued by a hundred vexations, dogged by avaricious office seekers, Lincoln kept worrying about Major Robert Anderson and the brave men in Fort Sumter. He was aware these staunch soldiers were faced with short rations, miserable quarters, isolation, the imminence of actual warfare.

Shortly after the inauguration, the President decided the government must move. By this time he had learned that Anderson's supplies could not last beyond April 15. The ring of hostile artillery looped about the fort was slowly garroting its defenders. Obviously, Anderson could not hold on much longer without food; he would be forced to surrender the bastion.

Voluntary abandonment of Fort Sumter was unthinkable to Lincoln. From a strictly legalistic viewpoint it would be tantamount to open admission by the government that secession had a legal basis, a point which Lincoln neither believed nor conceded. If he ordered Anderson to give up, the Union was forever doomed; the stock of the Confederacy would soar at such a victory and the Davis government would certainly get recognition from European powers. Retreat at Sumter would prove that the President did not consider the Union worth defending—and inevitably it would be a strong reason for other states to secede. Who could blame them for withdrawing from a Union too weak, too supine to enforce its own authority?

But hurling a force against the Confederate batteries to relieve the Sumter garrison was a most hazardous undertaking. The Confederate emplacements were strong. The siege of Fort Sumter should have been lifted many weeks before, when all the Confederate preparations had not yet been completed. Even now Lincoln could have ordered General Scott to send strong detachments of troops and naval units to slug it out with Charleston's shore batteries and hope the effort would be successful. But there was a big chance the attack might fail. Then the Union position would be untenable. A military fiasco would erase the waning prestige of the United States; the whole world would see that the Washington administration was moribund.

Even if the military expedition gained its objectives, reduced the Charleston batteries, routed the Carolina army, and relieved and reinforced Fort Sumter, the victory would belong to the Confederacy, for Washington would be blackened by an act of aggression. The Border States, now teetering on the brink, would be shocked into lining up with the Confederacy and Jefferson Davis would achieve his dream of emerging from the holocaust as the Father of his Country.

Lincoln had no intention of committing national suicide. He was too wily to fall into a pit of his own digging. Another way must be found to aid Anderson; a way that would not discredit the United States yet would not break faith with that devoted officer and his brave followers . . .

· 4 ·

After many years of obscure service, Major Robert Anderson suddenly emerged as a national hero by his defence of Fort Sumter. The gallant stand of the isolated garrison captured the imagination of the North. Before mail service was interrupted, thousands of letters poured into Fort Sumter giving moral support to faithful Bob Anderson. Hero worship was a new experience for him; he was not used to attracting public attention, and the adulation he was receiving would have made him blush had he been able to witness it.

In the North pretty young women carried his picture in lockets that hung on their bosoms. Wherever his likeness was displayed, women of all ages kissed it shamelessly. He was the sweetheart of both starry-eyed maidens and wrinkled matrons. Men lifted their glasses to him in every bar and restaurant. A popular song called "Bob Anderson, my Beau Bob," was sweeping the North, and in music halls audiences cheered wildly every time a performer sang it. Bob Anderson and his lonely men trapped in the stone bastion were likened to the martyrs of Valley Forge and Bunker Hill. A nation's hopes and prayers and love were centered on Fort Sumter—and if the North had needed a symbol around which every divergent group could unite, Bob Anderson provided that symbol.

Actually "Beau Bob" was as unlikely an individual as one could find to fill the role of national hero and to epitomize Union resistance to the march of slavocracy. He was a Southerner by birth, a native of Kentucky. His wife was a Georgian. He had been a cotton planter and had owned slaves. But these ties did not affect his devotion to his duty; they merely made his task a little more difficult.

A West Pointer—Class of 1825—Anderson had had thirty-five years of army service, mainly as an artillery officer. After all those years he was only a major; promotion came slowly in the Regular Army. But Anderson was not dissatisfied; he had enjoyed his career in a profession he had chosen.

Deeply religious, Beau Bob was almost the prototype of the perfect officer—fearless, dedicated, and scrupulous with his men. Next to God, duty was most sacred to him. During his ordeal in Fort Sumter, he had moments of wavering and doubt but never faltered in carrying out his orders; he was bound to hold the post, despite all odds, until properly relieved, driven out by force, or ordered to evacuate.

The idea of civil war sickened him; he could not bear the thought of fighting his own people. But Bob Anderson had given his oath to uphold the Federal government, and, despite his Southern origins, no divergent loyalties swerved him from his duty.

Fifty-seven years old at the time of Fort Sumter, Anderson had previously met both Lincoln and Jefferson Davis—more than a quarter of a century earlier, during the Black Hawk War. His contact with Lieutenant Jefferson Davis had been on official army business, yet he made an impression on the frosty young officer; many years later Davis recalled him with these words: "He is . . . a true soldier and man of the finest sense of honor."

Anderson's meeting with Lincoln had been both cursory and unnoteworthy. In addition to his other duties, Anderson was appointed mustering-in officer for volunteer troops. Among these was a detachment of Illinois men including Private Abraham Lincoln, who was later elected captain by the men of his company.

An extra touch of irony spiced the situation at Fort Sumter. Anderson had served at West Point as an instructor of artillery. A Creole from Louisiana, bearing the grandiose name of Pierre Gustave Toutant Beauregard, had been one of his star pupils. That same Beauregard, until recently Superintendent of West Point, now commanded the Confederate forces menacing Fort Sumter. He held his former teacher in high esteem and Anderson regarded his ex-student most cordially. If circumstances had been different, Anderson might have been well pleased by the skill Beauregard showed in his placement of the encircling cannon. It was a tribute to his own ability as an instructor of artillery.

While Anderson was holding Beauregard to a stand-off, Lincoln spent sleepless nights pacing the worn carpeting of his bedroom, shuffling back and forth in battered house slippers and a flapping, threadbare robe, as he wrestled with the problem of Fort Sumter. The President's gaunt cheeks grew more hollow; dark rings encircled his deep-set eyes and his shambling figure slumped more noticeably as if the burden of decision was wearing him down.

He probed and searched for an honorable solution; a solution that was neither surrender nor attack. At last, he hit on a scheme which seemed satisfactory. Lincoln proposed to send a flotilla of relief ships carrying nothing but food for the beleaguered garrison in Charleston Harbor. For humane reasons alone, nobody could object to such a venture. The Confederates could not claim force was being brought into play against them or that the shipment of foodstuffs was an act of provocation. Nevertheless, the plan showed the determination of the government not to yield the bastion supinely. If the Confederates regarded feeding valiant men as a warlike move and tried to hinder such an undertaking by force, the responsibility for what followed was theirs.

Having decided what to do, Lincoln went ahead resolutely. On March 29, 1861, he ordered Welles and Cameron to outfit a convoy which should depart from New York not later than April 6. This would bring the expedition off Charleston on April 11 or 12, three days before Anderson's rations were entirely depleted.

At last the cards were on the table. Lincoln stood pat against all opposition, even that he met in his own cabinet. There he received real support only from Montgomery Blair, the Postmaster General, who backed him by declaring: "Provisioning the fort would vindicate the hardy courage of the North and the determination of the people and their President to maintain the authority of the government."

The relief ships cleared New York on schedule and started the voyage to Charleston with the good wishes of the North behind them. Adhering to strict legality, Lincoln dispatched to Charleston one Robert S. Chew, a War Department clerk, with a message for Francis W. Pickens, governor of the state. And when he confronted Pickens, the clerk read him the following notification:

> I am directed by the President of the United States to notify you to expect an attempt will be made to supply Fort Sumter with provisions only; and that, if such an attempt be not resisted, no effort to throw in men, arms, or ammunition will be made without further notice, or in case of attack on the fort.

The little fleet cutting through the Atlantic swells carried more than bacon and flour and coffee for hungry men; the ships were taking with them the dignity and honor of a great nation.

Eager crowds scanned the newspapers to read about the results of Mr. Lincoln's gesture. None but the dissident and disloyal elements of the North questioned his motives and wisdom in taking the step. Generally the people chuckled over Old Abe's strategy. He had passed the hot potato right back to Jefferson Davis. What would the Rebel do now? Would he drop it—or burn his fingers?

FIVE

Mr. Davis

"He who makes the assault is not necessarily he who strikes the first blow or fires the first gun"—

JEFFERSON DAVIS, April, 1861

The battle's fought, the victory's won,
Old Abe's flag hauled down by Anderson,
Now the Border States no more will retard,
But wheel into line under Beauregard;
And with cannon, mortar and petard,
Take Washington with Beauregard!

Confederate song, 1861

· 1 ·

DOWN IN Montgomery, Alabama Confederate Congressmen and their wives were grumbling and showing extreme discontent. The city was much too small and unsophisticated for men and women used to living in the cosmopolitan atmosphere of Washington and being close to cities like Baltimore, Philadelphia, and New York. The inadequate housing, the lack of entertainment and the limited social life grew irksome. As a result demands were raised to move the capital to a more suitable city—logically, Charleston, the cradle of the Confederacy, should have been the unanimous choice.

But as on nearly every question, in those early days of the new republic, finding an area of complete agreement among government officials seemed an impossibility. Confederate leaders squabbled about all important matters, and the relocation of the capitol also became a subject for argument.

Dramatic events decided that controversy. Lincoln's message to Pickens and what followed solved many problems—including the new home for the Confederate capital.

On April 9, President Davis received from Governor Pickens a copy of Lincoln's message. An emergency session of the cabinet was immediately called on the Sumter crisis. Davis had decided on his course even before the meeting. To him, the mere dispatch of ships, even though on an apparently humane mission, was a warlike move. He deeply mistrusted the Lincoln government and, as he later wrote, felt that:

> ... remonstrances, patient, persistent and reiterated attempts at negotiations ... by ... South Carolina and by the Confederate States ... had been met by evasion, prevarication, and perfidy. It was evident that no confidence could be placed in any pledge or promise of the Federal Government ...

Thus, the Confederate cabinet met in an attitude of suspicion and distrust regarding Lincoln and his advisers. Davis' feelings about the Washington government found ready reception among his cabinet members. With only one dissenting voice, the cabinet echoed war talk. The lone dissenter was bluff Robert Toombs. He felt it would be wrong for the President to order General Beauregard's guns to fire on Fort Sumter rather than permit the food to be shipped in.

Toombs, once the most bellicose of anti-Unionists, foresaw the peril involved in bombarding the Fort. His eloquent plea for moderation was fraught with prophecy worthy of a Cassandra:

> The firing on that fort will inaugurate a civil war greater than any the world has ever seen . . . Mr. President, if this is true, it is suicide, it is murder, and will lose us every friend to the North. You will wantonly strike a hornets' nest which extends from mountains to ocean, and legions now quiet, will swarm out to sting us to death— it is unnecessary, it puts us in the wrong, it is fatal!

But, like Cassandra, Toombs spoke to men who listened with indifference; in their arrogance and smugness, they did not believe him. His colleagues regarded him as lacking the courage to fight for his convictions. After he had spoken, his remarks were ignored. The meeting continued and Toombs fell into a dark, brooding silence at this rebuff.

Presently the cabinet and the President came to a decision. A telegram to General Beauregard at Charleston was drawn up. It certainly clarified the intentions of the Confederate government:

> If you have no doubt of the authorized character of the agent who communicated to you the intention of the Washington government to supply Fort Sumter by force, you will at once demand its evacuation, and, if this is refused, proceed, in such manner as you may determine, to reduce it.

Thus, Beauregard, who was not noted for his even temper or his patience, was given virtual carte blanche to start the war at his discretion. The telegram was handed to a messenger boy who ran with it to the telegraph office across the street. Then Davis adjourned the meeting amid the jubilant congratulations of everyone but Toombs, who lumbered away, still smoldering with anger.

Davis himself had no qualms about issuing an order which rejected any settlement short of war. He understood the nature of his decision because some time later, he wrote:

> To have waited further straightening of their position by land and

naval forces, with hostile purposes now declared for the sake of having them "fire the first gun," would have been as unwise as it would be to hesitate to strike down an assailant, who levels a deadly weapon at one's breast, until he has actually fired. He who makes the assault is not necessarily he who strikes the first blow or fires the first gun.

Characteristically, Davis, the self-styled aristocrat, tried to explain the making of revolution with gentlemanly loftiness. His concept of revolt had nothing to do with masses and mobs and was motivated by only the most high-minded ideals. Davis was no ranting demagogue like Roger Pryor screaming for "the sprinkling of blood."

Even the launching of revolution must be couched in dignified terms. Davis simply disapproved of the action taken by Washington and determined to punish the Federal government. Davis reserved the right to doubt Lincoln's word, and thus rationalized his own position as one of righteous indignation rather than sheer warmongering.

Davis had acted with imperious dignity, but when his telegram reached Charleston, young soldiers, untouched by war, greeted the news with joy. They waved bowie knives and fired pistols in the air. Bands blared. People danced in the streets. Torchlight parades snaked through the city. The hour had come; there was going to be glory enough for all.

War was torchlight parades and singing; pretty girls in crinoline tossing flowers from balconies; it was carnival and Mardi gras too. The young men of the South saw themselves as crusaders marching off to a battle against an enemy that was tyrannical, perfidious, and evil. They felt they were White Knights girded for battle on the side of truth and purity . . .

· 2 ·

The gallant and elegant Pierre Gustave Toutant Beauregard, Brigadier General, C.S.A. observed all the niceties of military courtesy, as befitted a gentleman-cavalier. Ordered by President Davis to conduct the business as he saw fit, Beauregard at first fell back on military punctilios. He sent politely formal notes to Anderson requesting the surrender of the Fort and Anderson respectfully refused to comply. These exchanges continued until April 11. By then, watchers on Charleston rooftops and along the shore line were scanning the open water for signs of the Lincoln relief ships, which were due at any time.

By then, too, Beauregard's Creole temper began to boil, and the note he sent on the morning of April 11, although worded in politic terms, brooked no further equivocation. Two Confederate officers rowed out to the Fort under a flag of truce and handed an ultimatum to Anderson:

> I am ordered by the Government of the Confederate States to demand the evacuation of Fort Sumter . . . All proper facilities will be afforded for the removal of yourself and your command, together with company arms and property, and all private property, to any post in the United States which you may select. The flag which you have upheld so long and with so much fortitude, under the most trying circumstances, may be saluted by you on taking it down . . .

Sad-eyed Anderson knew the string had run out. But although surrender would bring him surcease, he could not honorably comply with the demand for capitulation, and he said so in his written answer which he handed to Beauregard's emissaries. As they were leaving, Anderson smiled wanly and said, "Gentlemen, if you do not batter us to pieces, we shall be starved out in a few days."

More discussion followed. Beauregard did not intend to commit an act of war without exhausting every possibility of avoiding it. Boats plied between the Fort and the shore. Much was made about preventing the useless "effusion of blood." Anderson was unwilling to risk lives in the defence of a hopeless position and asked for a period of grace until April 15, at which time his last rations would be used. He could then surrender without prejudice to honor and duty.

However, the game had been going on too long. General Beauregard could dally no longer. At 3:20 A.M., April 12, 1861, four Confederate officers solemnly presented the irrevocable demand of the Confederate government:

> By authority of Brigadier-General Beauregard, commanding the provisional forces of the Confederate States, we have the honor to notify

you that he will open the fire of his batteries on Fort Sumter in one hour from this time. We have the honor to be, very respectfully, your obedient servant,

James Chesnut, Jr.
Aide-de-Camp

Stephen D. Lee
Captain, C.S.Army, Aide-de-Camp

The Confederate party boarded its boat. As the craft was preparing to shove off, Anderson called out, "If we do not meet again on earth, I hope we shall meet in Heaven."

Soon the Confederate emissaries were at a battery commanded by Captain George S. James. Several men, prominent in the secession movement, were present at the redoubt. Among them was the firebrand, Roger Pryor. He was tendered the honor of firing the first gun at Fort Sumter. Pryor paled, backed away, and shook his head. "No. No. I could not do it. I could not start the war," he whispered hoarsely.

But, while Pryor shrank from the bloodshed he had advocated, one man on the scene did not. He was sixty-seven-year-old Edmund Ruffin, an archsecessionist and bitter Union foe for many years. He doffed his hat, let the breezes ruffle the white ringlets of his hair and grasped the lanyard with a firm grip. At exactly 4:20 A.M., a signal flare streaked across the dark sky. Ruffin yanked the lanyard. The cannon belched flame . . .

After enduring a bombardment of three thousand shells, over a period of thirty-six hours, Major Anderson struck his colors. He had neither food nor ammunition left in the fort. On Sunday, April 14, 1861, his men marched out in parade order, with the band playing "Yankee Doodle." The Stars and Stripes was saluted by a salvo of fifty guns. During the ceremony, a private was killed when a tenpounder exploded. He was the only fatality suffered in the battle. The flag was lowered and handed to Anderson as a keepsake.

The relief fleet which had arrived at the height of the bombardment hovered helplessly outside the harbor until the surrender. Then Anderson was permitted to load his men on board the ships. As the flotilla headed back towards New York, Anderson saw the Confederate flag fluttering over Fort Sumter.

The guns that pounded Fort Sumter into submission heralded more than the end of a tenuous peace. They marked the beginning of the demise of the very society and way of life for which the Davis government was risking all.

Jefferson Davis was confronted by a staggering task, for despite all its military swagger and trappings, his country was unprepared for armed conflict. It lacked the very instruments for making war: the rifles, cannon, ships; the knapsacks, bayonets, shoes, cartridge boxes; the bullets, gunpowder, shells, and bombs; even the necessary military organization was deficient. The South abounded with eager men who had to be trained as soldiers; it had courage and spirit. These were its major assets. Jefferson Davis did not flinch from the intricate complexities of his office. He strove mightily to create and sustain a nation, to impart and breathe into it his dedication and vision.

With the flimsy peace ripped away, events raced on at a frightening pace. No Secessionist, least of all Davis, could have anticipated the reaction throughout the North following the bombardment of Fort Sumter.

Southerners had clung to their belief that Yankees cared for nothing except money. They gaped at the fervor which swept Yankeedom now when the people learned about the occurrence in Charleston Harbor on April 12-14. Mass meetings and rallies assembled in every great city. Laborers, mechanics, artisans, craftsmen of all types pledged their skills to sustain the Union. Everywhere the Stars and Stripes was unfurled. People thronged squares to hear speeches and patriotic slogans. Bands played national airs. Churches were crowded with solemn worshipers praying for divine aid and begging the Lord's protection for President Lincoln, his generals and his soldiers. They were a devout people, these Yankees—Baptists, Methodists, Presbyterians, Catholics, Anglicans, Jews—and it was only natural for them to turn to God in this trying moment. They did more than pray.

The young, strong men—the lifeblood of the Union—trudged from fields and pavements to the enlistment offices in response to Lincoln's call for seventy-five thousand State Troops to serve a

112

The North responded to the outbreak of war with an outburst of patriotism. The troops marched off to bands, cheers, and flowers. (Above) New York regiments parade on Broadway as they head for transports to take them to the seat of the war.

In the beginning, war was fun, especially in Charleston, S.C., where it all began. Gentlemen of the city try out rifles at the Ordnance Bureau, prior to joining newly formed regiments.

period of ninety days, to put down "combinations too powerful to be suppressed by ordinary procedures of government." The young men came in such numbers that muster rolls had to be closed and avid volunteers turned away.

Patriotism and indignation had kindled a fierce fire in Northern hearts. As one Yankee volunteer put it, "This is Massachusetts agin South Carolina and, by God, we'll learn them secesh some respect . . ."

The act of firing on Fort Sumter had united the North as never before. With few exceptions, nineteen million persons spoke in one voice and shouted defiance at the makers of rebellion. Davis had been neatly caught in the trap Lincoln had baited. Nothing could erase the cold truth that the Confederates had started the war. But within the Confederacy responsibility for beginning hostilities seemed of minor concern. All nine million citizens of the new nation appeared to be solidly behind their President and the Cause.

At least, the Davis government chose to believe the people were united. But if there was some grumbling in various quarters, the dissatisfied were not considered worthy of attention; too much was happening to heed malcontents. As Roger Pryor had predicted, Virginia came over to the Confederacy. On April 17, the "Old Dominion" departed the Union; and with her, Virginia, the "Mother of Presidents," brought prestige, influence, and strength. Her troops went into action immediately. They seized the Federal arsenal at Harper's Ferry without a fight, but not until the guard had managed to destroy war matériel worth millions.

Three days later, April 20, Virginia forces menaced the Norfolk Navy Yard and its commander burned ships, stores, munitions and guns valued at thirty million dollars. He was an inept saboteur, however, and the destruction was incomplete. The powerful frigate *Merrimac* had been scuttled, but not put to the torch—and sat in the shallow water of her berth, virtually intact. One day she was to rise again.

With Virginia the Confederacy gained a stately, dignified warrior —the master of a fine estate at Arlington, Virginia, and a soldier of whom General Scott had said, "He is worth fifty thousand men." The soldier was Colonel Robert E. Lee. He had turned down an invitation to command the Union Army and had offered his services to the Confederacy. In his resignation, Lee wrote to General Scott:

"Save in defense of my native state, I never again desire to draw my sword."

So, Robert E. Lee, who did not believe in slavery, secession, or rebellion, found himself fighting for all three. The great soldier, who might have achieved immortality by defending the Union, won it as an enemy.

Long before fighting started in the field, the newspapers on both sides fought a bitter verbal war. The columns were filled with vivid stories of rape, pillaging and murder. Overzealous journalists described in gory detail scenes which existed only in their own fevered imaginations. Southern hacks told how lovely Secessionist beauties were handed over to howling, lust-ridden Five-Points gangsters in New York City and detailed luridly the indignities they suffered at the hands of "howling, hairy Abolitionists."

Northern newspapermen were no more restrained. One daily related in purple prose the atrocities committed on a beautiful— the victims were always beautiful—Northern woman, a schoolteacher in New Orleans, because she spoke in praise of Old Glory. The unfortunate young woman had been stripped naked, raped, beaten, tarred and feathered, and left to die horribly in a swamp.

Circulation-minded editors—both Southern and Northern— dumped truth out the window. Hyperbole and fiction ran rampant. According to them, the Yankees were arming the Sioux and sending drunken savages out on wanton scalping raids against Southern women and children. The Rebels, according to Northern sources, had given free rein to the Cherokees, promising a white woman to any warrior who took the warpath under Southern aegis.

It was quite a war in the papers, if not yet on the battlefield.

So-called eyewitness accounts received a big play. One Southern paper ran this story:

Old Lincoln sleeps with a hundred men in the East Room to protect him from the Southern army. He is expecting them to attack the city every night; he keeps a sentinel walking in front of his bed-room all night, and often gets so frightened that he leaves the White House, and sleeps out, no one knows where. These are facts. Mrs. Lincoln, a few nights since, heard whispering in the hall in front of her room; she rose from bed, dressed and sat up the remainder of the night, watching for the Southern army to blow up the White House as they are confidently expecting it.

In the South the revolution was still a novelty. The spirit of the rebellion ran high. The soldiers were fresh-faced and unscarred. The uniforms were bright, the sabers shiny, the boots polished. No one had yet seen a man torn by grapeshot or heard a wounded horse screaming in agony. The spring flowers were blooming; morning glories climbed trellises; the roses were in bud; the fields ripening. The rebellion was made up of a band of brothers standing shoulder to shoulder, united in opinion, resolve, and patriotism.

"Little Ellick" Stephens, who had fought against secession, but had become its ardent advocate, was not yet embittered against Jefferson Davis and the Cause. He made an impassioned speech in Atlanta, before a cheering crowd:

> Lincoln may bring his seventy-five thousand troops against us . . . but we fight for our homes, our fathers, our mothers, our wives, brothers, sisters, sons, daughters and neighbors! They fight for money! God is on our side . . , and who shall be against us? We can call out a million people, if need be, and when they are cut down, we can call out another, and still another, until the last man of the South finds a bloody grave . . .

This was the spirit of the South; flamboyant, bombastic; a combination of bravery and chivalry. Here was a new nation purportedly devoted to liberty and independence but, paradoxically, dependent for survival on the intervention of European powers, primarily England and France. The Confederacy, a republic born in the struggle against "tyranny," was turning to the tawdry Emperor Louis Napoleon of France and the imperialistic English Queen Victoria.

But this was only a part of the contradictions which enlaced the Confederacy. A new country allegedly concerned with individual freedom boasted that its cornerstone was slavery. A country who scorned its enemy as mercenary hailed cotton as king—cotton, the most prosperous business in the South.

With the secession of Virginia, the movement spread to include Arkansas, Tennessee, North Carolina, and Texas. The ranks of the seceded states were now filled. The war could go on.

From Virginia came an invitation to transplant the capital of the country to Richmond. The bored politicians in Montgomery were delighted; their wives even more pleased at the suggestion. If any Southern city symbolized the true culture of the South, it was the graceful city on the banks of the James River. There the first families flowered; it was the breeding place of aristocrats—not "scrub gentility," but the real thing.

Davis himself was dubious about the wisdom of the move. He felt Richmond was too far north and vulnerable to attack. But his Congress overruled him. The proximity of the capital to the potential fighting front was a morale factor, the representatives believed. The prestige of Richmond and of Virginia would make an impression on the vacillating Border States. Davis gave his consent finally, and during the last week in May, advance echelons went on to Richmond to prepare offices and lodgings for the government and its top personnel. Clerks and lesser employees would be transported to Richmond, but had to scrounge living quarters for themselves. The Confederate Congress recessed, after voting to reconvene in Richmond on July 20. And once Davis had completed his business in Montgomery, he and his family headed for the new capital, evoking wild enthusiasm at every stop en route.

Richmond was swarming with a motley assortment of troops. Hillbillies and small farmers who had never owned a slave, or a foot of ground, for that matter, marched in slovenly ranks beside crack regiments made up of rich planters and their sons. Virginia regiments, which numbered in their ranks some of the most illustrious names of the South, cheerfully pitched tents and slept in muddy hollows and damp fields.

Illiterate yokels in coarse butternut homespun mingled with elite gentlemen wearing finely tailored gray uniforms. The Confederate troops in the environs of Richmond and on the fields of Virginia made a democratic army which was the shield and buckler of a nation that stretched from the Potomac River to the Gulf Coast and out to the reaches where the Rio Grande rambled along the New Mexico border.

The new nation extended fifteen hundred miles from Chesapeake Bay to Kansas. From all over this vast area came the best young men, ready to sacrifice health and strength, and even life, in a Cause that was nebulous to most of them and in a war brought on by

HENRICO COUNTY JAIL, RICHMOND.

THE CITY OF

In May, 1861, the Confederate capital was moved to Richmond, Virginia, and that city became the symbol of the Southern Cause. An over-all view (above) depicts Richmond early in the war. Henrico County Jail, (top left) and buildings

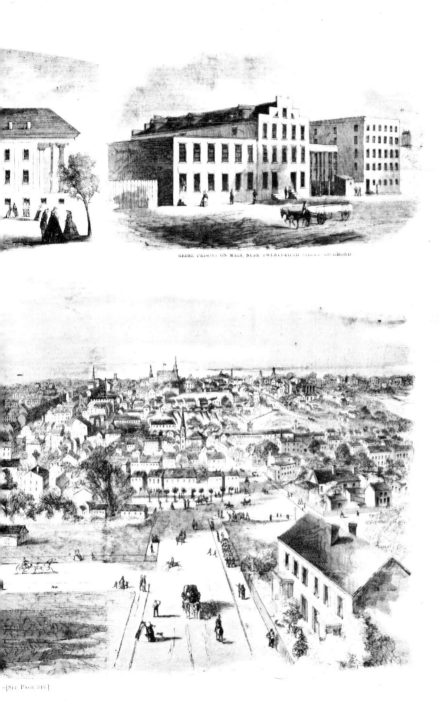

REBEL PRISONS ON MAIN, NEAR TWENTY-FIFTH STREET, RICHMOND

—[SEE PAGE 313.]

on Main Street served as prisons for Unionists and Northern sympathizers. The State Capitol building (center) was also the national Capitol.

others. Only a fraction of them were slaveholders; only a few had ever raised or even sold a bale of cotton. Nevertheless they were risking their lives for slavery and cotton, although this facet of the Cause was masked behind glowing words and eloquent phrases.

William Howard Russell, the correspondent of the London *Times,* on a tour of the Deep South, wrote: "I am not prepared to say they are right or wrong, but I am convinced that the South can be forced back only by such a conquest as that which laid Poland prostrate before Russia."

Richmond, which had hailed many heroes in its day, never had given anyone the reception it afforded President Davis on his arrival. Jubilant crowds milled around the railroad station to greet his train. Pretty girls strewed his path with flowers. Thousands lined the streets along the route to Capitol Hill, shouting their elation.

Smartly uniformed militia companies executed complicated drills for the edification of the President and his lady. The entire city was bedecked with bunting and flags, especially the Spotswood Hotel, which was to serve as temporary quarters for the Chief Executive and his family until a suitable house could be found.

The people of Richmond scrutinized their President and liked what they saw. Davis seemed to be born to the task he had assumed. He had the look and the bearing of an aristocrat, which pleased snobbish Richmond.

Varina, on the other hand, did not fare as well under the same severe inspection. She was a type almost unknown in Richmond society. A frank, outspoken woman, she did not observe the rules of female behavior demanded by Richmond's social arbiters. She could not adapt herself easily to the regimen established by the first families of Virginia such as the Byrds, Spotswoods, Custises, Lees, and Randolphs. Varina had grown accustomed to the social amenities of plantation life and the free atmosphere of Washington boarding-houses rather than the strict demands of formal society.

She had manners, graciousness, and bearing, but never quite felt comfortable in Richmond society. Too honest to gossip, Varina found herself surrounded by women who regarded tattling as a favored pastime. She had little talent for chitchat or playing the helpless fluttering female so typical of that city.

Varina knew more about politics than most men. She had opinions and expressed them. She was intellectually superior to most Richmond ladies and fairly attractive as well. They grew wary of her because she possessed qualities they envied. Soon enough, she became the victim of mean gossip and nasty backbiting. Small wonder she found living in Richmond none too congenial, for, as she said, the city was "more exclusive, more English and the people were more offish to strangers."

After a brief stay at the Spotswood, the Davises moved into the former residence of Dr. John Brockenbrough at the foot of East Clay Street, on the crest of a steep hill overlooking the shanties of a dismal slum known as "Butchertown." But the fashionable section of East Clay Street in which the Brockenbrough house stood was named Court End. The houses close by were on the elegant side. It was a fitting neighborhood for an Executive Mansion, and suited the Davises well. The citizens of Richmond secured the residence and wanted the President to accept the house as a gift, but in his scrupulous fashion, Davis insisted on paying rent for his living quarters. A modest annual fee was fixed.

The gracious atmosphere of Court End was often disturbed by the clamor and racket of "Butchertown" at the bottom of the hill. Drunkenness and immorality were rife down in the slum. Whores and thieves made it their headquarters. Police seldom ventured through those twisting streets and alleys. Filth, pollution, and misery made "Butchertown" a morbid pesthole.

Among the youths of this noisome slum, vicious resentment was harbored against the "swells" living in luxury atop the hill. The prime target of their hatred were the sons of the wealthy mansion dwellers. Sometimes, bitterness generated violence. A gang of teenagers known as the "Butcher Cats" made sorties up the steep slope and poured onto East Clay Street to beat and even rob any youngster who crossed their path. After several such raids, the Court End youths formed a defensive gang called the "Hill Cats."

Battles between these two groups intensified in ferocity. Sticks, stones, rocks, fists, and even pieces of iron pipe came into play. Broken heads and bloodied noses were commonplace in both camps. At last, after a particularly gory clash, President Davis decided to intervene. Since the "Butcher Cats" were admittedly the aggressors, Davis went down into "Butchertown" on a peacemaking mission. Once in the shabby street, he was surrounded by swarms of slum dwellers. He made a speech, addressing his remarks particularly to a group of ragamuffins who appeared to be the "Butcher Cats," judging by the marks of battle on their persons. Davis pleaded with them to cease their attacks and flattered them by calling them "the future rulers of the country."

The teen-agers listened respectfully enough and applauded the President when he had finished—but rejected his plea to end hostilities. One of the lads spoke up, saying, "Mr. President, we like you, but we ain't going to be friends with them Hill Cats."

Davis studied the determined young faces, accepted his defeat gracefully and trudged back up the hill with all the dignity he could muster. The "Butcher Cats" sent him off with three cheers and a tiger. In dealing with these boys, Davis revealed a side of his nature that only his wife and family knew. Unfortunately, as a public figure he never permitted himself to show the warmth and kindness of which he was capable. If he had been able to do so he would certainly have become a much more popular person.

Actually he never concerned himself about popularity. During his entire political career, he did not need to struggle for public favor. In 1845 the influence of his brother Joe Davis had been enough to send him to Congress. And after that, until he became the Confederate President, he had held only one other elective office—that of United States Senator. At that time, senators were not chosen by direct popular vote, but by the state legislature.

Nor did he have to curry the good will of the voters to become President of the Confederacy. A group of men in Montgomery had appointed him Provisional President; in the main, they were men of his caste and background. When he was voted into his permanent term of six years he ran without opposition. Unlike Lincoln who always had to fight for office, he was required to do so only once, during the Mississippi gubernatorial election of 1850. And then he was roundly beaten by Henry Foote.

Yet, in spite of this, no nation could have been led by a more dedicated Chief Executive than the Confederacy during Davis' stay in office. He was so intent on carrying out his tasks that nothing else held any meaning for him. As in the past, he was certain that his intellectual processes were so keen that he could find the proper course to pursue when faced with any problem on earth.

He had little time for pleasure and followed a Spartan schedule of work that played havoc with his frail health. As a result he became even more aloof and withdrawn than usual. He could not shed the cares of office for a single minute. This preoccupation kept him from enjoying any but official relationships with his colleagues and with Congressmen. It resulted in misunderstandings and unnecessary animosities. One of his associates, Secretary of the Navy Mallory, wrote of him:

> His relations with members of Congress were not what they should have been; nor what they might have been . . . Position and opportunity presented him every means of cultivating the personal good will of members by little acts of attention, courtesy or deference, which no man, however high his position, who has to work by means of his fellows, can dispense with . . . While he was ever frank and cordial to his friends and those whose conduct he approved, he would not and, I think, could not, sacrifice a smile . . . or a demonstration of attention to flatter the self-love of any who did not stand well in his esteem . . . By members of the Congress who had to see him on business, his manners to and reception of them were frequently complained of and pronounced ungracious and irritable . . . Though he listened patiently and heard all they had to say . . . and in return calmly and precisely stated his reasons against the proposed measure, he rarely satisfied or convinced them simply because in his manners and language there was an indescribable something which offended their self-esteem and left their judgement room to find fault with him . . . some of his best friends left him at times with feelings bordering closely upon anger . . . and with a determination hastily formed, of calling no more upon him; and many of them, embracing some of the most sensible, prudent, calm and patriotic men of both houses, were alienated from him more or less from this cause. It was of no use for his friends . . . to counsel him to adopt a different manner toward the members of the Congress and to see them socially, etc.; for he could not do this; it was not in his nature, and his restless, manly and turbulent spirit turned from what was to him the faintest approach to seek popularity; and he scorned to believe it necessary to coax men to do their duty in the then condition of their country . . .

While much of Davis's insociability was the result of poor health, he still found time to do many of the things he wished to do: daily walks, brisk rides to the camps, playing with his children—time that might have been more profitably spent in cultivating the good will of the government officials with whom he was barely cordial.

His behavior brought mild censure even from his loving and devoted wife. In her *Memoir,* Mrs. Davis wrote:

> He said he could do only one or the other—give entertainments or administer the government—and he fancied he was expected to perform the latter service in preference; and so we ceased to entertain, except at formal receptions or informal dinners, given to as many as Mr. Davis's health permitted us to invite . . . It would have been much better if the President could have met the Congress and State officials as well as the citizens socially and often, for the magnetism of his personality would have greatly mollified their resentments.

Davis was a hard, unrelenting worker whose mind was always on business. When others around him were gay, the President was somber. A proud man, he chose to ignore his enemies rather than strike back—and maintaining a dignified silence took its toll on him. His nature was so high-strung that he became ill for days if he ate even the simplest foods while under strain or excitement.

On the other hand, Lincoln had learned, years before, that tensions and stresses could destroy a man. He developed the art of storytelling and joking to relax himself and his co-workers. It was a habit Jefferson Davis might have emulated profitably . . .

· 5 ·

The capital city of the Confederacy was not entirely stylish and well-mannered; its people were not all aristocrats and gentlefolk. Richmond had a large working class. Among them were artisans and skilled craftsmen: mechanics, machinists, carpenters, blacksmiths, tool and die makers, and draftsmen; it was a working class capable of producing anything—luxuries and necessities. Among the many inconsistencies of the Confederacy, not the least was the strange spectacle of Richmond's strongly class-conscious workingmen supporting a war for the survival of slavery.

In 1861, Richmond was a city of 38,000 people—a population that was soon to nearly double in the ebb and flow of war. It was an industrial center with machine shops and ironworks.

At the foot of Oregon Hill on the banks of the Kanawah Canal stood the Tredegar Works, a mammoth plant, with sprawling red-brick buildings and tall chimney stacks poking skyward. It was one of the greatest ironworks in the country, and manufactured boilers for United States Navy frigates and heavy naval guns as well. Tredegar also produced locomotives and steam engines, iron pipe, and sewage ducts.

While Tredegar was the largest, other plants and shops also made equipment for both American and European railroads. Sugar refineries, woolen mills, and factories of bricks, brushes, cabinets, caps, carriages, dresses, guns, pistols, and a multitude of other products were located in and around Richmond. For a traditional Southern city, it was as bustling and active as any New England commercial center. Richmond had dozens of produce and livestock commission merchants, insurance companies, and banks, and it was rapidly rising in importance as a financial and business community.

The capital was a rarity among the cities of the Confederacy. Very few towns had any manufacturing facilities at all. For years the South had been getting most of its manufactured goods from the North. In fact, only 113,000 industrial workers could be counted in the entire South; but in the North, 1,300,000 people worked in plants and factories. Only 18,000 industrial establishments were set up in the Confederate States as against 110,000 in the North. The Yankees had almost as many industrial plants as the South had factory workers.

Only one out of eighty-two persons in the agrarian South worked in industry. But, despite the agricultural economy of the region, much of its fertile land was devoted to growing only one crop—cotton. So even in the production of foodstuffs, the South was not self-sufficient.

Davis was confident that he would win the war because the Southern cotton planters practically controlled the world's cotton supply. At the very outset of the conflict, Davis resorted to a game of economic blackmail. He ordered an embargo on cotton shipments to Europe. His price for lifting the ban was recognition and aid, especially from Britain and France, leading users of cotton in their great textile industries. Davis even hoped to bring about Franco-British intervention against the United States.

In practise, the cotton embargo created an effect quite opposite to that expected by Davis. The cotton mills of England and France were hard hit by the loss of American cotton—but the woolen and linen industries of both nations spurted to fabulous heights.

The workers in the Lancashire mills suffered greatly—thousands were out of work. But they demonstrated a solidarity that won the admiration of labor everywhere. These impoverished hands refused to work with Southern slave-grown cotton—and for all intents, went on strike and held their ranks so solidly that the manufacturers were forced to find other sources of supply. Soon a flow of Egyptian cotton permitted some mills to resume operations.

A few days after the war had begun, on April 17, 1861, Lincoln proclaimed a blockade of all Southern ports and harbors. At the time, the blockade was hardly effective. The Union lacked a navy capable of carrying out such an action. But Jefferson Davis's cotton embargo served the same purpose. By his own hand, Davis destroyed his country's greatest economic weapon. Cotton that could have been shipped to England and France without any Yankee interference was piled up in bulging warehouses all over the South. By the time Davis tried to rectify his error and lifted his embargo, it was too late.

At the very outset, Judah Benjamin had proposed to Davis that the Confederate government should buy up 100,000 bales of cotton at a fixed price and ship them to England. He advised that the money secured in this transaction be used to purchase arms and ammunition. Benjamin believed the war was going to be a long one. His foresight was ridiculed. The President and the cabinet scoffed at the idea that the North could not be whipped in short order. The combination of Franco-British assistance and Confederate valor would quickly defeat the Yankees and bring Lincoln to terms.

Thus, due to the mistaken policy of the Davis government, the cotton that might have secured independence for the Confederacy was piled up at the great southern ports; warehouses in New Orleans, Savannah, Mobile, and Charleston bulged with cotton. Ironically, 1861 saw a bumper cotton crop with a yield estimated at between four and five million bales, hardly any of which reached market.

Then, with several millions of bales in the storage bins of the South, the slogan "Plant no cotton in '62!" was raised. It was heeded by the cotton growers; the yield for 1862 amounted to a mere 500,000 bales. The planters had figured there was a sufficient supply of cotton on hand to meet any European demand. What had not been taken into consideration was the fact that Union military actions would put tens of thousands of bales into Federal hands. The Yankees could either confiscate or destroy it as they chose. Like lemmings, the planters had committed mass economic suicide . . .

In the hectic days of early 1861, a phantom haunted the South—the phantom of its own guilt about slavery. Even the most dyed-in-the-wool Southerner was subject to doubts about the moral right of the "peculiar institution." True, the economy of the cotton-growing states was based on slavery—but the bulk of the Confederate people were not slave-owners. Of the 5,000,000 whites in the South, only 385,000 owned any slaves at all. About 77,000 of them had only one slave; 200,000 had between two and ten; 61,000 had over ten but not more than twenty; 44,000 owned over twenty but not more than one hundred. Less than one-twentieth of one per cent of the total population, some 2,300 planters, were the Bourbons who held one hundred or more slaves. A half-million Southern farms were worked with no slaves at all, as against 306,000 which utilized bondsmen.

Most Southerners played no part in perpetuating the system of human bondage; and to a great number, slavery was an abhorrent practise.

Outwardly the Southerners appeared to accept the custom—but in fact many suffered a twinge of conscience over it. In the flowery words of a prominent Virginian, Mary Minor Blackford, who sent five sons into the Confederate Army: "Disguise it as thou wilt, Slavery thou art a bitter draught . . . I am convinced that the time will come when we shall look back and wonder how Christians could sanction slavery . . ."

Mrs. Blackford first wrote these prophetic lines in 1833, and she repeated them frequently throughout the war; she was not alone in her sentiments. Notable Confederates like Robert E. Lee, Joseph E. Johnston, Matthew Fontaine Murray, and A. P. Hill openly deplored slavery. Yet these men, and Mrs. Blackford, too, were able to rationalize their positions and support a Cause admittedly based on that institution.

But an even deeper contradiction than ambivalence over slavery plagued the South. Within the boundaries of the Confederacy were two separate and discordant nations. One contained a strange mixture of old-line Southern traditionists and the parvenu cotton planters. They had united against the North—and they stirred up the fires of war. From this grouping stemmed the image of the romantic South: handsome cavaliers riding off to battle with a song on their lips; the twang of banjos around campfires; drawling voices whispering gentle words of love; magnolia blossoms and pretty girls twirling parasols on wooded paths. This was the gallant, the courtly, the aristocratic South, bold and idealistic with a spiritual devotion to the Cause.

This was the nation and the class of Jefferson Davis. For him and his class, the war was being waged to retain the status of the privileged gentry. They neither understood nor cared about the masses of the South: the streetsweepers, the mechanics, the laborers, the poor dirt farmers, the men who drove horse cars and who marched off in ragged columns to spill their blood on mountain slopes and in swamps; to die of fever and wounds; and to be buried in unmarked graves, from the Chickahominy to the Rio Grande.

This was the chivalry of the South—genteel, well-mannered and wealthy; they were at opposite poles to the other elements within the Confederate nation. These were the nonslaveholding people, many of them poverty-stricken mountain folk with no love for the aristocratic government in Richmond. As a matter of fact thousands of these hardy men and women never wavered in their loyalty to the Union. The Cause of Jefferson Davis was not their cause. They owned no human chattels and had no interests threatened by the Yankees. Their hard-scrabble farms did not bloom with puffs of cotton bolls, nor did they live in gracious, porticoed homes overlooking gardens and fountains and broad expanses of ripening crops. They did not ride to the hounds on blooded Arab hunters; and when they shot game, it was for food—not sport. Their lives were grim, filled with arduous toil; the dreams and aspirations of the gentlefolk in Richmond meant nothing to them. The Old Flag was good enough for them.

Geographically, this dissident area of the South formed a huge peninsula pointing into the heartland of the Confederacy. It stretched from the Pennsylvania border into north Georgia and Alabama, reaching to a depth of five hundred miles and a width of two hundred miles.

Its eastern boundary was the Blue Ridge Mountains, its western, the Cumberlands. The vast region comprised nearly one-third of the land south of the Ohio River and east of the Mississippi, and contained western Virginia, east Tennessee, western North Carolina, northern Georgia and parts of Alabama.

The inhabitants of this expanse were by tradition, origin, custom, occupation, and manner the antithesis of the cotton planters and Bourbons. Mainly Scotch-Irish by descent, they were Baptist, Methodist, and Presbyterian—not Anglican.

While the North had its subversives and Copperheads, in the Southern hill country secret anti-Confederate societies like the Heroes of America were formed for the purpose of sabotaging the war effort. The mountaineers and dirt farmers disrupted recruiting, opposed conscription, encouraged desertion, and played a large part in the defection of 103,400 Confederate soldiers during the war. The Heroes of America resorted to terror tactics, bushwhacking, arson and assassination. Many of them joined the Rebel army only to go over to the Federals at the first chance. The activities of the Copperheads and the Knights of the Golden Circle in the North were neither as widespread nor as successful.

The unity of the South was a myth. Within its territory a secret civil war raged almost from the onset of the greater conflict. In a large measure it accounted for some of the Union successes in the West and in the mountainous regions of Virginia.

If the new nation had a dual personality, so did its President. On the one hand, Jefferson Davis was a devoted father, husband, and friend—a dedicated leader. On the other, he was a frigid, intransigent, and unapproachable executive. Some saw him as an opinionated, short-sighted public official. Others described him glowingly as an idealistic, modest man, long-suffering and patriotic.

All that was said of Jefferson Davis was true. The man was contradictory and the Cause itself was paradoxical. The Confederacy reflected this ideological clash.

Only the casualty lists evoked no controversy. No one could argue that pain and suffering and grief were not the same both North and South . . .

SIX

Mr. Lincoln

"I will hold General McClellan's horse if
he will only bring us success"—

ABRAHAM LINCOLN, October, 1861

Just before the battle, mother
I was drinking mountain dew
When I saw the Rebels marching,
To the rear I quickly flew.

Union army song

· 1 ·

MARY LINCOLN was not having a pleasant time in the national capital. The social set treated her formally, with the politeness demanded by her position and by the rules of protocol. Like Varina Davis, in Richmond, she was pilloried and slandered by wagging tongues. Much that was said against her stemmed from malicious gossip; Mrs. Lincoln was not a termagant, a fool, a Rebel spy, or an unfaithful wife.

Actually, she was a warm-hearted woman who suffered from mental instability and neurotic compulsions which drove her into temper tantrums, fits of jealousy, and frequent hysterical outbursts. At times, as though to reassure herself that she was the First Lady, Mrs. Lincoln went off on extravagant spending sprees, buying dresses she neither needed nor wanted, useless luxuries, and exorbitantly priced furnishings for the White House.

She ran up huge bills in New York stores and then fretted and brooded over them, darkly imagining she had bankrupted her husband and disgraced the family. Plagued by an irrational fear of poverty (Lincoln was a rather wealthy man), she resorted to strange, petty economies; once, she herself offered to do the housework in the White House if the Commissioner of Public Buildings, Major Benjamin Baker French, would pay her the salaries of the steward and housekeeper.

Between these disparate levels of behavior lay the real Mary Todd Lincoln: a strong-willed and determined woman, yet a loving wife and doting mother. She particularly idolized Robert, her eldest son, who was a senior at Harvard. Mrs. Lincoln worried constantly that he would join the army and wrote frantic letters pleading with him not to do so—a common enough plea of mothers in those days.

The White House was enlivened by the presence of the two other Lincoln boys, Thomas (Tad) and William Wallace (Willie). They were spirited lads, full of mischief. A family intimate gave this description of the boys:

Willie was a noble, beautiful boy of ten years, of great mental activity, unusual intelligence, wonderful memory, methodical, frank and loving, a counterpart of his father, except that he was handsome. He

133

was entirely devoted to Taddie, who was a gay, gladsome, merry, spontaneous fellow, bubbling over with innocent fun, whose laugh rang through the house, when not moved by tears. Quick in mind and impulse, like his mother, with her naturally sunny temperament, he was the life, as also the worry of the household. There could be no greater contrast between children.

Despite the strains and tensions of being the wartime First Lady, Mary Lincoln should have been satisfied with her role. She had attained to position and prestige of which she had never dreamed. Despite the gossip and the slander, Mrs. Lincoln still had much to enjoy in her White House life.

She decided to face her maligners and deriders with a façade of indifference. She carried herself with pride and reserve, but calmness only masked her anger at her derogators. Finally, Mrs. Lincoln resolved to teach them a lesson: she would force them to acknowledge her as the First Lady.

Although the War was daily growing grimmer, with fighting raging in the West and the memory of the disaster at Bull Run still fresh in everyone's mind, Mary Lincoln decided to hold a levee in the White House which would be the grandest party Washington had ever seen.

She sent five hundred invitations to the reception and supper to be held February 5, 1862. Reaction to the affair was explosive. Some who had not been invited protested bitterly that they had been snubbed without reason—as a result, three hundred more invitations went out. Others angrily criticized the President and his wife for holding a gala in wartime. The abolitionists were pronouncedly antagonistic and many refused to attend the party. Senator Ben Wade, the vituperative antislavery spokesman was one of those who rejected his bid to the occasion. Wade's note of refusal said bluntly: "Are the President and Mrs. Lincoln aware that there is a Civil War? If they are not, Mr. and Mrs. Wade are, and for that reason decline to participate in feasting and dancing."

The party was widely criticized in advance by the antiadministration press. Cartoons lampooned Lincoln as a henpecked husband and a tool of his wife's whims—he had announced that no public funds were to be spent on the party; he was personally footing all the bills.

Mary Todd Lincoln, the President's wife, was given to extravagance. She spent huge sums on clothes and personal luxuries. Her elaborate wardrobe (above) was often placed on public display.

This stylized lithograph of the Lincoln family shows Robert, Mrs. Lincoln, Tad, Willie, who died in 1862, and the President. In background is the Capitol with dome, a figment of the artist's imagination since the dome was not finished while young Willie was alive. (Bettmann Archive)

A vicious poem called "The Lady President's Ball" was widely circulated. The lengthy verse told of a dying soldier who expressed his feelings towards the woman who indulged in heedless extravagance and frivolity while thousands of boys were writhing in death throes on muddy battlefields.

Despite adverse publicity and criticism, Mrs. Lincoln pressed her party plans. She did not trust Washington caterers to carry out the arrangements and imported Louis Maillard, one of New York's most exclusive restaurateurs, to handle the cuisine and to design the decorations.

Several days before the party, Maillard swept into Washington with his retinue of pastry chefs, cooks, bakers, waiters, stewards, confectioners, butlers, and footmen. He descended on the White House and took over the ballrooms and the kitchens. Day and night the White House bustled. Carpenters were busy with hammering and nailing; cooks peered into steaming pots; bakers sent up clouds of flour as they kneaded and rolled mountains of dough; and in the midst of all the activity, Maillard capered and minced, pouted and fretted, until everything was done to his taste.

At last the great day came. All Washington was agog. The assemblage that converged on the White House was one of the most brilliant and glittering ever gathered in the capital. The entire corps of foreign diplomats attended in the uniforms of a dozen nations. A babel of many languages mingled in gay conversation. High-ranking army and navy officers and their ladies crowded the beautifully adorned rooms.

Mrs. Lincoln, wearing an exquisite white satin evening gown with a long train and low neckline, greeted everyone graciously as she stood on the receiving line beside the President. When Lincoln saw his wife in that dress for the first time, he had said, "Whew! Our cat has a long tail tonight. It would, perhaps, be in better taste if some of the tail were up closer to the head."

His jocular remark made his wife angry; the low-cut dress was daring, but in the latest Parisian style. As the guests began arriving, however, she regained her good humor. The night was her triumph, and she felt it was worth the effort and money that had been poured into it. In deference to the war, no dancing was permitted, although the Marine Band played popular airs. At 11:00 P.M. the doors of the state dining room were thrown open and the guests filed in to supper. Even the most sophisticated among them gasped at Maillard's table arrangement and the abundance of the elaborate repast. Rare wines and costly liquors were freely poured. Ten gallons of champagne punch sparkled in a huge punch bowl.

The buffet table held a ton of turkeys, ducks, geese, venison, partridges, pheasants, and hams. The decorations Maillard had created were both unique and exquisite. Nougat water nymphs formed the base of a fountain which spurted forth wine. Hives that swarmed with lifelike sugar bees were crammed with whipped-cream delicacies. Washington had never before known such an elegant party. Mr. Lincoln had come a long way from his humble youth to preside as host at such an occasion; and for Mary Todd Lincoln, the occasion marked the apex of her social ambitions.

But that magnificent affair was an endless ordeal for the presidential couple. That very afternoon Willie and Tad had been out in the rain, riding their ponies. Both boys had caught cold and were stricken with sudden fever. Willie, especially, seemed seriously ill. If it had not been too late, Mrs. Lincoln would undoubtedly have canceled the party.

As it was, Lincoln and his wife frequently slipped away from the festivities and hurried upstairs to look in at the sick children. The President grew increasingly anxious and deep lines of worry creased his face. He was a doting and overly indulgent father; the boys were the sum of his existence.

About 2:00 A.M. the party ended; the last carriages rolled away from the White House. Servants snuffed out the candles and doused the gaslights. But there was no sleep for the apprehensive parents who stayed all night at the bedsides of their fever-ridden sons.

The next morning their worst fears were confirmed. Both boys had typhoid; Tad's case was a mild one—but Willie's was serious. For two agonizing weeks, the anguished mother and father watched Willie slowly dying. Neither their prayers, their love, nor the best medical care could save him. On February 20, at 5:00 P.M., Willie Lincoln died.

The President staggered from the death room into the office of his secretary, John Nicolay. "Well, John—my boy is gone, he is actually gone!" Lincoln cried. He burst into tears and stumbled to his own office, where he sat weeping without restraint, his shaggy head bent, his lean body racked with sobs.

Mrs. Lincoln was prostrated. Malignant enemies accused her of heartlessness, saying that the White House had resounded with music and revelry as Willie lay dying. The canard was cruel and untrue. Even during the party she had seen to the comfort of her sons. The memory of that party haunted her forever. She never again gave another large reception in the White House. Except at state functions which she could not avoid, Mrs. Lincoln was rarely seen after that at festive occasions.

Willie's funeral was held on February 22, Washington's Birthday. It was to have been a gala day in Washington. Parades, fireworks and band concerts had been scheduled, not only to honor the first President, but also to celebrate signal Union victories in the West. The war was going well for the Union and the North had something to rejoice about. Instead, the city was decked in mourning. At the exact hour Lincoln should have been reviewing troops on Pennsylvania Avenue, he was following Willie's casket to Evergreen Cemetery. Mrs. Lincoln was too overcome to attend the services.

For months she suffered from shock; often she burst into sobs which gave way to hysteria. Once, according to an eyewitness, Mary Todd had a particularly violent weeping fit. The President took her gently by the arm and led her to a window.

Off in the distance, the rooftop of the insane asylum was visible beyond the banks of the Eastern Branch. Lincoln pointed to the building. "Mother, do you see that large white place on the hill yonder? Try and control your grief or it will drive you mad and we may have to send you there," he said, softly.

Mrs. Lincoln gradually regained control. But she refused to enter the guest room where Willie had died, or the Green Room in which the embalming had taken place. She could not even bear to look at his picture. The White House, to which she had aspired in the Springfield days, had become a dismal trap. She was surrounded here by spiteful people whom she distrusted. No matter what she did or failed to do, she remained the target of critics.

The only refuge the First Lady found from her misery was in visiting the military hospitals and helping relieve the sick and wounded soldiers. She performed this duty without fanfare; sometimes she brought along delicacies from the White House kitchen; sometimes she simply chatted with the men and gave sympathy where it was needed.

The soldiers were grateful to her and their appreciation was reward enough for Mary Lincoln. No matter what her enemies had to say against her, at least these soldiers knew the truth.

The President could not give in to sorrow over the loss of Willie; his responsibilities were too great. On the surface he appeared to recapture his composure rapidly, and carried out the normal functions of his office without revealing that he was heartbroken.

But, one night, shortly after Willie's death, a fire broke out in the stables near the White House. Lincoln dashed into the darkness, hurdled a boxwood hedge, and raced towards the stables where firemen were battling the blaze.

"Have the horses been taken out?" he asked.

"No, sir," someone replied. "They're all goners for sure."

Lincoln pushed by the men and yanked open a stable door. Flames licked out at him. He hesitated for a moment and then started to enter the blazing structure. The firemen seized and held him back.

A detachment of soldiers came on the double. The duty officer announced that the fire might have been an assassination attempt. The President was forcibly dragged to the safety of the White House.

He stood at a window of the East Room, tears running down his cheeks as he watched the fire destroying the stables and the horses. Later it was learned that one of Willie's favorite ponies had been in the stable. Lincoln had risked his life in a vain effort to save the animal . . .

· 2 ·

The war which was bringing so much grief into many thousands of homes overshadowed the sorrow of a single family—even the family of the President.

After the debacle at Bull Run in July, 1861, the military picture was a gloomy one for the North. The ensuing months brought some brightness, however. In the West, forceful action had saved Missouri for the Union. In the East, Forts Hatteras and Clark, North Carolina, had been captured; so had Port Royal, South Carolina. Dashing General George B. McClellan had gained victories in West Virginia—victories made sweeter because they had been wrested from the doughty soldier Robert E. Lee, who had not shown to ad-

Ten drummers in Zouave uniforms head the divisions of the Army of the
Potomac as it moves in awe-inspiring ranks down Pennsylvania Avenue in

Washington, D.C., prior to the invasion of Virginia in the late spring of 1861. Note unfinished dome of Capitol in background.

vantage in the field. Even in the South, he was regarded now as a has-been and called "Granny."

Following Bull Run, Lincoln realized he needed a commanding general capable of molding an army and leading it to victory. A young Winfield Scott would have been the perfect man—but "Old Fuss and Feathers" was at the end of the road. This war had to be fought by vigorous men, not by a magnificent ruin. The Union forces had been commanded at Bull Run by General Irvin Mc-Dowell, a capable and energetic officer. He deserved another chance, but the taint of defeat was on him. McDowell, the polished, educated soldier who loved music, landscape gardening, and architecture was no longer deemed suitable for high command even though the Bull Run fiasco was hardly his fault. He had been pressured into a battle by the politicians, long before he was ready to fight.

McDowell was not flamboyant enough to inspire men crushed by defeat. The new general had to have the verve and imagination needed to rekindle the spirits of the crestfallen Union army. Morale was at its lowest. Regiments had practically disintegrated. Washington was jammed with soldiers either absent without leave or simply unable to find their former units. Deserters skulked in alleyways or hid out in houses of prostitution. Drunken men in uniform staggered about the streets. Dirty, unshaven soldiers begged money for whisky. The more vicious turned criminal and mugged passers-by. The city was in a state of chaos and despair during those hectic days in July after Bull Run.

Only the regulars, and scattered regiments of volunteers, still behaved like soldiers. They manned the outposts, picketed the roads, and guarded the bridges. As the days passed, more and more absentees returned to their outfits. Shame and fear gave way at last to angry pride.

The Union army had marched off to fight a battle in a holiday atmosphere. Sight-seers had accompanied the troops acting like merry-making spectators attending a sporting contest. By late afternoon of that fatal July Sunday, McDowell's army, the glory of the North, was a broken rabble pouring panic-stricken back to the capital.

Not everybody ran. Not everybody threw away his weapons. Among even the rawest troops there were companies and regiments which marched off the field in disciplined ranks despite the disorder. Some of the regular army units coolly and competently covered the withdrawal; to them, a lost battle was no catastrophe but merely an incident of war.

The Confederates who had stumbled awkwardly to victory were not able to capitalize on their success. Confusion had spread from the highest to the lowest ranks. The exhausted Rebel troops could not be driven further and gave only token pursuit to the shattered Federals.

Recriminations, excuses, alibis, and accusations were heard everywhere in Washington. The volunteers blamed the regulars for what had happened. As a matter of fact, regular army artillerymen had broken from the front and driven their caissons to the rear at top speed for more ammunition. Green troops panicked because the inexperienced soldiers assumed the artillery was fleeing.

Regular army officers castigated the volunteers: "The dogs ran at the first shot," they cursed.

Critics lashed old General Bob Patterson for failing to hold Joe Johnston in the Shenandoah Valley and keep him from reinforcing Beauregard. Disgusted line soldiers knew whom to blame: the damned political officers who weren't worth a pinch of sheep dung except for whoring, drinking, and parading.

The men who had done the fighting summed it all up in the words of one bearded volunteer: "How the hell could we win? They sent us into battle with no-account officers who didn't know beans. They gave us lousy rifles that wouldn't shoot. We had bayonets that didn't even fit the rifles. The miracle was that we fought at all. And we didn't do so bad, neither. We danged near whupped them, didn't we?"

The Yankees had indeed come close to "whupping" the Rebels. Up until 3:00 P.M. victory had seemed certain. Then, all at once, the army was broken. But even at the moment when the Yankees were fleeing, an anguished Jefferson Davis, in the rear of his own troops, watched the walking wounded staggering back from the front line, saw decimated regiments running in panic, without guns or equipment. He stared aghast and later recalled: "All seemed lost, our lines broken, all was confusion."

Victory came to Jefferson Davis as he grappled with his own anxieties. Defeat came to Lincoln the same way. The President heard the news in the War Department and walked slowly from the building. An old friend took his arm, "Abe, for God's sake, tell us whether the news is good or bad!"

Lincoln looked at him morosely. "It's bad, Bob, damn bad." That was the first time anyone had ever heard the President use even the mildest profanity . . .

· 3 ·

Bull Run had a sobering impact on the North. To Lincoln, it · meant the struggle was going to be long and exhausting. He issued a call for 500,000 three-year volunteers and cast about for a general.

The President found him. Thirty-five-year-old General George Brinton McClellan—brilliant, fiery, and with a good Mexican War record. McClellan had entered West Point at the age of fifteen and a half, below the legal age for a cadet. In his case, the regulations had been waived because of his physique, mentality, and intellectual attainments. The prodigy warranted the confidence shown him. Out of fifty-nine cadets, McClellan was rated second in his graduating class.

"Little Mac" had observed all the European armies and witnessed the fighting in the Crimean War. At the outbreak of the Civil War, McClellan had been serving as president of the Ohio and Mississippi Railroad at Cincinnati, with a salary of $10,000 per annum. He was a man to whom success had become commonplace. McClellan returned to the army after the attack on Fort Sumter; with a force of 18,000 men he had been campaigning in West Virginia where he won for the Union its only victories in the Eastern theater.

On the whole, McClellan seemed an excellent choice to revitalize the army. Lincoln gave him unusual powers and a free hand, and on July 27, only a week after Bull Run, McClellan had command of all Union forces in Virginia and around Washington. He stepped into the breach manfully at the nation's most critical hour. Very quickly Washington became aware that a strong hand was holding the reins. McClellan soon demonstrated that he had talents beyond running a railroad and designing the cavalry saddle that bore his name.

Patrols of regulars swooped through Washington rounding up stray soldiers and sending them back to their regiments. The saloons

At the first battle of Manassas, in July, 1861, green Union troops under McDowell fought raw Confederates under Beauregard. The tide of battle favored the Union at first (above).

Before the day was over, the Federals were fleeing from the battlefield in wild disorder. An artist here depicts the disastrous rout which almost wrecked the Army of the Potomac.

and bars were cleared of military personnel. Incompetent officers were peremptorily dismissed from the service. Bivouac areas were neatly laid out and proper order was restored in all army encampments. With limitless energy, "Little Mac" made the commissary and the quartermaster provide sufficient clothing and ample food for the troops. He instituted a severe regimen of drill and training. The fields and meadows in the environs of Washington and across the Potomac in Virginia resounded with the cadenced tread of squads, platoons, and companies learning the rudiments of soldiering. A surge of confidence engulfed the whole country from the President to the sweating privates awkwardly performing the evolutions of army drill.

Shortly after McClellan's promotion, Lincoln received a letter that underlined the depths to which Northern morale had been shaken by Bull Run. The communication was written by Horace Greeley, the eccentric editor of the New York *Tribune*. Greeley had penned the missive at midnight on July 29. The envelope was noted for Lincoln's attention as "In strict confidence and for your eyes only." Greeley said:

> Dear Sir: This is my seventh sleepless night—yours too, doubtless— yet I think I shall not die because I do not have the right to die, I must struggle to live, however bitterly. You are not considered a great man, and I am a hopelessly broken one. You are now undergoing a terrible ordeal, and God has thrown the gravest responsibilities on you. Do not fear to meet them. Can the rebels be beaten after all that has occurred, and in view of the actual state of feeling caused by our late awful disaster? . . .

These were strange sentiments from the man who recently had been composing bloodthirsty editorials against the South and its "nest of traitors."

For weeks, the *Tribune* had featured a banner line over its masthead: "On To Richmond!" it proclaimed in large, bold letters. Greeley had been among the loudest to call for action. Now he was bawling for peace; in this remarkable letter he begged Lincoln to seek an immediate armistice, to call a peace conference, and to disband the armed forces. He said:

> The gloom in this city is funereal—for our dead at Bull Run were

Striking a Napoleonic stance, Major General George B. McClellan imitates his personal hero. "Little Mac" had all the earmarks of a great military leader, but he never could achieve the success he confidently promised the nation.

many, and they lie unburied yet. On every brow sits sullen, scorching, black despair.

Greeley swore to back any compromise measures the President might propose. He closed his craven letter, "Yours, in the depths of bitterness."

Lincoln did not even deign to answer Greeley. He characterized both the contents and the author in one word: "Pusillanimous." Lincoln knew Greeley represented only a panic-stricken minority. He had too much respect for hard-grained Yankees to believe that one blow could destroy their will to fight. Because he was of the people himself, the President knew how to judge their mood; he was positive Bull Run would only make the Northerners angry. He was right.

The ordinary citizen read the news, rolled up his sleeves, spat on his hands, and headed for the nearest recruiting office. The Secesh wanted war—now, by Jiminy, the slavers were going to get a bellyful.

Machine-shop forges glowed twenty-four hours a day. Heavy hammers pounded molten metal into gun barrels. The North flexed its muscles, gathered its strength, and set to work creating a war machine that would grind the rebellion into dust.

· 4 ·

Lincoln acted resolutely, swiftly and firmly; he far exceeded his constitutional authority in many of his acts, but what he did had to be done and the legalities could be straightened out later. In areas where secessionist sentiment ran strong, he suspended the writ of habeas corpus. Known secessionists were thrown into jail, under military jurisdiction and without formal charges. Because he thought the legislature of Maryland might vote for secession, Lincoln arrested the entire body. Stern, undemocratic, and repressive measures were employed, as the dangerous situation warranted.

In addition, Lincoln had called up troops without consent of Congress and had launched a war while the legislature was in adjournment. He had also proclaimed a blockade of the Southern coastline, increased the size of the regular army, authorized the expenditure of Federal funds, and taken numerous other actions not normally within the scope of the executive branch.

His enemies called him "despot" and "tyrant." Charges of dictatorship were made. Lincoln knew better than anyone else that his conduct had been extralegal; but he also knew that if he had not moved as he did the United States was doomed and the Union would have been forever dissolved. He never denied he had overreached the powers allotted to him by the Constitution, and when Congress convened on July 4, he said:

> These measures, whether strictly legal or not, were ventured upon, under what appeared to be popular demand, and a public necessity; trusting then, as now, that Congress would readily ratify them.

Those who had sneered at Lincoln as not strong enough to maintain the presidency had already learned how badly they had underestimated him. In the interests of national security, he had the courage to move vigorously. Despite some opposition, Congress simply had to rubber-stamp their approval of Lincoln's drastic steps.

At his behest, the Administration worked out an over-all concept for the prosecution of the war. This master plan was the one which directed all the thinking and orientation of the armies and the navies. It was a good one and had three important facets. In the East, an army was to cross the Potomac, drive Beauregard and Johnston from Virginia, and capture Richmond. On the Western Front, an army would march South through the friendly regions of Missouri, Kentucky, and Tennessee, break the Rebel line from Bowling Green to Corinth, open the Mississippi, and slice the Confederacy in two. While these land operations were being carried out simultaneously, the Navy was ordered to close Southern ports from Cape Charles to the Gulf, patrol the rivers and cooperate with the land forces in every way possible.

The strategy had been temporarily thwarted in Virginia but, elsewhere, it was being successfully followed. Coastal areas in the Carolinas had fallen to the Federals. The blockade was starting to have important, if not total, effect.

At the beginning of 1862 the North was full of optimism for the Union cause. Everywhere—except in Virginia—victory seemed at hand. And the situation there was soon to change, everyone believed.

A tumultuous demonstration of military fierceness in New York City, by Billy Wilson's Zouaves, a regiment of Tammany Hall adherents which displayed

more fervor in patriotic meetings than on the battlefield. Such demonstrations were typical of patriotic ardor early in the war.

McClellan was building the greatest army the world had ever seen—the Army of the Potomac. No one doubted that in the spring, "Little Mac," the Young Napoleon, would launch an overwhelming offensive to sweep the Secesh out of Virginia, capture Richmond and end the rebellion in jig time.

While such pleasant prospects made interesting table talk, Union hopes were rising on more than speculation. The year had started with a victory at Mill Springs, Kentucky, and the emergence of a first-rate Union combat General—George H. Thomas. A Virginian, Thomas had remained loyal. Some radical congressmen suspected him because of his Southern background, but "Pap" Thomas rammed these suspicions down their throats at Mill Springs by beating the Confederates under General Felix Zollicoffer who was killed in the battle. The battle was not a big one but it opened the road into East Tennessee and boosted Federal morale.

The most important Union successes of the war came in February of that same year. A stoop-shouldered, forty-year-old Brigadier General named Ulysses Simpson Grant who had resigned from the Army some years back, and had failed at every civilian occupation to which he turned, emerged an unlikely hero and rose from obscurity to national renown as the conqueror of Forts Henry and Donelson.

These crucial Rebel bastions guarded the Kentucky-Tennessee border. Fort Henry sat on the Tennessee River and Fort Donelson on the Cumberland, about twenty miles apart. Early in February, it was decided to move against these two strong points.

Grant loaded fifteen thousand men on transports and, escorted by a flotilla of gunboats under Flag Officer Andrew Foote, went up the Tennessee to attack Fort Henry. The redoubt looked formidable, even impregnable—but its strength was merely on the surface. Not only was the fort undermanned, it was also half flooded. The Rebel engineers who had erected the bastion had chosen its site unwisely. Water seeped in and weakened the foundations. The river's backwash inundated part of the works.

When the attack got underway, Grant landed his troops some distance below the fort to invest it by land. While the infantry was still floundering in the boggy bottom lands, Foote moved his gunboats up to Fort Henry's walls and commenced a furious bombardment. The Confederate commander struck his colors and surrendered to Foote after briefly withstanding the naval barrage. Jubilation over the capture was somewhat lessened when the victors discovered that the bulk of the fallen stronghold's garrison had been safely evacuated to Fort Donelson.

Taking Donelson proved more difficult. The Confederates fought bravely and furiously. The United States gunboats were heavily damaged by the fort's cannon and the naval units had to be withdrawn.

The job was left to Grant and his soldiers. On February 15, the General ordered an all-out attack against the works. The fighting was heavy. At one point during the engagement volunteers serving under Brigadier General C. F. Smith, a crusty regular, faltered as they ran into Confederate rifle fire. Smith, who was sixty years old and had been in the army almost forty years, was riding at the front of his troops. He spurred back to the wavering men. Leaning out of his saddle, he bellowed: "Damn you, gentlemen! I see skulkers! I'll have none here. Come on, you volunteers, come on! This is your chance. You volunteered to be killed for love of country, and now you can be. You damned volunteers—I'm only a soldier and don't want to be killed, but you came to be killed and now you can be!"

After loosing that blast, Smith wheeled his horse and without so much as a backward glance, rode on towards the earthworks amid the whining bullets, his huge white mustache bristling fiercely. Although dozens of sharpshooters took pot shots at him, he was unscathed. Inspired by the brave old soldier, the volunteers jumped up and charged. They swarmed through the abatis and went over the breastworks to drive out the Rebels with bayonet, gun butt, and fists.

Smith's bold charge slammed the door on the Confederate garrison. General Gideon Pillow, the Southern commander, was trapped and knew it. Fearing a Federal firing squad if captured, Pillow passed the command down to the next in rank, General John Floyd, and fled from Fort Donelson. Floyd, who had been Secretary of War under Buchanan, felt equally certain the Federals would hang him for his treasonable acts while in office. So he promptly passed the buck to his subordinate, General Simon Bolivar Buckner, and joined Pillow in flight. Buckner, who had known Grant in the old army, was left with the unappealing chore of surrendering the post and its garrison. He asked Grant for terms and received the historic reply: "No terms except an unconditional and immediate surrender can be accepted. I propose to move immediately on your works."

Buckner grumbled and thought Grant unchivalrous for treating an old friend so poorly—but he surrendered 13,828 soldiers, a mountain of supplies and equipment, guns and munitions. Fort Donelson's fall gave the North its first major victory and affected the entire course of the war in the West. It also marked the rise of Grant. The "failure" from Galena, Illinois, had become the toast of the nation. Folks claimed that his initials, U.S., stood for "Unconditional Surrender." At last, old Abe had found himself a real general. Grant was the sort of man the people understood. He wasn't a plug hat. He'd had his share of life's hard knocks. He was supposed to have a weakness for liquor. But, best of all, he was a plain, tough soldier who spoke the only language Rebels understood. He had the right idea. No terms for Rebels. Surrender, or we'll blast you to hell.

· 5 ·

As if the stresses of actual warfare were not sufficiently taxing for Lincoln, two crises developed. One had international repercussions; the other took place within the President's own cabinet.

In November, 1861, the Confederate government sent two envoys, James M. Mason and John Slidell, on missions to England and France. The men slipped through the blockade, and on reaching Nassau, took passage for Europe aboard a British packet boat, the *Trent*.

The U.S.S. *San Jacinto*, a sloop-of-war, commanded by Captain Charles Wilkes, was on patrol duty in the Caribbean. Spies advised Wilkes that the Confederate agents were on the *Trent*. Wilkes stopped the British vessel and in spite of the protests of the ship's officers put a boarding party on her and forcibly removed Mason and Slidell.

The rash captain was hailed as a hero throughout the North. Radical and abolitionist members of Congress cheered his illegal act. Let the traitors feel the weight of the Federal government, they cried. If the British didn't like it, they could lump it. So Mason and Slidell were locked up in gloomy Fort Warren, near Boston—and there they languished while a dangerous storm arose over their imprisonment. The reaction to the Trent Affair in England was one of outrage and anger. Lord Palmerston, the pro-Confederate Prime Minister, beat the war drums; British troops were sent to Canada; and, for a time, a war between Great Britain and the United States seemed inevitable.

Secretary of State Seward favored provoking the British into a conflict. He still believed that involvement in a foreign war would bring back the Confederates. But Lincoln convinced him that the United States had enough war on its hands. The President felt it was suicidal to tackle Great Britain as well as the Confederacy.

Lincoln had his way. "One war at a time," he cautioned. In the Trent case, he pointed out, the American position was palpably wrong. The War of 1812 had resulted from similar acts carried out by the British: the boarding of neutral vessels on the high seas. So now before the war flames took hold, Lincoln put out the fire. He said:

> I fear the traitors [Mason and Slidell] will prove to be white elephants. We must stick to American principles concerning the rights of neutrals. We fought Great Britain for insisting by theory and practise on the right to do precisely what Wilkes has done. If Great Britain shall now protest against the act, and demand their release, we must give them up, apologize for the act as a violation of our doctrines and thus forever bind her over to keep the peace in relation to neutrals and so acknowledge that she has been wrong for sixty years.

Lincoln's astute manipulation of the potentially explosive predicament not only prevented a clash with the world's greatest sea power, but also twisted the British Lion's tail. By accepting the American apology and the release of Mason and Slidell, who were permitted to continue their interrupted journey, the British tacitly admitted their own wrongdoing over the years. No British man-of-war ever again interfered with a neutral ship on the high seas.

The public appreciated Lincoln's maneuverings. Old John Bull had been given his comeuppance. The President's popularity rose a few notches. Northern unity was cemented a bit more securely and Seward's admiration of his chief mounted. Even Lincoln's opponents had to give "Old Abe" grudging credit.

But with the Trent Affair settled, Lincoln had to call on all his political sagacity to solve an unpleasant mess in his own cabinet.

Unsavory Simon Cameron, who had been forced upon Lincoln, started living up to his dubious reputation. He displayed undue fondness for placing military contracts with Pennsylvania business men. One cynical dealer in military supplies smugly remarked, "You can sell anything to the government at almost any price you've got the guts to ask." He might have added, "Providing you're a Pennsylvanian and can prove it to Cameron."

Contractual arrangements with the War Department were so abusive and the goods purchased of such inferior quality, that a leading magazine printed this satirical verse:

> I, Lieutenant-Colonel Graham,
>   of the Twelfth depose and say,
> That the coats contractors gave us,
>   were of shoddy cloth of gray;
> Only for a day we wore them,
>   and they came to pieces then.

The scandalous war contracts pointed to chicanery in the War Department. On one occasion, the government sold condemned car bines at $2.00 each. The faulty weapons then passed through several hands and were finally resold to the government at $22.00 apiece. All the principals were Pennsylvanians.

But this was not the worst that happened. An even more outlandish swindle was foisted on the government. Horses had been purchased for equipping cavalry units outfitting in Louisville. The quality of Kentucky horseflesh was world renowned. However, the War Department agents did not procure the mounts in the Blue Grass State. Instead, they bought 1,000 animals in Pennsylvania at bonus prices. Added to the original outlay was the cost of transporting the horses to Louisville. The total figure was so high that pure-blooded Arabian chargers could have been secured at the same prices.

When the horses were unloaded at Louisville and examined by Army veterinaries it was found that the government had been hoodwinked. Of the 1,000 animals in the shipment, 485 were blind, spavined, ringwormed or otherwise diseased. According to one veterinary, "They must have scoured the boneyards for these nags."

There were other difficulties brought on by the Secretary of War.

Cameron, an advocate of a high protective tariff, was loath to buy arms abroad. He let out large orders to local manufacturers—most of whom, coincidentally, were located in his home state. The domestic factories were not prepared to meet the demand for large quantities of guns and ammunition.

The thousands of recruits swelling the armies could not be equipped and the Secretary of War was forced at last to look to additional sources to fill the Army's needs. By the time his agents approached European armament manufacturers, the Confederates had pre-empted most of the foreign output and only the dregs of continental production were available to the Union purchasing commissions. Consequently, obsolete and defective Belgian, Austrian, French, and British weapons were bought up at fabulous prices—often with tragic consequences. Entire regiments took to the field with arms which failed at crucial moments.

In all fairness, no evidence was ever produced to indicate that Cameron had profited personally from these outrageous deals. But he was so attuned to backroom politics that he treated the national emergency like a patronage plum. And, although he now occupied an exalted place, he could not forget his ward-heeling past.

Lincoln, irked by his colleague's antics, was unable to shake off the Pennsylvanian without arousing the ire of the abolitionists and Radicals within his own party. Wily Cameron had ensured the support of these extremists by his outspoken stand against slavery. There was no way of ascertaining whether the sentiments he expressed were sincere or if he was simply playing the abolitionist side of the street for his own devious purposes.

Cameron well knew Lincoln disliked slavery. But he was also aware that the President favored prudent action on the knotty problem; he knew too that this prudence had engendered Radical and abolitionist opposition to Lincoln. The Secretary of War capitalized on the impasse and almost beat Lincoln at political gamesmanship. He came out bluntly for arming the slaves and enrolling them in the military forces. It was a master political stratagem.

The cagey Pennsylvanian played his trump card by using the Negroes. Many slaves had come into Union hands either as runaways, contrabands, or by other means. In December, 1861, at the time of Lincoln's message to Congress, Cameron submitted the following in his annual report:

If it shall be found that the men who have been held by the Rebels as slaves are capable of bearing arms and performing efficient military service, it is the right and may be the duty of the government to arm and equip them and employ their services against the Rebels under proper military regulation, discipline and command.

This blatant declaration met with instant enthusiastic response from those who wanted drastic action. By cloaking the statement in the respectability of an official report, Cameron made it seem he was expressing official governmental policy.

Without advising the President of his intentions, Cameron had his declaration distributed to all postmasters and ordered them to hand it to the press in their various localities. Some papers ran the item, but once it had been brought to Lincoln's attention, telegrams were hastily sent to the postmasters recalling Cameron's statement.

Lincoln was justly angered at the Secretary for this trick. He was heard to say explosively, "This will never do! Cameron must take no such responsibility. That is a question which belongs exclusively to me!"

The Chief Executive knew the time had come to ease out the undesirable cabinet member. Cameron must be purged in a way which would neither impugn him nor arouse the resentment of the Republican Party's extremists. This was a situation which called for tact and diplomacy. Lincoln had to hide his distaste of Cameron and make it appear that the change was at the Secretary's behest.

Cleverly estimating his own position, Cameron let out hints that he was wearied of his cabinet post and would prefer another assignment, preferably a foreign mission. In January, 1862, a fortuitous solution was found.

Cassius Marcellus Clay, United States Ambassador to Russia, resigned to accept a commission as a major general. The post was open and, while Russia was far enough away to assure Cameron's removal from the political scene, a major ambassadorship was no small honor to bestow upon him. Lincoln quickly exploited the opportunity. On January 11, about a month after the controversial "slave-arming" report, Lincoln sent a crisp note to the errant Secretary:

My Dear Sir:
As you have more than once expressed a desire for a change of posi-

Gideon Welles, Secretary of the Navy.

tion, I can now gratify you consistently with my view of the public interest. I therefore propose nominating you to the Senate next Monday as minister to Russia.

> Very sincerely, your friend,
> A. Lincoln.

The appointment caused a great deal of comment. The antislavery press excitedly defended Cameron. But his old antagonist, Thaddeus Stevens, could not resist saying, "Cameron, Minister to Russia? Ugh! Ugh! The Czar had better lock up his silverware every night!"

Horace Greeley, who blubbered so shamefully after Bull Run, had regained his composure. He wrote a laudatory editorial on Cameron, explaining away the corruption in the War Department in these words:

> Cameron has been surrounded and pressed upon by troops of noisy well-wishers who would have scorned the idea of selling their God for thirty pieces of silver so long as there was the faintest hope of making it forty. These have bored him into signing contracts by which they have made enormous profits at his expense as well as the country's . . .

Many journals took this line in clearing Cameron of chicanery. The New York *Evening Post* praised him for his position on slavery and while admitting there had been corrupt and grafting practises in the War Department, baldly stated that Cameron had "no participation in these robberies."

However, all the press was not so kindly disposed towards the Czar of Pennsylvania. The influential *Leslie's Weekly* said:

> Mr. Lincoln has a wide reputation as a humorist. The nomination of Mr. Cameron to St. Petersburg, which is a long way on the road to Siberia, looks as if he were also addicted to practical joking. It would be no joke for the ex-Secretary of War, however, if the Czar were to take his appointment as a hint to "pass him on" to that land of penance, and the companionship of that goodly company of army contractors and speculators whose exploits in the Crimean War failed to receive the imperial approval!

Thus, stormy Simon Cameron departed for the Russian shore. Even in his leaving, he managed to turn one more deal. Two days

Early in 1862, Lincoln appointed **Edwin McMasters** Stanton as Secretary of War to succeed wily Simon Cameron. **Here,** Stanton meets the leading officers of the army in his office.

after he had been advised of his removal from office, but before his successor had taken over, Cameron approved a contract for an unlimited number of swords and sabers to be delivered within six months by a Pennsylvania firm.

And on the eve of his departure, he got off a parting shot at Lincoln. Cameron observed to a foreign diplomat that the outlook for the United States was dark and unfavorable. "We want a great man —and have not got him," he said.

· 6 ·

Lincoln's choice to succeed Cameron was a unique personality, Edwin McMasters Stanton. That the President should select the forty-seven-year-old prominent lawyer as one of his closest advisers was proof of his willingness to set aside his own feelings for the welfare of the nation. Certainly Stanton had never given the President any reason to like him. He had often gone out of his way to deride Lincoln.

About six years earlier, both men were engaged as attorneys in a large-scale lawsuit. The first time Stanton saw Lincoln he remarked peevishly, "Where did that long-armed creature come from and what can he possibly expect to do in this case?" Lincoln, already awed by Stanton's legal fame, overheard the remark. Flustered and embarrassed, he fled from the courtroom, followed by Stanton's snickering.

Stanton had made no effort to hide his contempt of the President. He was a friend of McClellan and acted as the General's legal adviser. He often expressed his feelings about the administration to McClellan, especially the disdain he felt for Lincoln. He once told the General: "Lincoln is the original gorilla. Du Chaillu was a fool to wander all the way to Africa in search of what he could so easily have found in Springfield, Illinois."

In spite of all this Lincoln felt that Stanton was right for the post vacated by Cameron. The President knew him to be an energetic, skillful administrator. Stanton had the ability to drive men and get things accomplished. Lincoln was aware that Stanton often entertained both himself and others at dinner parties with his jibes at the President; none of this mattered to the Chief Executive. He had already tamed Seward, Chase, Cameron, and Bates. He felt capable of handling Stanton as well.

One thing was certain. As Secretary of War, Stanton would not tolerate the crooked contractors, jobbers, and speculators who had grown rich off infamous contracts. Their holiday at the expense of the soldiers and the nation would be over. Once in office, Stanton would drive out the chiselers, prod the generals, and make certain the troops had proper clothing, food, and weapons. The new Secretary was peevish, petty, and arrogant—but he was also determined to crush the Rebellion, grimly efficient, and fervently devoted to the Union.

When the appointment was announced many of Lincoln's friends in Washington were genuinely alarmed. They feared the dynamic new Secretary of War might overshadow the President and take over control of the government. Lincoln listened to them, grinned and eased their concern with a story: "We may have to treat him as they are sometimes obliged to treat a Methodist minister I know out West. He gets wrought up to so high a pitch of excitement in his prayers and exhortations that they are obliged to put bricks in his pockets to keep him down. We may be obliged to serve Stanton in the same way, but I guess we'll let him jump awhile first."

Lincoln not only kept his unpredictable Secretary of War under control—he also gained his loyalty and respect. The President's talents for winning over people were seldom more successfully demonstrated than in his management of Stanton.

The man Stanton had once deprecated as a "long-armed creature" became, for him, the living symbol of the nation and the Cause he loved. Lincoln had no follower more faithful than his strange and moody Secretary of War.

Not only his eccentricities, but also his appearance marked Stanton as an "odd horse." He had long, untidy black whiskers, bushy black hair, and popping near-sighted eyes which glared from behind thick spectacles. He was stocky and barrel-chested; when he stared vehemently, his eyes, magnified by the lenses, made such a fearful impression that even the toughest army officer was cowed. His temper was fearful; his tirades, shattering. No one around him dared shirk or malinger.

Edwin McMasters Stanton had been born in Steubenville, Ohio, on December 19, 1814. His boyhood was hard and bitter. He had to work from the time he was thirteen. His father died in 1827, leaving no money and many debts. Young Edwin rolled up his sleeves and pitched in to help support his mother, brothers and sisters. No job was too difficult for him. No hours too long. He was tireless and dedicated. Due to his efforts, the Stanton brood survived.

He doggedly worked his way through Kenyon College in Gambier, Ohio, where he studied law. One of his many jobs while in college was as a clerk in a book store. There, he met pretty Mary Lamson, the daughter of an impoverished Episcopal clergyman. After his admission to the bar in 1836, he married her.

Stanton was a successful lawyer from the moment he hung up his shingle in Cadiz, Ohio. He was scrupulously honest in money matters although he charged exorbitant fees for the day. He was in the practise of law to make a good living and expected to be well paid for his services. On one occasion, he charged a farmer $1,000 to win a $2,000 claim. The client protested this was exorbitant. "Do you think I would argue the wrong side of a case for less?" Stanton coldly asked.

He took on cases which other lawyers had refused as hopeless. Stanton defended criminals, embezzlers, forgers, murderers—anyone who could pay. In this, he was motivated not only by mercenary reasons, but also by the firm conviction that every man was entitled to the best possible representation in court.

He had a morbid fear of death and his actions sometimes bordered on the psychotic. Before his marriage to Mary Lamson, Stanton had a sweetheart named Anne Howard. The girl died suddenly from a violent attack of typhoid fever. He had seen her alive only that morning. By evening she was in her grave—a precaution customary with victims of the dread disease. Stanton was beside himself with grief. Believing she had been buried alive, he obtained a court order to exhume her so he could see the corpse for himself.

Then too he later grieved so deeply over the death of Lucy, his first child, that a year after her demise, he had the baby disinterred and cremated. He kept the ashes in a metal box on the mantelpiece in his study for many years.

His wife, Mary, died in 1844 as the result of childbirth. By then, Stanton was one of the most prominent lawyers in the country and had pleaded many cases before the Supreme Court. He was so stricken by her death that he refused to allow her to be buried in any but her wedding clothes. "She is my bride and shall be dressed and buried as a bride," he cried.

Despite his strange ways, Stanton cleaned up the mess in the War Department. He drove out the contractors and chiselers. Nobody was safe from his righteous anger. Military arrests on suspicion of treason mounted. When direct action was needed, Stanton never hesitated.

A typical incident took place in 1862. He received a telegram from Harper's Ferry urgently requesting cannon of a large caliber. A similar message arrived at the Arsenal. Stanton hurried there after hours and learned that the guns were scheduled for shipment the following day. Acting on his own authority, Stanton ordered the Arsenal doors opened, organized a work party and even added his own weight in dragging out the field pieces. He supervised loading them onto drays, accompanied the shipment to the railroad station, commandeered a train, and watched the cannon placed aboard the train and sent off to Harper's Ferry.

The next morning, the Arsenal Ordnance Chief brightly reported to Stanton that he would have the guns shipped that very day. The Secretary of War glowered at him and thundered, "The guns are already at Harper's Ferry and you, sir, are no longer in the service of the United States."

This was the man Lincoln had wisely placed in the War Department. Stanton soon made a host of enemies. He demanded that everyone must do his best and felt free to attack those he believed were not giving their all for the Union. Yet, no one had cause to complain about his sternness—he demanded even more of himself . . .

· 7 ·

General McClellan spent the fall and winter of 1861 bringing his troops to combat readiness. Reinforcements poured into the Army of the Potomac, and by November the army had attained 168,000 effectives. It was no longer a band of hastily mobilized volunteers in variegated uniforms. The colorful garb of the militia regiments no longer enlivened the camps—except of the Zouaves. The troops wore blue blouses and light-blue kersey trousers. The ordinance had been standardized; infantrymen were armed with Springfield .52 caliber muzzle-loading rifles instead of a weird assortment of weapons; recruits went through rigorous tactical training; Regular Army officers kept sharp tabs on the military niceties, and the Army of the Potomac emerged as a spit-and-polish, crisply drilled, razor-sharp army.

Droves of cattle clomped across the Long Bridge to feed the troops in Virginia. Warehouses bulged with hardtack, shoes, shirts, underwear, socks, caps, blouses, trousers, knapsacks, swords, scabbards, bayonets—everything and anything troops needed for a supreme effort in the field.

A generous government had given "Little Mac" plenty of men and matériel for military success. He seemed the perfect leader for such an army. The flaw that marred him was not readily apparent. He looked and acted like a man of purpose and resolution. He had made the clumsy recruits feel like soldiers.

They had learned to march in perfect cadence, to charge across open fields without losing alignment, to conduct themselves in a military manner; they were instilled with pride of outfit and in the Army of the Potomac. All this McClellan had helped impart to them. He had inspired the callow lads from cities, villages, shops, and farms with a bit of his own verve and dash. He evoked cheers from his troops when he galloped past, followed by a trim, sparkling retinue of staff officers which included many foreign noblemen. The only obstacle to complete victory lay within McClellan himself. He lacked that indefinable spark which could sweep on to triumph in battle.

Additional honors and responsibilities were piled on him. In November, 1861, the weary old warrior, Winfield Scott, retired with pay. On November 3, at 4:00 A.M. in the predawn blackness, the Young Napoleon and his dapper staff, with a squadron of cavalry, galloped to the railroad station and saluted ceremonially as the aged soldier was helped into a special car of the waiting train that would carry him to West Point where he had chosen to live out his days.

Scott's retirement removed what McClellan had considered a hindrance. He had not enjoyed cordial relations with the former General-in-Chief. Now the way was cleared for him to earn the gratitude and adulation of his country. If ever a man had opportunity to earn immortality in a nation's history, that man was George Brinton McClellan. Yet he displayed admirable humility in the moment of his potential glory. In a modest letter to his wife, he described Scott's departure, and added: "He was very polite to me and sent various kind messages to you and the baby; so we parted . . . It may be that someday I, too, shall totter away from Washington, a worn out soldier, with naught to do but make my peace with God."

After Scott had left, Lincoln appointed McClellan to the highest command. The thirty-five-year-old Golden Boy was now General-in-Chief. During a conference with Lincoln at the White House, the President said, "I should be perfectly satisfied if I thought this vast increase in responsibility would not embarrass you."

"It is a great relief, sir! I feel as if several tons were taken from my shoulders today. I am now in contact with you and the Secretary. I am not embarrassed by any intervention," McClellan promptly replied.

Lincoln had wanted avidly to hear just these words. They buttressed his own faith in the brilliant young soldier. "Draw on me for all the sense I have, and all the information. In addition to your present command, the supreme command of the Army will entail a vast labor upon you," Lincoln told him.

"I can do it all!" McClellan cried.

He meant to do it all. Yet that undetectable flaw within him was both corrosive and paralyzing. He was like a magnificent painting done with exquisite technique and wondrous detail but executed on a flimsy canvas which had neither the strength nor tensility to sustain the painting. McClellan burned for victory: one bold, glorious thrust that would smash the rebellion. He knew how to gather and train forces to strike the blow; yet could not bring himself to carry it through. He did not hesitate because he lacked confidence. This was a man who was a stranger to failure.

Nor was it a dearth of courage that fettered him. His bravery and coolness under fire had been outstanding in the Mexican War. His fearlessness was further demonstrated while on a hunting trip in the Northwest. He had fired at a charging panther but missed his shot. Instead of running for safety, McClellan had grappled with the beast and skulled it with his rifle butt.

Perhaps he had no genuine desire to send this glittering army of his into the ghastly destruction of war; perhaps he was haunted by the dreadful vision of his men lying torn in windrows of death on the battlefield. Despite his timorous approach to war, McClellan continued training and polishing, until the Army of the Potomac was a model of precision and mechanical perfection, like a fine watch. He had created what seemed to be a military juggernaut. His army sparkled with military pomp and growled with martial fierceness; but it was still untried in battle. All through the perfect days of autumn when the roads into Virginia were hard-packed and all the conditions were ideal for an advance, McClellan had not budged and the Confederate flag flew mockingly from Munson's Hall within sight of the capital.

Pressures began mounting on "Little Mac." The North was roused once more by cries of "On to Richmond!" When McClellan responded to the demands for action by holding reviews and parades, the ordinary citizen began questioning the abilities of the Young Napoleon. What good was the Army of the Potomac, the taxpayers wanted to know. The men were eating three square meals a day; the troops were costing over $1,000,000 daily just to be kept in the field—and the Rebels were not being hurt at all. Senators and Congressmen began propounding the question: when will the Army of the Potomac do some fighting?

Once the country had recovered from its initial infatuation with McClellan, the people could observe the General realistically. There was much about his comportment to regard with displeasure and distrust. For one, he did not live in the field with his men, but kept an elegant house in Washington. These luxurious headquarters were guarded day and night by elite troops—a praetorian guard, his critics called it. Then, too, McClellan preferred high-born foreigners on his staff—the Prince Salm-Salm, the Comte de Paris and other dashing Continentals. The General held lavish parties in his Washington home and often roistered into the small hours with his staff at midnight oyster and champagne suppers.

McClellan proved too aristocratic, too arrogant for the unsophisticated American taste. In the days following Bull Run, he had admirably fitted the needs of those dark hours. He was the hero personified—reckless, handsome, gallant, and unshaken by adversity. Now some of his glamor was fading. What had seemed desirable in a General was growing irksome. The Radicals and "Hard War" Congressmen became more insistent that McClellan should make a move; the only military results he had achieved were highly negative: a few inconsequential skirmishes and a disastrous reconnaissance at Ball's Bluff in which President Lincoln's friend Senator Baker had been killed.

In the summer months, McClellan had been above reproach; as winter drew on, the honeymoon ended. Carping newspapers needled him mercilessly, especially about his predilection for surrounding himself with a staff of foreigners. Typical of such comment was this excerpt from a New York newspaper:

> The Prince de Joinville's two sons are admirable additions to General McClellan's staff, and both speak English so well that I can almost understand what they say. Two Arabs are expected here tomorrow to take command of the Irish brigades, and General Blenker will probably have two Aztecs to assist him in the German division.

McClellan reacted to such critical barbs with outraged pride and growing bitterness. He felt that he was being crucified by stupid and ignorant men; those who disagreed with him, McClellan dismissed as witless and crass. He extended this contemptuous attitude to the President himself. In his meetings with Lincoln, to be sure, the General carefully observed protocol. He always addressed the Chief Executive as "Your Excellency"—but in a dozen ways he showed his disdain of Lincoln.

A shocking example of McClellan's insolence and incivility towards the Chief Executive occurred one night when Lincoln, accompanied by Secretary of State Seward and his personal secretary, John Hay, went to the General's house for an evening conference. They were informed by a servant that the General-in-Chief was attending a wedding but was expected home shortly. Hay recorded the event in his diary:

> We went in, and after we had waited for an hour, McC. came in and without paying any particular attention to the porter who told him the President was waiting to see him, went upstairs, passing the door to the room where the President and the Secretary of State were seated. They waited about half-an-hour, and sent once more a servant to tell the General they were there; and the answer coolly came that the General had gone to bed.

Hay reacted furiously to this rebuff; he felt it was a blatant attitude of military disrespect for civilian authority. Lincoln calmed him, saying, "This is not a time to stand on etiquette and personal dignity." He believed that the country needed the haughty soldier. "I will hold General McClellan's horse if he will only bring us success," Lincoln added.

The President's humility only amplified McClellan's scorn; he actually hid from Lincoln to avoid meeting him, claiming the President's visits were tiresome and boring. McClellan several times stayed away from his own house and took refuge, on occasion, in Stanton's home. During one of these interludes he wrote his wife: "I have not been home for some three hours, but am concealed at Stanton's to dodge all enemies in shape of 'browsing' Presidents, etc. . . ."

The Army of the Potomac, numbering 160,000 splendid troops was confronted by a Confederate army one-third its size at Manassas. Almost inconceivably, McClellan refused to concede his superiority in men and equipment. He chose rather to believe the outrageously inaccurate intelligence reports of Allan Pinkerton, the detective, who headed up the Union intelligence service. Pinkerton was a first-class operative, but his milieu was capturing criminals, not military spying. His information was totally erroneous. According to him, the Rebels under General Joe Johnston enjoyed an almost two-to-one numerical advantage.

Pinkerton's faulty arithmetic gave him an excuse for not taking the offensive, and McClellan accepted it without reservation. Surely, even the idiots who made up the Administration could understand the danger of attacking a well-entrenched enemy with twice as many troops.

This McClellan was a complex man. He believed he was persecuted by the politicians; they were frustrating him in everything he was trying to do. He claimed to be working on the details of a campaign that would destroy the enemy in one decisive stroke. This complicated strategy needed time to be perfected and he had to be left to his own resources to accomplish it; but the unfeeling civilians persisted in their interference.

In a bitter letter to his wife, he wrote: "I . . . only wish to save my country, and find the incapables around me will not permit it . . . Their reply to everything was 'Impossible! Impossible!' . . . I was obliged to attend a meeting of the cabinet at 8 P.M. . . . and was bored and annoyed. There are some of the greenest geese I have ever seen—enough to tax the patience of Job . . . I am becoming daily more disgusted with this administration—perfectly sick of it."

The pettish General complained he had to deal with "unscrupulous, false men." Nevertheless time that might have been spent fighting the enemy he frittered away in drill. His troops were primed for battle, but McClellan stood fast. The approach of winter removed any hope of a major campaign in the East now. The General was aware of the disappointment his failure to engage the enemy had aroused. His daily letters to Mrs. McClellan became more peevish. Late in November, he wrote: "I am thwarted and deceived by these incapables at every turn . . . I have one great comfort in this—that is, that I did not seek this position, as you well know; and I trust that God will support me and bear me out. He could not have placed me here for nothing."

Divine intercession, however, was not forthcoming; the Army of the Potomac was commanded by George B. McClellan and God gave him neither the strength nor the determination to carry out his mission. Once, rumors of impending action swept through the vast encampments of the Army. At a full-scale review, McClellan had ringingly declared: "Soldiers! We have made our last retreat. We have seen our last defeat. You stand by me and I will stand by you, and henceforth, victory will crown our efforts!"

The soldiers threw their caps in the air and cheered lustily. Everyone looked for action, but instead of fighting, the Army was ordered into winter quarters. The huge war machine dug in and waited. Now the latrine gossip spoke of the big offensive coming in the spring of '62, which was to be the year of total victory. "All quiet along the Potomac" became a household phrase in the disappointed North.

Even Lincoln became impatient with McClellan's inaction. He accompanied a group of visiting dignitaries to the Army's camping grounds. The party stood on a rise overlooking the vast panorama of tents, cabins, hutments, and sheds; hundreds of cook fires twinkled in the dusk; sentries paced silently to and fro; snub-nosed cannon were aligned row on row in the artillery parks. It was an impressive scene and a visitor murmured, "So this is the Army of the Potomac!"

"No, sir. It is not the Army of the Potomac. It is General McClellan's bodyguard," Lincoln said wryly.

SEVEN

Mr. Davis

"After a series of successes and victories
we have recently met with serious disasters . . ."

JEFFERSON DAVIS, February, 1862

Sitting by the roadside on a
  summer day,
Chatting with my messmates passing
  time away,
Lying in the shadows underneath
  the trees,
Goodness, how delicious, eating
  goober peas!

       Confederate army song

GRAY WAS THE dominant color in Richmond that first winter of war —drab, monotonous gray. The skies were dismal and sunless. The winter proved to be one of the worst and coldest in many years. The cold bit through the stoutest overcoat and the wind rattled against doors and windows. Sleet and snow glazed the streets with a slick layer of ice and dray horses slipped on the treacherous cobblestones.

War was becoming real and it did not take an astute observer to notice signs of discontent or to hear mutterings of dissatisfaction. Few smiling faces were seen in Richmond's streets. Men walked quickly, hunched against the cold, hurrying to their jobs in factories, shops, mills, and government offices. Women carrying shopping baskets skidded along the icy walks, with worried frowns—there was much to worry them. Food prices were soaring; in some instances they had risen almost 100 per cent since April, 1861. The strangling blockade was taking its effect: coffee was almost unavailable at $1.50 per pound; tea cost $10 per pound; butter, 75¢; meat, 50¢, with decent cuts growing scarcer. Housewives clucked in dismay. How did they expect one to feed a family at such prices?

While there was no actual want as yet, the pinch was becoming severe, with the average worker earning about $20 per week. The families of soldiers bore the brunt of the hardships—a private's pay of $13 per month was hardly better than a dole.

Clothes were getting shabby. People who had taken pride in their stylish dress began to look dowdy. Men who had disdained to wear cobbled shoes now walked on soles little better than cardboard. Shirt cuffs were frayed and trousers mended. Chic ladies no longer wore chic gowns. To replace even essential items presented grievous problems: ladies' shoes were $15 a pair; men's boots, $30. Household items, pots, pans, dishes, sheets, blankets, pillowcases, towels, tablecloths had quadrupled in price. Rents were rising at a fantastic clip.

The boastful exuberance that had followed the Federal debacle at Bull Run was no longer in evidence. Richmond had borne the full impact of that battle. The human wreckage that had flooded back from Manassas gave proof that victory could be bitter. Hundreds of crippled and wounded men, gray-faced sacrifices, showed the people of Richmond that war demanded a steep price.

The capital's aspect had changed considerably. Its once-leisurely pace had been stepped up hectically. Factory chimneys belched smoke and sparks all through the night and hammers clanged incessantly at the Tredegar plant. The wharves and railroad depot teemed with traffic; drays, lorries, vans, and carts rumbled at all hours, hauling guns and supplies. Every incoming train disgorged passengers on government business. Other elements also poured in: whores, thieves, speculators, gamblers, and sharpers.

Brothels burgeoned everywhere—in shanties and in grand town houses. A gambling parlor run by a Virginia dandy named Johnny Worsham drew the elite. A man could lose his money playing cards, dice, or roulette at Worsham's, and the place was crowded with eager gamesters every night. Despite the blockade, Worsham had no trouble keeping his bar stocked with expensive whiskies, French champagnes, and fine brandies. The buffet table was heaped with caviar, lobsters, oysters, candied hams, terrapin, turkey, roast beef, and wild fowl. The shortages and stringencies of war brought no hardships to Richmond's monied pleasure-seekers.

As in every war, a class of newly rich evolved. Contractors and wholesalers, dealers in the goods of war, lived riotously and lavishly. Splendid equipages drawn by blooded horses rolled through the city carrying beefy profiteers and plump courtesans. The silken prostitutes of Richmond fared well on the money of the profit makers . . .

This was the winter of Confederate discontent. The summer soldiers lost heart in the wintry blasts. In the summer, the war had been a grand lark; but the part-time patriots had learned that the Yankees meant business. Up North they were raising and training an army of 500,000. The forces of the Union were being readied to engulf the South. The Yankees were building a special navy for operations along the rivers that were the back door to the heart of the Confederacy.

The enemy was not making any secret of his plans. New Orleans was one prime target; the recapture of the Mississippi to its mouth was another. Abe Lincoln was not going to spare men, equipment, or money to seize the river and slice the Confederacy in half.

Most alarming to thinking Southerners was the rate at which enlistments were falling off. Since the early Confederate victories, a feeling of overconfidence had spread across the South and nothing had happened to dispel it. The volunteers who had signed up for short terms—three, six, nine months—went gaily home when their time was up.

Hell, hadn't they trimmed the abolitionists and sent the damn blue-bellies yelping back to Lincoln? If the Yankees dared another try, the boys said, they'd drop their plows and take up soldiering again. But everyone knew the war couldn't last. The Yankees just didn't have the guts for fighting.

An avalanche was threatening to crush down on the South, but the planters sneered at the danger. England and France, they thought, would soon realize King Cotton was the almighty power—and they'd stop hemming about intervention. Optimistic feeling about aid from Europe ran so high that the Davis administration took no steps towards expediting the manufacture of heavy equipment and medical supplies. The authorities chose to believe the Union blockade would soon be broken and all the matériel the South needed would come pouring in . . .

Richmond had become accustomed to its role as the national capital. Jefferson Davis and his family settled into the Executive Mansion without difficulty. Varina Davis was adept at homemaking. She added charming touches to the already gracious Brockenbrough house. Her family was growing. There were three children now, and Mrs. Davis was expecting a fourth in December.

Despite his cares of office, Davis managed to spare an hour or so a day for his young ones. The house echoed with the gleeful laughter of the children playing with their father. While his reluctance to delegate authority usually kept the President working late in his study, life was not unpleasant for the Davises. Sometimes the war seemed far away from the capital, an irksome job that must be finished before the advantages of independence might be enjoyed.

Yet, even before the winter set in, clouds of trouble dampened the euphoria in which the South was basking. Even the tone of the newspaper advertisements boded a bleak future.

A dry-goods merchant announced he had quantities of excellent quality gray cloth suitable for uniforms at prices "very cheap for the times." A druggist listed certain shortages of such vital medicines as quinine explaining that "the usual avenues through which our supplies are obtained now being closed."

Even more significantly, in certain areas with Secessionist sympathies there was a poor turnout of volunteers. One regiment of Maryland volunteers, for example, was unable to fill its roster.

But even had hordes of patriots swarmed to the colors, weapons were lacking to arm them. The Confederate Ordnance Department issued a plea for all who held captured United States arms as souvenirs to turn them in—rifles, revolvers, and even swords, in any condition, were urgently needed. The shortages were worse than the authorities dared to reveal. A regiment of the Fort Henry garrison was armed with flintlocks harking back to the War of 1812.

The aura of well-being that permeated the South gave a false impression. Serious trouble was brewing. Disharmony spread among the leaders and the first defection among the original Davis cabinet appointees took place in July, 1861. Robert Toombs quit his office and took the field as a Brigadier General of Georgia Volunteers. He preferred the hazards of the firing line to governmental intrigues. He was replaced as Secretary of State by a Virginian, R. M. T. Hunter, formerly President of the Confederate Senate.

Then Leroy P. Walker, the bumbling Secretary of War, turned in his portfolio in November, 1861. His departure was barely noted and not regretted. The outspoken Toombs had once described him in this scornful way: "He . . . is so inept that if a Napoleon should seek a commission in the Confederate Army, Walker would refuse him . . ."

In a surprising move, Davis brought Judah P. Benjamin from the Attorney General's office to the more important War Department. The smiling Benjamin soon became the object of vicious slanders; anti-Semites attacked him for his Hebrew origin; he was accused of enriching himself in the inflated commodity market. Unfounded charges that Benjamin and a clique of traitorous Jews were manipulating food prices spread through Richmond. These manifestations of anti-Semitism came from only a bigoted minority in the South. Benjamin was not popular, but his lack of public favor stemmed from personality rather than race. Many honestly felt he was the President's evil genius. Only the most narrow-minded believed him a profiteer and a traitor. Benjamin was a snob, a chauvinist and an arrogant intellectual, but he was devoted and ardently loyal to the Southern Cause . . .

When the mass exuberance and optimism of midsummer vanished, it was replaced by carping and quibbling on all levels. Mean and petty feuds flared up in the highest echelons of the government. The President was not without blame for some of them. Once Davis had decided a subordinate disagreed with him, he severed relations with the dissenter no matter how trusted or valuable the man might have been. This unbending attitude Davis often carried to extremes.

In one case, at least, a slur about Varina brought on the resignation of a competent and responsible officer. The Confederate Quartermaster General, General Abraham Charles Myers, had proved to be a first-rate administrative official. He performed prodigies in supplying the troops. But when the beautiful Mrs. Myers scornfully referred to Mrs. Davis as an "old squaw" at a private dinner party, the tale came back to the President. General Myers was placed on the block; Davis pressured him out of office.

His successor, General Alexander Robert Lawton, whom the President had known at West Point, turned out to be a bungler. His mistakes and inefficiency were costly to the Confederate war effort. But because Davis regarded him as a friend, he would brook no criticism of the Quartermaster General and refused to remove him despite clamor from all sides.

As if the Yankees were not trouble enough, the hot-blooded Southerners seemed incapable of maintaining peaceable relations with each other. Arguments often ended violently. Congressmen had fist fights on the legislature floor. An opponent hurled an inkstand that split William Yancey's cheekbone. Henry S. Foote, the President's old antagonist, was threatened by a Senator from Alabama who tried to stab him with a bowie knife. Later, Foote traded punches with another Senator and at some time after that, a third solon clouted him over the head with an umbrella in a restaurant.

·   2   ·

The unseemliest feuds Davis conducted were those with some of his most important generals. Outstanding were the ugly controversies he had with Joe Johnston and P. G. T. Beauregard. One unsubstantiated story traced the bad feeling between Davis and Johnston to a dispute over a girl they had known at West Point. Whatever the reason, the antipathy came to a head on August 31, 1861, when Davis sent a list of five officers to the Senate for confirmation as Generals.

Johnston had every reason to expect he would be the top-ranking General in the Confederate Army. He based his assumption on newly passed legislation which provided that Confederate rank should be based on commissions formerly held in the U.S. Army. In 1860, Johnston, a Colonel in the United States Regulars, had been appointed Quartermaster General; this brought him automatic promotion to Brigadier General, the rank called for by his position. Yet when Davis submitted his recommendations to the Senate, the nominees were rated as follows: (1) Samuel Cooper; (2) Albert Sidney Johnston; (3) Robert E. Lee; (4) Joseph E. Johnston; (5) Pierre Gustave Toutant Beauregard.

Johnston had been the only officer of the rank of General at the time of his resignation, but Davis chose to ignore this fact. The President claimed that Johnston's star had been awarded for a staff position which carried no line command. Yet had Davis been consistent, top-ranking Samuel Cooper would have been much farther down the list, because all his promotions above the grade of captain had come in staff positions. Davis could not rise above personal prejudice in a matter like this. He simply did not like Joe Johnston and was incapable of treating him with impartiality. It was no coincidence that the two highest-ranking generals, Samuel Cooper and Albert Sidney Johnston, had been the President's closest friends at West Point. Davis' loyalty to devoted associates too frequently outweighed his sense of fair play.

When the listing of the generals was officially announced, Joe Johnston, a man of no small temper, flew into a fury. He wrote a blistering 1,800 word letter to Davis—a scathing denunciation accusing the President of ignoring both justice and legality in denying him his rightful place as ranking General.

Davis' reply to the bitter letter was a masterpiece of frigid brevity; the answer consisted of only thirty-nine words:

Sir:
    I have just received and read your letter of the 12th instant. Its

language is, as you say, unusual: its arguments and statements utterly one-sided, and its insinuations as unfounded as they are unbecoming. I am &c- Jeff'n Davis

This icy note did not make Johnston any happier. The breach between the men continued not only throughout the war, but also for the rest of their lives. Years later, Davis wrote his friend, L. B. Northrop:

> Joe Johnston, I see, is to have an office under the new administration, so that the rewards for treachery have not ceased with radical rule.

The Presidential clash with Beauregard was handled with the same tactlessness and undiplomatic harshness which the Chief Executive had displayed towards Johnston. Beauregard was the hero of the Rebellion in the eyes of the Southern people. At first, he had amicable relations with Davis—but the cordiality waned shortly after the first battle of Bull Run when Beauregard charged he had been thwarted in his opportunity to capture Washington by both Executive interference and a breakdown in the Confederate supply system.

At the time, it was commonly believed that Washington could have easily been captured, and Beauregard's allegations caused a sensation. Beauregard was a man addicted to bombast. While it was true that the Confederate supply system left much to be desired, many of the flaws could be excused. Beauregard knew that the chain of supply had never been tested in full-scale battle before Bull Run. Plenty of mistakes were made under fire. And even Beauregard, the professional soldier, contributed to the blunders of that hot July Sunday.

"The Grand Creole" had no justification for charging the Executive with interference. Mr. Davis, although present, swallowed his desires for military glory and took no part in directing the army at Bull Run. The honors and the errors belonged to Beauregard and Joe Johnston.

Davis was annoyed at Beauregard's statement, but showed admirable constraint in his official rebuke of the popular hero. In turn, Beauregard took his chiding in good grace and made his apologies to Davis.

But shortly afterwards, for his own undisclosed reasons, Beauregard raked over the old coals. In October, 1861, he released a verbose report of the battle. The document rang with self-praise; the General spared no adjectives in describing the role he had played in the victory. By no accident, a Richmond newspaper secured a copy of the report and ran a condensed version of it before President Davis had read the 9,000-word document.

Understandably, Davis was angered by the General's brashness and immodesty. This time he lambasted Beauregard unmercifully. The President told him that his account of the battle was in fact an attempt "to exalt yourself at my expense." The cold fury of this rebuke chilled forever the excellent association Davis had enjoyed with the Grand Creole.

Davis was not a man to forget or forgive a hurt, and he never pardoned Beauregard. He intended either to drop the General or at least to keep him from ever again holding important command. However, Davis could not readily achieve that. The people worshipped Beauregard and such a man was not easily shelved. Still, Davis never stopped trying to even the score. His chance came in June, 1862.

Beauregard then commanded the Army of Tennessee, but was in poor health. Under doctor's orders, he decided to spend some time in Bladen Springs, Alabama, for rest and recuperation. In mid-June, Beauregard temporarily turned over his command to General Braxton Bragg. He left his army with a certified medical disability certificate from his chief surgeon, and on June 14 notified the War Department of his actions. He had, however, neglected to clear this enforced leave with the Richmond authorities. Adjutant General Cooper immediately notified the President of Beauregard's actions. Since the General's leave was unauthorized, Davis had the excuse he needed to give the Grand Creole the axe. He arbitrarily relieved Beauregard and gave permanent command of the Army of Tennessee to his own good friend, Braxton Bragg.

The sacking of the Confederacy's first hero aroused furious protests. Beauregard was not only popular with the masses, but also enjoyed powerful support in Congress. He could not be sidetracked with impunity. The President's motives in taking this drastic step were sharply questioned and his prestige damaged.

In September, Senators Edward Sparrow and Thomas Semmes of

Louisiana handed Davis a petition signed by fifty-nine Senators and Representatives protesting Beauregard's dismissal and urging the President to restore him to command.

According to Semmes, Davis waspishly said, "So far as giving Beauregard command of Bragg's army is concerned, that is out of the question. Bragg has arranged all his plans . . . and to put a new commander at the head of the army would be so prejudicial to the public interests, that I would not do so if the whole world united in the petition."

No reasonable basis existed for Davis' confidence in Bragg. The General was totally unequal to high command. He was criticized from every quarter; even his own officers voted for his removal. But the arrogant and vain streak in Davis—the perverse strain that did not permit him to concede that he could make a mistake—forced him to hold on to Bragg. He ignored those who demanded the reduction of that officer, although only military disaster seemed bound to result from Bragg's continued presence in a crucial command post.

Lacking the grace to concede that his judgment in elevating Bragg had been faulty, Davis found other reasons for the universal dissatisfaction over Bragg and expressed them in a letter to the General on August 5, 1862: "You have the misfortune of being regarded as my personal friend, and one pursued therefore with malignant censure by men regardless of the truth . . ."

Such bickering and disagreement tended to weaken the Confederacy. The Cause that had been born in a blaze of unselfish idealism was being consumed by smoldering resentments. Disgust with Davis was expressed openly—even on the battlefield. At the Second Battle of Bull Run in August, 1862, Robert Toombs galloped to the head of his brigade, waved his sword and shouted, "Go it, boys! I am with you again! Jeff Davis can make a General, but only God Almighty can make a soldier!"

The strong preference Davis showed towards West Pointers roused animosity among officers who had not graduated from the U.S. Military Academy. There was intrigue, hatred, and jealousy in almost every facet of Confederate military and political life.

Davis, who only months before had been greeted by pretty girls strewing flowers in his path, was now the target of disapprobation. It was a bad time. Men who should have known better viewed each

other with suspicion and mistrust. The flaws in the Confederacy
were flaws in performance, human errors committed by men strug-
gling to function under impossible odds and difficult circumstances.
They made understandable and excusable errors of judgment. But
the founders of the Confederacy believed they had been ordained
to carry out a vague, God-given mission; and like all men dedicated
beyond logic to a Cause, they had no realistic view of their purposes
or even why they were fighting. Davis clung stubbornly to one view.
His detractors disagreed not only with him, but with each other as
well.

The defects inherent in the Confederacy did not lie with the
youths who died sublimely for the Stars and Bars. They sacrificed
everything for a Cause that did not sustain them. The incipient nation's ultimate fate was brought on both by the hammering of the
enemy—and the cancer of its own disunity.

From the earliest days of its existence, there were influential
men in the Confederacy who had neither the perception nor the patience to realize that storms and setbacks were unavoidable in
achieving the independence that was the goal of their revolution.
Among these were several newspaper editors who disliked Davis
because he was frequently brusque and uncivil to the press.

E. A. Pollard and John Moncure Daniel of the Richmond *Examiner* were two of the foremost Davis-baiters. Daniel struck at the
President at every turn. Once he editorialized:

> Had the people dreamed that Mr. Davis would carry all his chronic
> antipathies, his bitter prejudices, his puerile partialities, and his dot-
> ing favoritisms into the presidential chair, they would never have al-
> lowed him to fill it . . .

At the height of this ill-feeling, the Confederacy suffered a suc-
cession of military setbacks. The loss of Fort Henry and Fort Donelson were particularly serious; as a result, Kentucky was irrevocably
gone and Tennessee thrown onto the defensive. The press screamed
for somebody's scalp; Albert Sidney Johnston, who had failed to
hold the forts, was a logical scapegoat. Davis refused to sacrifice
him. "If Sidney Johnston is not a general, I have none to give you,"
the President stoutly maintained.

When the anti-Davis bloc saw him standing by Johnston, they

turned against the second presidential favorite deemed responsible for the reversals—Secretary of War Judah P. Benjamin. By striking at Benjamin and Johnston, the critics were really striking at the President himself.

"Benjamin must go! Turn the Jew out of office!" came the outcry.

Davis would listen to none of this. When the opposition demanded that Benjamin's conduct of the War Office be subjected to an investigation, he regarded this as an impugnation of his own integrity. Instead of admitting to Benjamin's errors, Davis publicly praised him—at the same time announcing that R. M. T. Hunter had tendered his resignation as Secretary of State.

Then on March 18, 1862, Davis further enraged his enemies by appointing Judah Benjamin in Hunter's place. This was an almost unbearable affront to the anti-Davis men. The Jew was being promoted instead of being thrown out. Benjamin was actually running the foreign policy of the government!

Davis had openly defied the opposition; those who had merely disapproved of him up to now became his sworn enemies; those who had disliked him now despised him. Edmund Rhett, editor of the Charleston *Mercury* ranted: "Jeff Davis is conceited, wrongheaded, wranglesome, obstinate—a traitor . . ."

Former Congressman Lawrence Keitt, lately resigned from the legislature to fight in the army, expressed himself positively in a letter home: "It . . . seems that things are coming to this pass: to be a patriot, you must hate Davis . . ."

Some of Keitt's ex-colleagues felt even more strongly; it was not uncommon to hear the President denounced in the corridors of the Capitol in pungent words—the least unpleasant of which were "idiot," "imbecile," and "stubborn fool."

The image of a second George Washington in the Confederate White House had certainly grown dim and blurred . . .

· 3 ·

The worst weather of the miserable winter of 1862 came on February 22. Richmond was battered by rain, snow, and sleet. The streets were deep in slushy mud. It was not a day to be out-of-doors, but crowds splashed towards Capitol Hill. A steady flow of carriages sloshed through the streets. Despite the weather, the occasion was a gala one. This was the Confederacy's first birthday, and the provisional government was giving way to the permanent one.

Although Davis was not as popular as he had been in the beginning, no one of any stature had risen to oppose him as a candidate for the presidency. As a result, the electorate had reaffirmed both Davis and Stephens for the regular six-year term in accordance with the Constitution.

Those voters who wished to show disapproval towards the Davis program had boycotted the polls. But the forces against the President were not sufficiently organized to beat him with ballots—and lacking any other choice, the people had overwhelmingly cast their votes for Davis and Stephens.

So, on this stormy day, the crowds had turned out to watch the inauguration. A rumor started that the defenders of Fort Donelson had routed Grant and a big Confederate victory was in the making. It was welcome news and raised the spirits of the Inauguration Day crowds.

Jefferson Davis, the leading actor of the day's events, was suffering from acute physical pain. The ebb of Confederate fortunes and the constant discord within the government had left a mark on him. His old ailments had recurred; the sight in his left eye was failing and he was tortured by excruciating neuralgic twinges. He was unable to eat and teetered on the brink of serious illness. Sheer will power alone kept him from surrendering to these physical frailties.

He appeared at the Capitol on the stroke of noon, the appointed hour, a soberly dressed, stiffly upright man on whose taut, hollow-cheeked face were written the signs of his ordeal. His lips were bloodless, his cheeks drained of color; his striking black eyes glowed with a fevered light, and he moved rigidly into the old Virginia House of Representatives for the ceremonies. Rain pelted the windows as the procession started outside.

Capitol Park was thronged with people huddling under umbrellas, strips of canvas, pieces of oilcloth, and sodden newspapers. The great crowd peered through the rain beyond the magnificent bronze statue of Washington which dominated the square. A covered platform, draped in soggy bunting, had been set up for the President to take his oath of office as the first permanent Chief Executive of the Confederate States of America.

(By an odd quirk, at the moment Davis stepped onto the platform Abraham Lincoln was riding in a carriage behind the hearse carrying young Willie Lincoln to the cemetery. North and South, Washington's Birthday was being celebrated in agony.)

A drenched army band played a march. The Presidential party slogged across the rain-swept walk from the Capitol and mounted the platform as the band played "Dixie." Bishop Johns, Coadjutor Bishop of the Episcopal Diocese of Virginia, invoked a prayer. The oath was administered to Davis and the President turned to face his people. He had nothing encouraging to tell them. Shortly before his arrival at the Capitol, he had learned the truth about Fort Donelson —the optimistic rumor had been cruelly wrong.

His demeanor was grave as he begged for "the Divine support I need so sorely." The audience shifted uncomfortably in the driving rain, straining to hear his uninspiring speech. He briefly reviewed the history and the background of the Confederacy. Then he went on to say: "At the darkest hour of our struggle, the provisional government gives way to the permanent government . . . after a series of successes and victories we have recently met with serious disasters . . ."

His words were sobering and cheerless. A shudder ran through the assemblage. The situation seemed hopeless; but from the atmosphere of universal despair epitomized by the foul weather, the people gathered strength for the future. It was a standing joke in Richmond that one half of the nation disagreed with the President and the other half felt he was wrong. Yet when he had finished his remarks, in which he had manfully refrained from making excuses and had offered no explanations for mistakes, a cheer went up.

It was an exalted and magical moment. For that brief time, men forgot their differences and recaptured the spirit that had impelled them to strike out for Southern independence. The Cause was a glorious one again and they voiced the faith still alive within their hearts. Cries of "God save our President!" rang out. The shouts must have gladdened Davis, and his face softened in the flicker of a smile. He turned from the platform. The band played "The Bonnie Blue Flag" and the crowd slowly dispersed.

Varina Davis delighted everyone by telling of an amusing experience on her ride from the Executive Mansion to the Capitol. Her carriage moved slowly through the rain and glancing out the window, she noticed four dignified Negro footmen attired in black broadcloth and wearing white gloves and top hats walking two abreast on each side of the carriage. Her coachman slowed the horses to the deliberate pace of the marchers. She called up to her driver and asked why the men were walking at the carriage side. He gave her an aggrieved glance and answered, "Well, ma'am, you told me to fix everything like it ought to be and this here's the way we do in Richmond at funerals and sich-like."

The anecdote brought laughter at the reception in the Executive Mansion that night. Nothing could change Richmond, the guests chuckled. The affair was a success. The elite of the city turned out in all its finery. While none of the ladies wore the latest gowns from Paris, there was some good wine and food and sparkling conversation. No one present seemed to bear the President any ill will, although some of his most violent critics were there. Comradeship and devotion to the Cause temporarily overshadowed the pettiness and acrimony of the preceding months.

Varina had never been more gracious. Even the stiff-necked Richmond snobs were captivated by her wit and charm. She moved radiantly from group to group spreading regal elegance. Davis himself showed little animation. The tidings of Fort Donelson oppressed him, but no one could tell from his impassive bearing that he carried with him the most crushing news of the war. Outwardly, the President seemed calm; his manner was flawless, a model of hospitable reserve.

The affair must have been an ordeal for him; against the background of lilting music, the clink of glasses, the laughter and conversation, he heard the groans of the wounded and the dying and the tread of defeated troops marching through the mud to surrender. The night was kept out by the cheery blaze of lights that illuminated the high-ceilinged rooms of the Brockenbrough mansion. Rich damask curtains were drawn across the windows—but even in that grand place, Davis was haunted by the faces of his defeated soldiers standing in the freezing rain.

He cloaked his inner feelings, smiled and bowed, shook hands with friends, and accepted the abashed congratulations of his enemies. He showed himself to the guests with the dignity expected of a leader, even in the bleakest hour . . .

· 4 ·

Many Richmond institutions suffered change, but none were altered as drastically as the police force. The wartime police, supervised by a stout, gray-haired old man named John Winder, had become the bane of the city.

Winder, formerly a Major in the United States Army, was the son of the General who had lost the Battle of Bladensburg to the British in 1814, a defeat which led to the sack of Washington and disgrace for the Winder family.

John Winder had lived a pettish life dominated by his father's failure; he was driven by a compulsion to erase the ignominy of his name. Now, with the star of a Brigadier General on his collar, Winder had been placed in charge of the Richmond police and had turned that once easygoing force into a ruthless, secretive organization reminiscent of the political police in Czarist Russia. The regular police were augmented by a band of plainclothes detectives— Southern sympathizers recruited from the slums of Baltimore, Philadelphia, and New York. They were coarse, tough, and unfeeling men hired as a secret service to counteract the work of Federal agents. Instead, they were used as Winder's private army to hound the people of Richmond.

Among his duties, Winder had been ordered to stamp out the crime wave which had plagued Richmond since the coming of troops and outsiders to the capital. A flood of unsavory people had swarmed into the city and an outbreak of felonies alien to the formerly well-mannered city had erupted. Once Richmond had been a place where householders seldom bothered to lock their doors; now whole areas were unsafe after dark.

Rowdyism reached frightening proportions. Numerous bordellos abounded in places with names like Locust Alley and "Ram Cat" Alley, between Main and Clay Streets. Every night the police swooped down on the unfortunate women who catered to army enlisted men. These females were no beauties wearing crinoline and lace. Lank-haired and dirty, in soiled calico dresses, these unlovely sluts were dragged before the Mayor's Court, night after night, and sentenced to jail.

The raids, the arrests, and the jailings did little to stem immorality. Richmond was a city practically in the front lines of a terrible war. The barriers had to come down. Thousands of homesick soldiers were jammed into the city, with nothing to do and no place to go. These young men let loose with awesome abandon. Saloons and restaurants were scenes of vicious brawls. Bawdy, drunken women staggered through staid residential districts hanging on to their whisky-soaked men. Fist fights boiled up into gun duels. Richmond had been a civilized city, long unaccustomed to such frontier violence.

Winder cracked down hard on criminal offenders, but the situation worsened. The choleric General did stamp out one aspect of Richmond's unhappy situation. The number of men wearing military uniforms and insignia without any right to do so had reached scandalous proportions. Winder handled this abuse in typically despotic fashion. Anyone in military dress, regardless of rank, could be stopped by his patrols. If the man had no pass from his unit commander—or was wearing the uniform illegally—he was in for a bad time.

Winder's detectives gave their prisoners a beating at the slightest provocation. The two prisons he ran—"Castle Thunder" and "Castle Godwin"—were filled with inmates who showed the aftereffects of a questioning by the secret service detectives: broken noses, black eyes, missing teeth, and smashed jaws.

If Winder could not outwit the Northern spies or control crime in Richmond, he did manage to clear the streets of bogus soldiers. The unauthorized wearing of uniforms ended abruptly. Few were foolhardy enough to court a session with Winder's men by strutting around in a gaudy uniform.

The dreary winter ended, and early in March, Davis morosely stated, "Events have cast on our arms and our hopes the gloomiest shadows." He had good reason for such pessimism. The military situation in the West was bleak. Defeat followed defeat. The Confederates had been badly beaten at Pea Ridge, Arkansas. Island Number Ten in the Mississippi was under heavy siege. The picture could not have been blacker.

In this unhappy period, President Davis, who had recently joined the Episcopal church, called for a national day of fasting and prayer, on March 3. He also wired General Lee, who was at Savannah, to return to the capital. Lee, still under a cloud as the result

Brilliant, sickly Alexander H. Stephens, Vice-President of the Confederacy, was often at odds with Jefferson Davis on questions of domestic policy involving states' rights.

of his failure in West Virginia, was then serving as military adviser to the President, an administrative post.

The President's proclamation of a devotional day was greeted by the Richmond press with cynicism. Vitriolic John Daniel who had authored many attacks against Davis, sardonically editorialized:

> When we find the President standing in a corner telling his beads and relying on a miracle to save the country, instead of mounting his horse and putting forth every power of the government to defeat the enemy, the effect is depressing in the extreme. When the ship springs a leak, the efficient captain does not order all hands to prayers, but to the pumps . . .

The comradeship of Inauguration Day quickly disappeared. The rumblings against Davis grew louder. The new Congress that met in February, 1862, held many men who openly opposed the President. Varina Davis admitted that the Congress was unreceptive to her husband. She wrote later: "Now, for the first time, there appeared to be an organized party in opposition to the administration . . ."

But the antiadministration Congressmen were no "loyal opposition." A strong faction actually wanted to displace Davis. According to Thomas R. R. Cobb, a cabal was actively plotting the overthrowal of the President. Cobb unequivocally stated: "Davis would be deposed if the Congress had any more confidence in Stephens than in him . . ."

It was not surprising that Stephens too was falling out of favor. "Little Ellick" appeared to have lost any desire to engage in governmental functions. He stayed at his Georgia home brooding about the plight of the Confederacy. And while he did not yet actively oppose Davis, neither did he do anything to help the beleaguered President.

Among the major criticisms of Davis, extreme dissatisfaction was expressed over his attitude towards the war. From the very outset, the President had decreed a defensive role for the Confederate forces. In his opinion, he was carrying on a war to force an "invader" from his country; his aim was to hold his lines and make the enemy assaults so costly that the disheartened Yankees would sue for peace.

When his defensive policy had met with success, Davis was hailed as a military genius. He was the father of his country, a great man.

But once the Yankees cracked open the Confederate defenses, Davis was called a blunderer surrounded by incompetents. His every move was disparaged. Extremists demanded that the Confederate armies should carry the war to the Yankees; they did not consider the realities—that the Rebel armies lacked both the equipment and the manpower for a prolonged offensive into enemy territory.

The arch Davis-baiter, John Daniel, was one of the chief spokesmen against the concept of a defensive war. He wrote: "The policy of monotonous defense which has been perseveringly pursued by the authorities of the Confederacy has been the subject of universal regret among the Southern people, of annoyance to our generals and of disease and death to our armies . . ."

The President's failure to adopt an aggressive concept brought him censure even from men who worked closely at his side. His own aides joined the universal grumbling. One of them. T. O. W--¹· ton, said: "There is general discont is pursued. It is thought by the be: to the State and the Cause and th tense . . . All the blame falls on . with the whole responsibility for th emy . . ."

In the face of this furor, Davis remained unshaken in his determination to defend every foot of his nation rather than take the offensive. This strategy of maintaining a defensive line spread the Confederate forces dangerously thin in many places. The foes of the President claimed that not only was he endangering the nation, but by forcing his way on Congress, Davis was in fact setting up a virtual dictatorship.

As proof of his despotic aims, the anti-Davis men pointed to the hasty passage of an ordnance allowing the President to suspend the writ of habeas corpus anywhere he deemed this drastic action necessary. The authority had been granted him at a secret session of Congress on February 27, 1862. Since the establishment of military rule was left to the President's discretion, the law gave him limitless power. Because Norfolk and Portsmouth were under Federal attack, Davis placed those two cities under martial law. Early in March, he ordered it also in Richmond and Petersburg. Civil rights were revoked and the military took over.

To the highly individualistic Southerners, the very idea of martial law was odious. The people who had rebelled against a government they had termed tyrannical, deeply resented knuckling under to rigid military regulations. The loss of basic civil rights and the suspension of habeas corpus created great animosity among the plain citizens. The fact that this stringent action was a necessity of war and had been legalized by the Congress made little difference to them.

The malcontents pointed out that Lincoln had been attacked as a "despot" when he declared martial law and lifted the writ of habeas corpus in the territory between Washington and New York. Now, Davis was doing the same thing. Did that not brand him a "despot" as well?

Davis vainly explained the difference between his acts and Lincoln's; the Yankee President had carried out these restrictive measures on his own authority by extraconstitutional means. Davis had been duly authorized by the Congress in accordance with the constitution. Lincoln's were the methods of an autocrat—the Confederate way was the democratic way.

This might all be true, the people said, but it made damned little difference whether you were legally and morally right if you had to live under the thumb of an Army commander and all your liberties were taken away. The people hated martial law—and they blamed Jefferson Davis for having imposed it on them.

General Winder administered the military rule in Richmond. His bully boys enforced the law with vigor. Only those with wealth and position could feel safe from arrest—Winder's men were not overscrupulous, and they had an appetite for bribes.

Anyone seeking to leave the environs of Richmond needed a passport. Winder was authorized to issue passports, but so was the War Department. The two offices worked at cross purposes; on many occasions persons refused a passport by Winder were granted one by Benjamin. A vehement feud grew up between the two men.

Winder claimed Benjamin was favoring Jews in granting passports and that "foreigners" were getting preferences over Southerners. The vitriolic General insinuated Benjamin was abetting Northern spies, trading with the enemy, and making huge sums by operating a smuggling ring. Benjamin made unflattering countercharges against Winder and a bitter controversy raged between the officials.

Obviously it was wrong to have passports issued by two authorities. Davis finally decided that Winder should have exclusive power in the matter. No one liked John Winder except the President; he mistook the General's spitefulness for vigor, his viciousness for zeal. Again, Davis had chosen the wrong man; and once more remained blind to the faults of his choice.

Once he had been granted the power by the President, Winder tightened the thumbscrews in Richmond. A purported pro-Unionist, John Botts, was summarily arrested and held incommunicado for eight weeks in a Negro jail. He was finally released for lack of evidence or any specific charge. This was no isolated case. Hundreds of "enemy agents" were rounded up on the flimsiest excuses. Hysteria, ill will, and fear played a large part in these undemocratic excesses.

Stanton, the Yankee Secretary of War, and his secret police— under notorious Lafayette C. Baker—conducted similar excesses. In the name of freedom and democracy, ugly autocratic repressions were being carried out on both sides of the Mason-Dixon Line.

Winder set up a passport office at the corner of 9th and 15th Streets in an old warehouse. His bullies abused the applicants. Blackjacks and locust sticks were freely used on anyone who protested the treatment he received. A person making too much of a fuss was arrested as a "Yankee disrupter" and thrown into jail. Corruption was a cancer in the police system. Passports could be purchased for a price.

Around this time a law was passed prohibiting the sale of whisky except for medicinal purposes. Only apothecaries were permitted to sell alcoholic beverages. A brisk and lucrative bootlegging trade evolved. Winder's detectives grew rich peddling liquor permits and avaricious doctors freely sold prescriptions to buy whisky for medicinal purposes.

Winder did make one honest effort to crack down on a growing abuse. The cost of food was rising so high that he issued an ordinance regulating the prices of dairy products and meat. Food dealers refused to obey the law. They closed up shop rather than sell at prices lower than they could squeeze from the desperate public. As a result, Winder's attempt to curtail profiteering failed, and when the markets reopened, the cost of living rose even more . . .

· 5 ·

On April 16, 1862, still another grievance was added to the roster of complaints against President Davis. The Confederate Congress now enacted a conscription law. The Draft Act came only ten days after the terrible slaughter at Shiloh or Pittsburgh Landing, Tennessee. This battle, which raged April 6-7, was the bloodiest military clash ever fought on the American continent up to that time. What at first had been hailed as an overwhelming Confederate victory proved to be just the opposite. The Southerners had been forced from the field and the grand soldier, Albert Sidney Johnston, killed in action on the first day.

General P. G. T. Beauregard had taken his place but the hero of Fort Sumter was not up to the demands of that battle. Instead of winning a great victory, the Confederacy suffered 10,000 casualties and lost more than 1,000 prisoners.

As if this calamity had not been enough, Island Number Ten fell to Union troops and gunboats on April 7. The Mississippi was in Federal hands all the way to Vicksburg. While the South still mourned its losses, the grieving populace was shocked by the conscription bill.

The law required all able-bodied males between eighteen and thirty-five to register for military service. Volunteers who had enlisted for less than three years would be retained in the Army for that period, dating from the start of their original mustering in.

States' rights advocates were horrified at this move by the central government. Previously the various states had supplied troops as requisitioned by Richmond. Now the tyranny of conscription was being foisted on them. The protest against the draft reached dangerous levels. The governors of several states, especially North Carolina and Georgia, opposed the law so heatedly that they verged on treason.

To foil the Richmond government, Joe Brown, Governor of Georgia, enrolled thousands into a paper State Guard and claimed these men were exempt from further service. He even went to the extent of seizing a shipload of arms consigned to the Confederacy because it had been landed at Savannah. He averred that it was now the property of Georgia.

The conscription law was neither popular nor fair; the burden fell on the poor, for the bill provided that a substitute might be furnished any draftee who could pay the government $300. This practice was also followed in the North when the United States draft law was enacted. Among the masses on both sides of the Mason-Dixon line, the slogan "A rich man's war and a poor man's fight" became widespread. Another discriminatory clause in the Southern draft act was the so-called "twenty nigger rule," which provided that a man who owned twenty or more slaves was exempt from service and allowed to stay home and supervise them.

While such economic and social factors made the law objectionable, the main resentment to it stemmed from its violation of states' rights, the cornerstone of the Confederacy. A private in a crack cavalry regiment, Hampton's Legion, wrote his feelings about the draft to his planter father, on April 13, 1862:

> The conscription bill . . . militates so strongly against the sovereignty of the state and is so gross an usurption of authority that I should be greatly shocked to see it passed unchallenged by my State . . . I trust, however, that before this infamy is consummated, the sky will grow so bright as to relieve the wretched triflers in Richmond from the panic which dictates such unconstitutional measures . . .

As a matter of fact the law had not been conceived by President Davis. It had evolved after suggestions from his military adviser, Robert E. Lee, and the commander of the Army of Northern Virginia, Joe Johnston. But the blame fell on Davis; he was being censured for what the people considered an "administration measure."

Lee and Johnston had offered conscription as a solution to the army's shrinking manpower. The urgency was great. In March, 20 steamers had disgorged thousands of Federal troops at Newport News. The reluctant Yankee General-in-Chief, George B. McClellan, had at last made his move. "Little Mac" was carrying the war to the Peninsula with Richmond as his goal.

Even the dullest person knew the most critical moments of the struggle were at hand. Many, faced with conscription, chose to evade the stigma of being drafted by volunteering. Throughout the South, recruitment spurted and the Confederate armies swelled to almost 400,000.

Yet despite conscription, thousands found loopholes in the Draft Act and avoided service. The law provided exemptions for druggists, so every general storekeeper stocked up with patent medicines to qualify as a dispenser of pharmaceuticals. Other professions not subject to service were school teachers, divinity students, and ministers. The sudden rush into those occupations easily matched the rush to the colors.

Down in Crawfordsville, Georgia, Vice-President Stephens took the stand that opened the final rift between him and Davis. The "outrageous" conscription act forced him into open opposition to the President's program and policies. In a speech, he said: "We should have called for volunteers for the war, and no doubt they would have come. It would have been better to rely upon soldiers thus recruited . . ."

The atmosphere of pessimism was oppressive. The cruel losses mounted. The morale of the people was shaken. Late in April, when New Orleans fell, Mary Boykin Chesnut, a stalwart Rebel, gloomily confided to her diary: "New Orleans is gone and with it the Confederacy."

Recrimination fell upon everyone who held a position of leadership. Joe Johnston was mercilessly criticized for the brilliant retreat he conducted before McClellan on the Peninsula. Johnston, probably the best defensive fighter in either army, refused to trade his soldiers' lives for ground. He kept withdrawing to the powerful bastions before Richmond, forcing McClellan to extend his supply lines, while shortening his own. But when he pulled out of the Williamsburg area, Robert Toombs wrote to his friend, Stephens:

> McClellan was there with his whole army, a good deal less I think, than ours, and we could have whipped as easily there as anywhere else. But as usual we burnt up everything and fled, were attacked in the retreat, and left in the hands of the enemy some ten or twelve hundred of our killed, wounded and sick, and that after a decided victory. That is called generalship!!

A despairing Alabaman penned these words:

> I am almost on the verge of madness . . . So far the people have done everything, the Government little, and this little in the wrong direction . . .

One of the South's most loyal and dependable men, Herschel V. Johnson, overwhelmed by dejection, sent a letter to a friend which contained this melancholy passage:

> You ask me if I have confidence in the success of the Southern Confederacy. I pray for success but I do not expect success . . . The enemy in due time will penetrate the heart of the Confederacy . . . and the hearts of our people will quake and their spirits will yield to the force of overwhelming numbers . . . The enemy is superior to us in everything but courage and therefore it is certain if war is to go on, until exhaustion overtake the one side or the other side, that we shall be the first to be exhausted . . .

In Richmond, a creeping fear crawled like a poisonous snake, slithering from street to street and house to house. Not everyone surrendered to despair, however. Each Federal victory brought secret exultation to the thousands of Negroes who even then believed a triumphant North would assure them of freedom.

And even in the capital of the Confederacy there still remained staunch Unionists. They too, rejoiced silently. All of them were not tacit in their feelings. On the walls and fences of Richmond hastily scrawled chalk slogans mysteriously appeared: "Union men to the rescue!"; "Now is the time to rally around the Old Flag"; "God bless the Stars and Stripes!"

To the fears of a military debacle were added the terrors of an uprising within Richmond itself. Rumors circulated that the Yankees had smuggled thousands of fanatics into the city—grim, ruthless men who had come in with the flood of refugees. The rumors made them veterans of the Kansas border wars, cold-blooded killers of the John Brown breed who would steal out one night to spread arson and death.

Richmond was a frightened city, but the men who crouched in their rifle pits on the Peninsula remained unshaken. The war was real to them—not whispers in the dark. The men in gray knew how to handle their job. They kept calm. They fought, marched, countermarched, and died, trusting in Joe Johnston and lemon-sucking, sanctimonious "Stonewall" Jackson.

EIGHT

Mr. Lincoln

"In giving freedom to the slave we assure freedom to the free,—honorable alike in what we give and what we preserve—"

ABRAHAM LINCOLN,
Second Annual Message to Congress,
December 1, 1862

So we're springing to the call
from the East and from the West,
Shouting the battle-cry of Freedom;
And we'll hurl the rebel crew
from the land we love the best,
Shouting the battle-cry of Freedom!

Union war song

· 1 ·

IN THE SPRING of 1862, the landscape danced with color; the sun shone and the winter miasmas were burned away in its warming rays. The countryside grew rich and verdant. On every side were smiling faces and high hopes.

Now "Little Mac" would tree the Rebs. Soon the Confederate armies in the Valley and in Virginia would be smashed and demolished; the Confederate government, scattered and in flight. The bells of victory would be ringing all through the North and the war triumphantly ended. This was the dream of millions.

The outlook was so optimistic that, on April 3, Edwin Stanton ordered recruiting halted in all the loyal states. There were men enough under arms to do the job of crushing the rebellion. A few more blows and the war would surely be over.

McClellan moved on Richmond, but he was not a scythe of vengeance cutting a swath through the enemy country. He advanced timidly and cautiously, still obsessed by the idea that he faced incredible odds. He kept demanding more troops, more cannon, more horses. But despite his timorousness, the Federals reached the outskirts of Richmond.

The military delays and McClellan's hesitancy made Lincoln short-tempered. He had grown dubious of professional soldiers. At the war's outset, he had held the West Pointers and Regulars in awe. He keenly felt his own ignorance of military matters. Now he was learning that generals were human beings like everyone else. Many of them merely knew enough to put up a good bluff. They adroitly explained their errors with convincing excuses, always placing the blame for failure on factors beyond their control—the weather, the terrain, the lack of roads. In a pinch, they did not hesitate to blame the inadequacies of a hapless colleague.

Lincoln also grew skeptical of army intelligence reports. He was convinced that the most optimistic were exaggerated, and the pessimistic, merely blinds for some boneheaded blunder.

He demonstrated this attitude during the Valley Campaign in May when General Irvin McDowell sent a dispatch stating that one of his officers had not been able to locate any enemy troops to the east of the Blue Ridge Mountains.

Lincoln peevishly wired back to McDowell: "You say General Geary's scouts report that they find no enemy this side of the Blue Ridge. Neither do I. Have they been to the Blue Ridge looking for them?"

Lincoln's insistence on complete reports from his Generals—especially McClellan—gave rise to a joke:

Obeying instructions, McClellan gave him full reports of daily happenings. One day he sent the President a telegram: "Have captured two cows. What disposition should I make of them?"

The answer came: "Milk 'em, George. (Signed) A. Lincoln."

McClellan did not use all his energies running the campaign on which he had embarked. He gave time and thought to matters not normally within the scope of an army commander. The Young Napoleon frequently offered gratuitous advice on political affairs; he gave his unsolicited counsel to the President, Congress, and the Cabinet in voluminous letters. Since he believed only he could save the country, McClellan felt his wisdom was needed . . .

But not even McClellan could indefinitely forestall a full-scale clash. Joe Johnston, who had retreated across the Peninsula, stood with his back to Richmond. The time had come for him to fight. On May 31, he turned on McClellan, and all that day and the next, smashed at the Federals south of the Chickahominy in the savage battle of Seven Pines, or Fair Oaks.

At first Johnston drove back the Yankees, but McClellan brought reinforcements across the river and regained his ground. The struggle ended indecisively, with the contending armies in approximately the same positions they had held before the fighting. Early in the battle, Joe Johnston received a severe wound and was succeeded by "Granny" Lee. The Army of Northern Virginia had, at last, found its man of destiny. Never again did anyone use the derogatory "Granny" in reference to Robert E. Lee. "Marse Bob" his soldiers called him; they were devoted to the gracious aristocrat who embodied all the noblest qualities of Southern chivalry.

Lee was an ambitious man, but possessed of both dignity and taste. He was no self-seeker, nor was he conceited and vainglorious. McClellan lacked precisely the qualities Lee had in plentitude.

Yet Little Mac, in his first major test at Seven Pines, did not fare too badly. He had held his positions and carried out the admonition Lincoln had wired him while the fighting was in progress: "Stand

Confident Union troops stream onto the Peninsula from their transports, to launch the spring offensive of 1862.

The march on Richmond, which started with such high hopes, ended in defeat for the Yankees. Here the Army of the Potomac retreats in the rain after the battle of Malvern Hill.

well on your guard, hold all your ground, or yield only inch by inch and in good order."

But even though McClellan had not been beaten by Johnston and Lee, Seven Pines almost ruined him as a general. He had never fought such a large battle before and was unnerved by the numbers of wounded men and mangled corpses. The war had come full circle for Little Mac. Now it was not the cheers of his troops drawn up on parade; it was not galloping importantly to and fro, trailed by his dapper staff officers; it was not striking poses to make female hearts flutter; it was not oysters and champagne at midnight, nor the plaudits and acclaim of a nation.

War was sheer horror.

McClellan, the perfectly endowed soldier, showed his greatest military defect. He cared so deeply for his troops that he could not bear to throw them into battle with the detachment a general needed for success.

Lee, too, loved his men. But, when necessary, he did not shrink from using them. Victory comes to the general who can control his emotions and not be haunted by the killed and the wounded. Lee was a professional soldier; McClellan, a dilettante at war.

Little Mac preferred to win victory by flashy maneuvers, not hard fighting. Joe Johnston's kind of war was to his taste: a bit of action and few casualties. Lee was a different breed of soldier; he hit hard and pressed on. Troops were his tools. If men were killed by the hundreds or the thousands, that was part of war's hazards. He was not a man for mourning; he was a man for action.

After Seven Pines, McClellan again nagged for reinforcements. He soon became his old self: strutting, cocksure, arrogant. He made boasts but did nothing. When Lincoln prodded him to take another crack at Richmond, McClellan complained that the rainy weather was hampering him by bogging down his wagon trains and artillery. To this Lincoln commented: "The rain and mud does not appear to bog down Lee. General McClellan seems to think, in defiance of the Scripture, that Heaven sent its rain only on the just and not on the unjust."

McClellan was quite conscious that he was playing a leading part in a drama with a world-wide audience. He had the opportunity to go down in the annals of military history as one of the greatest of generals. No man had ever commanded an army of more than

Robert E. Lee, the aristocratic Virginian, was the greatest of the Southern generals. A master strategist, Lee was beloved by the men of the Army of Northern Virginia whom he commanded from 1862 until the bitter day when he surrendered.

100,000 on the American continent. His troops had been given the best the government could furnish. He stood at the pinnacle of his career—and the spires of Richmond rose out of the mists only four miles away.

A daring thrust might have brought him glory and victory. Little Mac was just not man enough to meet the challenge. The old fears oppressed him. He believed he was outnumbered and that his army faced total annihilation. As the weeks slipped by, Lincoln, realizing that the suspension of recruiting had been premature, called on the states to enroll 300,000 new soldiers for three years. Lincoln was dubious of McClellan's reports about Confederate numbers. Yet the government could not afford to take chances. A disaster to the Army of the Potomac might spell the end of the Union. If McClellan asked for men, he must be given them.

Down on the Peninsula, Little Mac's confidence in himself waxed and waned. At times, he was excessively humble; at others, insufferably arrogant. The new recruiting program got under way in the North and volunteers came to the colors—but these raw men were hardly soldiers. Reinforcements for McClellan had to come from the troops in the field.

Stanton was frankly reluctant to hand additional units over to McClellan. He had grown to distrust his former client. The War Department could not refuse to support the General, however. Stanton decided to send McDowell's corps to Little Mac—but with strings attached. The corps was to come as an independent force. McDowell would be under McClellan's command but not under his control. He could be withdrawn at any time.

McClellan's response to this offer was a haughty rejection of the proposed reinforcements. He telegraphed Stanton: "If I cannot control all the troops I want none of them, but would prefer to fight the battle with what I have, and let others be responsible for the results . . ."

The General's insolence was staggering. He believed his stature permitted him to bargain with the government as an equal. He seemed to be cracking under his responsibilities. His letters to his wife made so many references to his fearlessness, determination, and faith that it was obvious he had serious doubts about himself.

McClellan's military activities creaked to a halt. While he did nothing, the enemy was busy. Jeb Stuart sent his cavalry on a ride around the Army of the Potomac in a daring and imaginative raid. Stuart's men burned, damaged, or captured tons of stores and came away practically unscathed.

In the Valley, "Stonewall" Jackson raised a whirlwind, defying and defeating McDowell, Frémont, and Banks, eluding 60,000 Union troops and by a series of forced marches combining forces with Lee before Richmond. But even with Jackson's seasoned men, Lee's army numbered only 85,000—yet this did not prevent him from striking out at McClellan's 100,000 on June 26.

The historic Seven Days' Battle was under way. The terrible fighting was to continue unabated for a week. At the end of the first day, McClellan wired Stanton: "I have seen too many dead and wounded comrades to feel otherwise than that the government has not sustained this army. If you do not do so now the game is lost. If I save this army now, I tell you plainly that I owe no thanks to you or any person in Washington. You have done your best to sacrifice this army."

Colonel E. S. Sanford, the military censor, happened to receive this particular message. He realized the implication of the last sentences in the telegram. He saw them as treasonable and intended by McClellan "to reach the public as a means of shifting the causes of his defeat from his own to other shoulders." Sanford deleted the offending phrases on his own authority. The President saw only the censored telegram. His reaction to it was prompt, and he wired the troublesome General: "Save your army at all events. Will send reinforcements as fast as we can . . . of course they cannot reach you today, tomorrow or next day . . ."

The Army of the Potomac retreated through the mud and rain toward its new base at Harrison's Landing at the mouth of the James River, where Navy gunboats could help hold off the pursuing enemy.

The fighting raged without letup and the Federals fell back to the crest of Malvern Hill. It was a classical defensive position the weary Army of the Potomac men held. Their artillery was planted in tiers to sweep every inch of the gentle slope. The infantrymen dug like moles and quickly erected a series of formidable breastworks. Lee came on in the fever of victory. He ordered an attack against the positions on Malvern Hill. The assault was one of the few military blunders he ever made. Nothing could stand up to the deadly Union artillery fire. Lee lost 5,000 men in minutes. The Confederates withdrew. The Army of the Potomac crept down from the crest of Malvern Hill, stunned at its easy victory over Lee. The men knew the Rebels were badly hurt. A counterblow now could shatter Lee, and the casualties suffered by the Federals in the Seven Days would not have been wasted.

Any general other than McClellan would have seen his opportunity and grasped it. He was not one for launching counterthrusts, however. The Young Napoleon was satisfied to have extricated his army in one piece. Instead of ordering counterattack and pursuit, McClellan resumed his retreat to Harrison's Landing. The columns obediently stumbled off through the darkness of a rain-swept night.

In at least one case, the order to retreat brought vociferous denunciation. General Phil Kearny, the one-armed commander of the First Division, Third Corps, heard the order with disbelief. Kearny was a colorful man. He had lost his arm in Mexico leading a daring cavalry charge. General Phil had led a romantic, adventurous life; he had fought with the French Foreign Legion in North Africa, was a veteran of the Franco-Austrian War in which he saw action at Solferino; and had also participated in several Indian campaigns out West. The General was no newcomer to war.

On receiving the word to move his troops towards Harrison's Landing, Kearny loudly proclaimed to his staff: "I, Philip Kearny, an old soldier, enter my solemn protest against this order for retreat; we ought, instead of retreating, to follow up the enemy and take Richmond. And in full view of all the responsibility of such a declaration, I say to you all, such an order can only be prompted by cowardice or treason . . ."

· 2 ·

After the failure of the highly vaunted Peninsula campaign, Lincoln said, "I was as nearly inconsolable as I could be and live."

The situation was not entirely black. While McClellan had failed in his purpose on the Peninsula, the Army of the Potomac had shown its mettle. The Union soldiers were the equal of Lee's best troops. Despite the retreat, the Federals had inflicted greater casualties on the Rebels than they themselves had suffered.

Safely ensconced at Harrison's Landing, protected by the big guns of the Navy, McClellan interpreted his retrograde movement as a

Abraham Lincoln of Illinois as he appeared in the closing days of the war.

great victory. Had he not drawn the enemy from Washington and borne the brunt of the foe's fury? He made glorious promises again. He had saved the country and now he would win the war!

Once more, he assumed the role of national leader, the man of the hour. He was going to tell the fools in Washington how to conduct the war and what was needed for victory: "To accomplish the great task of capturing Richmond and putting an end to the Rebellion, reinforcements should be sent me rather much over than much less than 100,000 men . . . I doubt whether there are today more than 50,000 men with their colors . . ."

After reading McClellan's latest demand, Lincoln showed that all the travail had not robbed him of his sense of humor. He said: "Sending more men to that army is like shoveling fleas across a barn-yard—not half of them get there. If I gave McClellan all the men he asks for they could not find room to lie down. They'd have to sleep standing up."

Lincoln and Stanton paid the Army of the Potomac a visit at Harrison's Landing. The President questioned McClellan and his corps and divisional commanders; Stanton spent a busy day totting up unit duty rosters. When Lincoln and the Secretary compared notes, they discovered a startling fact about the Army of the Potomac—its strength. McClellan had present for duty 86,500; 34,000 more were absent with leave; 3,700 absent without leave. A little simple addition showed that "Little Mac" had somewhat more than 12,000 men under his command—more than double his own gloomy total of 50,000.

If its General was downhearted, the Army of the Potomac did not behave like a whipped army. The severe fighting had not dampened the men's ardor as demonstrated by the ovation they tendered Lincoln as he rode past to review the troops. The President did not present an imposing figure on horseback. He sat his mount neither gracefully nor with dignity. Yet he was always welcomed and respected by the men in the ranks.

A soldier of a Connecticut regiment described Lincoln in the saddle, as follows:

> It did seem as though every moment the President's legs would become entangled with those of the horse he rode and both come down together, while his arms were apparently subject to similar mis-

haps . . . That arm with which he drew the rein, in its angle and position resembled the hind leg of a grasshopper—the hand before, the elbow way back over the horse's tail.

The removal of his hat before each regiment was also a source of laughter in the style of its execution—the quick trot of the horse making it a feat of some difficulty, while from the same cause, his hold on it, while off, seemed very precarious.

But the boys like him, in fact his popularity with the army is and has been universal. Most of our leaders and rulers fall into odium, but all have faith in Lincoln. "When he finds out," they say, "it will be stopped . . . I don't believe they'll be able to pull the wool over old Lincoln's eyes . . ."

When Lincoln arrived at Harrison's Landing this time, McClellan committed one of the strangest acts of his inconsistent military career. As the President stepped off the steamer that had carried his party down from Washington, McClellan handed him a long letter which Lincoln read in the General's presence. After thanking McClellan for the opportunity to see it, Lincoln placed the letter in his pocket. His subsequent actions offered no hint about his reaction to its unusual contents.

We know now that McClellan said many things in that remarkable letter; he even surpassed his previous arrogance. He presumed to provide the President with a blueprint for running the war and the administration of the country.

The war, according to McClellan, should be "conducted on the highest principles known to Christian civilization." Private property should not be violated. The General further warned Lincoln that "radical views, especially on slavery" would cause mass unrest among the troops; the Army of the Potomac would never fight to make the Negroes free. McClellan said much more in his unique document; it contained advice on political affairs, foreign relations, finances—and, in short, told the President how to manage his entire office.

Without question, McClellan was convinced he had acted in the best interests of the United States. He wrote Mrs. McClellan: "I have written a strong, frank letter to the President . . . If he acts upon it, the country will be saved . . ."

Yet he also anticipated that the epistle would arouse so much presidential wrath that it might bring on his own downfall. In preparation for this expected martyrdom, McClellan said, in one of his daily letters to his wife: "I will send you a copy tomorrow [referring to the Lincoln letter] as well as other important letters which I wish you to keep as my record. They will show, with the others I have, that I was true to my country, that I understood the state of affairs long ago, and that had my advice been followed we should not have been in our present difficulties . . ."

The belief that he was destined to be sacrificed by the "incompetents" in Washington—the President included—grew to be an obsession with McClellan. He alerted his wife to this eventuality, by writing her: "The President, of course, has not replied to my letter, and never will. His reply may be, however, to avail himself of the first opportunity to cut my head off . . ."

George B. McClellan could not purge himself of the delusion that fate had chosen him as the instrument by which the United States would be rescued in its darkest hour. Once, as he rode through a bivouac of cheering soldiers, he told an associate, "How these brave fellows love me and what a power that love places in my hands! What is there to prevent my taking the government in my own hands?"

His companion soberly replied, "General, don't mistake those men. So long as you lead them against the enemy, they will adore you and die for you; but attempt to turn them against their government and you will be the first to suffer."

Ugly whispers rose about Little Mac's loyalty and motives. The word "traitor" was often used to describe him; and rumor persisted that McClellan was playing the game of certain politicians who had stated that, "It is not on our books that McClellan should take Richmond." Coincidentally, just prior to Lincoln's call at Harrison's Landing, the General had been visited by Fernando Wood, the devious Mayor of New York City, whose loyalty to the Union was highly questionable. Wood was accompanied by a prominent Democrat politician. McClellan and his guests had discussed politics, and the suggestion was made that the General might consider the possibilities of becoming the Democratic Party's candidate for the Presidential elections in 1864.

However, military necessities forced General McClellan to temporarily set aside his personal ambitions. Harrison's Landing was located in swampy, low-lying country. With the onset of summer, sickness spread in the ranks. Obviously the huge force could not remain inactive in that unhealthy atmosphere.

Prior to this Lincoln had reluctantly concluded that McClellan could not "do it all," and in the spring of '62 General Henry W. Halleck, known in the army as "Old Brains," had superseded him as General-in-Chief. Halleck decided to evacuate the troops to the former lines along the Potomac. The manpower and matériel spent in the fruitless Peninsular Campaign had been wasted. The men who had defeated Robert E. Lee at Malvern Hill were marched back to the environs of Washington.

The people heard the news and wondered why there was failure when all the signs had been of success. They were more angered than frightened and made the only response they could. More able-bodied men went off to become soldiers. The recruiting drums were sounded and the men came, "from Mississippi's winding stream and New England's shore." Three hundred thousand strong, they came. The war had not yet exacted its full quota of blood . . .

In Washington, the intimations that McClellan had sabotaged the campaign for his own purposes grew louder. According to the radicals and the abolitionists, he desired the country in grave danger so he could take over the government, set himself up as military dictator, negotiate a peace with the slavers and rule the United States. It was widely known that McClellan was no foe of slavery— and in some quarters, that was synonymous with treason.

Stanton did not conceal his virulent sentiments towards the discredited General: "This fellow with his gang is as busy as the devil impressing on the men he is murdering to no purpose, that the abolitionists at Washington, as he calls us, have abandoned them to death in the swamps of the Chickahominy. We are today in more peril from the Army of the Potomac than the rebels at Richmond . . ."

Stanton had somewhat overstated his case. The Army of the Potomac was not traitorous; and neither was McClellan. He was simply a man with too much conceit and not enough talent to do the job assigned him. He had neither the moral fiber nor the heart of a great soldier.

Although he had failed in the main objective—to crush the rebellion—McClellan had succeeded signally in another area. He had molded the mighty Army of the Potomac. That army could have performed miracles. Its leadership had unfortunately not been up to the standards of the men.

Little Mac had strutted and fretted long enough. Now he was relieved of command in the field and sent to Alexandria for orders. The Army of the Potomac was broken up piecemeal to form the new Army of Virginia under General John Pope. While McClellan, with a comparative handful of troops remained on guard along the Potomac, to defend Washington . . .

· 3 ·

The new General, John Pope, like his predecessor, gave the impression of greatness. He was stalwart and handsome, spoke grandiloquently, and had a record of victory behind him in the West; it was he who had captured Island Number Ten.

Pope had courage in combat, but was a boastful and tactless man who had a weakness for distorting the truth. He lost the confidence of his newly acquired army even before leading it into battle. He issued to the war-weary troops a proclamation which he considered a strong and stirring call aimed at rousing them to enthusiasm. He declared "I have come to you from the West where we are used to seeing the backs of the enemy." He bragged that his headquarters had been "in the saddle."

The response to this ringing statement was anything but fervid. Cynical, battle-hardened infantrymen knew a phony when they heard one. They resented the comparison between their performance and that of the Western soldiers. His declaration that his headquarters were in the saddle evoked the jibe, "John Pope's headquarters are in his hindquarters." And the catch phrase "as big a liar as John Pope" swept through the Army.

Pope's unpopularity affected all ranks of the army from privates to corps commanders. McClellan had been purged, but his influence remained strong. The troops, despite all that had happened, still believed in him; they felt he had been given a bad deal. These veterans knew how McClellan had transformed them from raw recruits into skillful soldiers; they were Little Mac's men and they wanted him back. Many of the generals, too, had been close friends of the deposed commander. They had known Pope in the days before the war and held him in low regard. It rankled them to serve under him.

Despite the dissension his presence was causing, Pope went ahead formulating plans and campaigns for his Army. Like McClellan, Pope was full of ideas about how the war should be conducted. The General was a "hard-war" man. He told his troops to live off the countryside in enemy-held territory. Instant destruction was ordered for any house from which a Federal soldier was shot. Any male non-combatant within Union lines was subject to immediate arrest. Those refusing to take an oath of loyalty to the Federal government were to be summarily expelled beyond Federal lines. Pope meant to show the Rebels the consequence of making war against the Federal government. According to the standards of the day, he was an un-civilized barbarian—but he was sincere in his desire to carry out punitive measures against Rebels. Pope was a petty man, and like all small people, was overwhelmed by his own righteousness.

He was the only Yankee general toward whom Lee ever expressed any real animosity. "Pope must be suppressed," he said. To aid him in this purpose, he called on the general he termed, "my right hand"—the eccentric military genius, "Stonewall" Jackson.

Braggart Pope had little chance against a team like Lee and Jackson. The unfortunate Union general tangled with Lee at Manassas on the same ground where the disastrous battle of Bull Run had been fought in July, 1861.

Lee had worked cleverly, sending Jackson on a raid through the Bull Run Mountains to destroy Pope's base at Manassas Junction. Believing he had only to contend with Jackson, Pope was confident of victory when he came to grips with the Rebels on August 30. He wired jubilant telegrams to Washington, claiming victory. But Lee united his divided forces on the battlefield and sent "Old Pete" Longstreet's 30,000 veterans smashing at Pope's flank. The Union army crumpled and fled in disorder reminiscent of the first Bull Run.

Only McClellan and his friends were able to take satisfaction from the defeat. Throughout the battle, Little Mac had sat smugly behind the fortifications of the Potomac while Pope's army was being ground to bits a few miles away. Some of his enemies felt this was the Young Napoleon's revenge; they charged that he wanted Pope destroyed at no matter what cost to the country.

The Rebels gained a tremendous victory at Manassas; Pope lost

14,000 men of his 80,000, while Lee lost 9,000 killed and wounded out of 54,000 effectives. The hybrid Army of Virginia which Pope had boasted he would lead to victory had been shattered in one overwhelming defeat. As a result of the defeat, the following evening, September 1, Phil Kearny was killed at Chantilly, Virginia, while leading a rear-guard action. His loss was a grievous one. The North had too few generals of his caliber. Kearny and thousands of other brave men were dead. As always, the Yankee soldiers had fought bravely and spiritedly—only to be betrayed by the bickering and jealousies of their leaders. Selfishness and politics had sacrificed the lives of the bravest.

McClellan was guilty in large measure for the defeat at Manassas, although he was not even present on the field. His power was felt in the reluctance of subordinates to obey Pope. The cat's-paw of the debacle was Major General Fitz-John Porter, a friend of McClellan and a Democrat. He was accused of flagrantly flouting Pope's orders. A general court-martial cashiered him. The case against Porter was flimsy, but the administration meant to make someone pay for the failure and his fate served as a warning to career soldiers that the government and not the military was supreme.

Lincoln was chagrined by the defeat. He had placed much faith in Pope and the setback upset him. He spoke despairingly to General M. C. Meigs, the Union Quartermaster General, who recorded the conversation in his diary. According to him, Lincoln said: "Chase says we can't raise any more money; Pope is licked; McClellan has the diarrhoea. What shall I do? The bottom is out of the tub! The bottom is out of the tub!"

Meigs consoled the distraught President. In his version of the conversation: "I told the President to meet his generals with Stanton, fix the bottom back in the tub, rally the army and order an advance at once. This seemed to brace him up a little and he went on to the War Department; but for the moment he was completely discouraged and down-hearted. Stanton on the other hand, was more full of power and vehement energy than ever."

The wounded men from Manassas streamed back into Washington. Public buildings were turned into temporary hospitals. The capital girded for last-ditch resistance. The Treasury was barricaded with hundreds of barrels of cement. Squads of hastily mobilized militia and government clerks drilled in the streets and parks. Important documents were readied for shipment to New York.

According to one observer of the frantic scene: "The Government ordered arms at the Arsenal and money in the Treasury to be shipped North . . . a gun boat with steam up, lay in the river off the White House, ready to carry the President . . ."

A call went out for volunteer nurses to handle the casualties but the response was poor. The treatment of the wounded was abominably mishandled. Medical supplies were stolen. Bands of drunken male nurses staggered about the collecting stations where wounded men lay unattended in the rain. Yet there were also instances of great heroism and sacrifice; dedicated nurses ministered to the broken men; bloodstained surgeons worked all night without sleep. As a whole the nation responded to the agonized cries of the wounded and rallied to their support.

Supplies of bandages, lint, medicines, liquor, and food poured into the capital. Once more, the North had proved its devotion to the Union. Even in this time of despair, the spirit of the people could not be crushed.

Pope was quickly relieved of his command and ordered to the Northwest to subdue hostile Indians. Lincoln agreed reluctantly to his banishment. He insisted that Pope had not been afforded a proper chance. He said: "Pope did well, but there was an army prejudice against him, and it was necessary he should leave. We had the enemy in the palm of our hands on Friday, if our generals who were vexed with Pope had done their duty; all of our present difficulties and reverses have been brought upon us by these quarrels of the generals . . ."

A decision had to be made. The army was leaderless. Pope's command—the Army of Virginia—was consolidated into the Army of the Potomac. Now a general who could regain control of the demoralized men had to be found.

Lincoln turned once again to McClellan, believing he alone could reorganize the Army. The Young Napoleon was appointed to command all the troops in Washington. The President was not pleased to make that choice, but no one else had as much influence with the troops. McClellan might not have been much of a fighter—but he could ready soldiers for combat.

Lincoln was fully aware of the dangers involved in returning Mc-

Clellan to power. He expressed his feelings to Gideon Welles, the Secretary of the Navy, who recorded them as follows in his voluminous diary:

> I must have McClellan to reorganize the army and bring it out of chaos, but there has been a design—a purpose in breaking down Pope without regard of consequences to the country. It is shocking to see and know this, but there is no remedy at present. McClellan has the army with him.

Angry protests were registered over McClellan's reinstatement. Three cabinet members—Chase, Stanton, and Smith—circulated a petition demanding the removal of McClellan from command of any army. They lashed out viciously at Little Mac—and painted a dire picture of the country's fate if McClellan was not shelved immediately. Despite the pressures on him, Lincoln remained firm. He gambled on McClellan and the Army of the Potomac.

McClellan acted swiftly and decisively, for once. When he took over, the army was a disorganized armed mob. Regiments, brigades, even divisions and corps had lost organization. Then, the word went out that Little Mac had returned. Miraculously the scattered brigades reformed. Divisions and corps regrouped. The Army of the Potomac lived again.

When word came that Lee had marched his rugged soldiers over the Potomac and into Maryland, McClellan went after him. The armies grappled in the mountain passes and on September 17, 1862, met head-on near the quiet Maryland village of Sharpsburg on Antietam Creek. The battle was long and bloody. Cannon and rifles racketed for fourteen consecutive hours. The toll was high on both sides; but when the fighting ended, Lee's torn legions stumbled back into Virginia. Yet once again the Army of the Potomac did not pursue him.

McClellan gladly let Lee escape without another battle and the North went wild with joy over his empty victory. Little Mac was satisfied with himself. He had come back into popular favor and once more was being hailed as the country's savior. He smirked at his detractors and swaggered with pride. Without him, the country would have been lost, he believed.

But the people wanted more than succor. They wanted the enemy battered into submission, and as the weeks passed after that bloody

September day when McClellan had been Lee's match, everyone realized Little Mac had not really changed.

He let his army grow stale and lose its fighting edge. Reviews and parades replaced combat. As in the past, McClellan wrote bitter letters demanding reinforcements. He listed dozens of excuses for not moving southward, until Lincoln finally lost all confidence in the man. McClellan had to be permanently discarded. "He has got the slows," Lincoln said of him.

On a snowy November day, Stanton peremptorily relieved McClellan of his command. The General was ordered to Trenton, New Jersey, to await assignment. Not since the American Revolution had that region seen any military activity. Stanton had finally consigned McClellan to the scrap pile.

The Army of the Potomac was handed over to General Ambrose E. Burnside, an honest and competent soldier who was most unwilling to replace his friend, McClellan. Burnside regarded himself as wholly inadequate for command of an army. He personally rated his ability at the brigade or divisional level, and possibly saw himself as a capable corps commander, but nothing more.

He accepted his assignment with an attitude of awaiting predestined failure. A month later, Burnside lived up to his own estimation of his military talents by leading the Army of the Potomac to ghastly slaughter at Fredericksburg. It was during this battle that Lee, watching the Union soldiers being mowed down, said, "It is good that war is so terrible or we might grow too fond of it."

· 4 ·

Although the Battle of Antietam was no clear-cut victory, it gave Lincoln the opportunity to make public a policy which changed the nature of the war. Less than a week later, he assembled his cabinet at a special meeting. He gave no hint that anything unusual was in the making. The cabinet members were not surprised when the President opened the session by reading an excerpt from the humorist Artemus Ward. Lincoln customarily prefaced even the most solemn meetings with a joke or a story.

Artemus Ward was a comical writer, and everyone but Stanton laughed at the passage. Stanton was noted for his lack of humor.

Frenzied cheers and wild enthusiasm greet Major General George B. McClellan
as he gallops past his men for the last time in November, 1862, having been

relieved of command. Behind him rides his ill-starred successor, Major General
Ambrose Burnside.

He constantly wore a martial frown as though this was more fitting for the Secretary of War than a smile.

When he had finished reading, Lincoln set aside the book, removed his eyeglasses, and faced his cabinet. "Gentlemen, I have, as you are aware, thought a great deal about the relation of the war to slavery . . ."

By the second year of the Southern rebellion, the war and slavery were becoming one. In the North, abolitionism was growing more popular. Its speakers were no longer in danger of being lynched or tarred and feathered. Sentiment was rising against the "peculiar institution." Not all the popular feeling against slavery resulted from moral indignation. To the average Yankee, slavery symbolized the South, and as the war grew more bitter and the casualties rose, the mass feeling turned against all things Southern, especially slavery.

In any case, the Negro had injected himself into the conflict. Colored people came to the Federals in droves, wherever Union troops penetrated Southern territory. The young and the old came, whole families in a black tide.

The Union military men had never expected to encounter such a large-scale social upheaval. The authorities handled the Negro question in accordance with the personal feelings of the area commanders. Some gave the runaway slaves back to their masters; others sheltered and fed them; and in many places the Negroes were put to work for the army, digging trenches, driving wagons, as cooks and servants. In numerous cases, Negroes proved invaluable as guides for invading Yankee troops.

In this period of change the Negroes had grown tired of being slaves. They wanted the dignity due them as human beings—the rights of freemen. And to many in the North, especially the soldiers who were coming into daily contact with the Negroes, the feeling spread that unless something grand and important was done about slavery, the war would somehow have no meaning. When the best young men of the country were giving their lives in battle to save the Union, they at least deserved to die for a cause that would mean a positive advance. It was growing clearer to many that no reunion could be consummated with a slaveholding South. The abomination of slavery had to be wiped from the national scene forever.

On April 16, 1862, slavery had been abolished within the District of Columbia. The administration no longer had to apologize for permitting the practise to flourish within sight of the Capitol. This had not been the first attempt to eliminate slavery as a wartime measure. On August 30, 1861, General John Charles Frémont had emancipated the slaves in Missouri. His action was revoked by Lincoln a few days later on that ground that it was premature and would offend the Unionist slave-owners in the Border States.

Less than a year later, on May 9, 1862, General David Hunter had proclaimed emancipation throughout the military area known as the Department of the South. Lincoln voided that order, too, although Hunter was a good friend; the President felt the nation was not yet ready to fight a war dedicated to the abolition of slavery.

Yet Lincoln was awake to rising abolitionist sentiment. And he was not a man to ignore either his own sense or the temper of the people. As the war's fury spread, the time was coming when steps could be taken to end slavery, with the support of the people at home and, even more important, the soldiers at the front.

To the delight of the abolitionists, Congress voted in June to exclude slavery from the territories. This legislation, at one stroke, settled the decades of controversy which had created the Missouri Compromise and the Kansas-Nebraska Act.

The time was at hand, Lincoln felt, to commit the administration to Negro freedom. Slaves owned by men in rebellion against the Federal government would simply be declared free men. Under any circumstances slavery could no longer be tolerated as it was.

Lincoln arrived at this decision on military and not humanitarian grounds. He felt that a commitment for emancipation would help the Union war effort. He had no illusions about equality for the Negro. In his opinion, Negroes should be colonized in a country where they could have more of a chance for social and economic betterment. Even with slavery ended, Lincoln foresaw terrible problems facing the Negroes in America; he had no false hopes that emancipation was a panacea.

Despite his concern over the Negro question, Lincoln never lost sight of the fact that the preservation of the Union was the major issue of the war. He clarified this stand in a letter to Horace Greeley who was now ranting about immediate freedom for the slaves, and about making this noble goal the primary war aim. On August 22,

1862, in response to an "Open Letter To The President," which appeared in the New York *Tribune,* Lincoln wrote Greeley:

> . . . I would save the Union . . . If there be those who would not save
> the Union unless they could at the same time save slavery, I do not
> agree with them. If there be those who would not save the Union un-
> less they could at the same time destroy slavery, I do not agree with
> them. My paramount object in this struggle is to save the Union, and
> it is not either to save or destroy slavery.
>
> If I could save the Union without freeing any slave, I would do
> it; and if I could save it by freeing some and leaving others alone, I
> would also do that. What I do about slavery and the colored race,
> I do because I believe it helps save the Union, and what I forbear,
> I forbear because I do not believe it would help save the Union . . .

Both Lincoln and the earnest men who pressed him to act on the Negro, realized that the status of the United States would be immeasurably aided in Europe by an emancipation of the slaves. Neither Great Britain nor France could morally intervene against a nation fighting to eradicate a universally detested institution.

As far back as July, the President announced to his cabinet that he intended to make some pronouncement of a governmental policy regarding the slaves. He stubbornly persisted in the feeling that mass colonization was the best solution for the social problem presented by free Negroes. Before signing the bill for compensated emancipation covering the District of Columbia (the three thousand slaves in the District were to be purchased from their owners for not more than $200 each) Lincoln had sought a provision that a steamship ticket to either Haiti or Liberia should be given any slave, so freed, who expressed a desire to migrate to those Negro republics.

And now, when he had informed the cabinet of his intentions about the slaves, Lincoln awaited an opportune moment to make his desires public. He felt the moment had come after Antietam. He told his cabinet, in part: "The action of the Army against the Rebels has not been quite what I should have best liked. But they have been driven out of Maryland, and Pennsylvania is no longer in danger of invasion. When the Rebel army was at Frederick, I determined, as soon as it should be driven out of Maryland, to issue a proclamation of emancipation, such as I thought most likely to be useful. I said nothing to anyone; but I made the promise to myself and—to my

Maker. The Rebel army is now driven out, and I am going to fulfill that promise . . ."

He then read the proclamation. It had, in the words of one commentator, "all the moral force of a bill of lading." The main point it made was that after January 1, 1863, all slaves in states or parts of states in rebellion against the United States, "shall be thenceforward, and forever free." The measure was being taken, the document was careful to explain, as a "military necessity."

The press printed this preliminary proclamation two days later. Response ranged from enthusiasm to bitterness; among the bitterest was General McClellan. He wrote his wife that the President's action and other troubles, "render it almost impossible for me to retain my commission and self-respect at the same time."

The Democratic Party excitedly stated, "The war for the Union has become a war for abolition." Treasonable Copperheads stirred discontent with the slogan that this was now a "war for the nigger."

Nevertheless Lincoln received heartening support in his stand. Sixteen Northern governors aligned themselves solidly behind him. The reaction abroad was encouraging. Among the working classes of Europe Lincoln's decision brought acclaim. In England, John Bright, an influential member of Parliament, who had been a staunch supporter of the Union, spoke for millions when he said, "I applaud the proclamation."

The South received the news with frenzy. Lincoln was labelled a coward, assassin, and murderer; his intent, it was claimed, was to instigate a Negro insurrection; his proclamation was a call for the slaves to kill, burn, and rape. A number of Confederate Congressmen declared themselves in favor of running up the black flag and giving no quarter to enemy prisoners and wounded on the battlefield. Fiery General Beauregard telegraphed a friend that after January 1, 1863, he hoped to strangle all abolitionist prisoners. The Richmond *Examiner* cried: "What shall we call Lincoln? Shall we call him Lincoln, the Fiend?"

The abolitionists, on the other hand, were disappointed by the Proclamation. The weakness of it, they pointed out, was that it did not deal with slaves under Union control, but only with those in the areas not yet subdued. In loyal sections, slaveholders could still retain their bondsmen. Still, they felt Lincoln had taken a giant step towards expunging slavery.

The course of the war was indelibly changed; the Negro had been given a place in the struggle. Before peace came, he was to play an even more vital role. He would march and fight in army blue and show the whole world that Negroes had the courage to battle and die for liberty.

Lincoln knew the future was a hard one. The war was far from finished. New problems were brought into the open by the Emancipation Proclamation. It had taken great strength and moral fiber to issue the edict. The President had carefully waited for the right pyschological moment; if he had come out with the Proclamation too soon, as had Hunter and Frémont, the public would not have accepted it. Lincoln explained his position in these words:

> A man watches his pear-tree day after day, impatient for the ripening of the fruit. Let him attempt to force the process and he may spoil both fruit and tree. But let him patiently wait, and the ripe pear at length falls into his lap . . . I have done what no man could have helped doing, standing in my place . . .

While he wavered and was often uncertain about the status of the Negro in America, Lincoln had deep understanding that, after all, the problem had to do with human dignity. He clung to his Negro colonization plan, not in order to sweep them from the national scene, but to protect them from the ignominy they were bound to suffer as freemen—social discrimination, mistreatment, denial of economic opportunities and little chance for education.

Only after mature deliberation did Lincoln decide that the Negro's plight could not be solved by segregating him in a distant land. The Negro belonged in America. He was part of the national heritage. Negroes had died in the Revolution; Negro sweat and muscle had helped push the borders of the country westwards.

At last, Lincoln saw all this. He dropped his colonization scheme and grappled with the task of creating a country in which men of all faiths and all races could live in peace as neighbors. Lincoln was no zealot; but he hated the indignities of slavery more sincerely than did the most fanatical abolitionist. His devotion to the Union was entwined with the eradication of slavery. The Union could exist without slavery—but not with it. As a patriot, Lincoln had to oppose the institution. He loved his country, and human bondage was an ugly sore marring the face of the land. He classed it with unemployment and want; with disease and illiteracy. These were feudal chains dragging the nation down, and must be broken. No American need be illiterate in the land of enlightenment. No American need be jobless, his children hungry in the land of plenty. And no American need be enslaved in the land of freedom.

The war had gone beyond restoration of the "Union as it was." It had become a social revolution, a class upheaval. The old Southern planter aristocracy was moribund; it could not survive in the new age. The era of the machine was dawning; capitalism was emerging as a vigorous and purposeful way of life. The time was over when one man could own another's labor and his freedom as well. Freedom was no longer for sale to the highest bidder; only labor was sold at the auction block.

Many battles had yet to be fought. No presidential decree could wipe out hatreds, bigotry, and fear. But the step had been taken and the unemotional words of the Emancipation Proclamation changed the destiny of the United States until the end of its history.

The Negroes hailed it as the "Jubilee" and together with the shells and bullets, the Proclamation helped destroy the Southern "chivalry" that had caused the rebellion. With the moving yet simple eloquence that characterized his speeches, Lincoln gave voice to the spirit which motivated the North in December, 1862, when he delivered his Second Message to Congress:

We know how to save the Union . . . in giving freedom to the slave, we assure freedom to the free—honorable alike in what we give and what we preserve. We shall nobly save, or meanly lose, the last, best, hope of earth. Other means may succeed, this could not fail. The way is plain, peaceful, generous, just—a way which, if followed, the world will forever applaud and God must forever bless.

NINE

Mr. Davis

"Let us, then, not despond, my countrymen, but relying on God, meet the foe with
fresh defiance, and with unconquered and
unconquerable hearts . . ."

JEFFERSON DAVIS,
last proclamation, April 5, 1865

Ye Cavaliers of Dixie!
Who guard the Southern shore,
Whose standards brave the battle storms
Which o'er our borders roar
Your glorious sabers draw once more . . .

Confederate war song

THE MASS suffering of the Confederacy was pinpointed in the individual agony of Private Edward Cooper, 24th Alabama Volunteers. C.S.A. Cooper, a farmer, had small holdings near Birmingham. He owned no slaves but believed in secession. He detested Yankees and loved his wife, Mary; his son, Eddie, five; and his daughter, Lucy, eight.

Even before the war, life had not been easy for the Coopers. Edward Cooper had worked hard on his land, and barely managed to take a living from the soil. He had plans: one day, he'd buy up the bottom acres; maybe get a herd of cattle and go in for a little dairy farming. With any luck, he'd pull together money enough to buy himself a nigger or two—then, he'd be out of the "mudsill" class.

But instead of realizing his dream, Edward Cooper went off to war. After two years of fighting, he'd had his bellyful of the army. He was sick of the suffering and the killing.

In Richmond, Davis made fancy speeches. He talked about noble ideals and high purposes; he used big words and called the soldiers "knights in a glorious cause." The soldiers didn't feel or look like knights, in their ragged uniforms and torn shoes. They ate moldy bread and maggoty meat. They suffered from scurvy and dysentery. Malaria cut them down, and so did measles and pneumonia. They died in swamps and woods, sometimes with a Yankee bullet in their guts or torn to pieces by a shell.

Cooper endured all this, hating the shoulder straps, the army, and the war. He fought the Yankees without hatred; only a bitterness remained. They were aliens who had come to free the niggers. Cooper, personally, had no bad feelings against niggers; they were all right in their place, which was to serve white folks. But he could not bear the thought that if a nigger was a freeman, he might even own land—and then he'd be on the same level as any white man. An intolerable idea.

Cooper longed to see Mary and his kids. He hadn't even been home in two years. He yearned to walk in the soft earth of his fields again; to smoke a pipe on the back porch, sitting in his old cane rocker, listening to the crickets and watching the glimmering fireflies twinkling in the darkness. It was so little for a man to want: peace and his own family.

During the years a lot of the lads in the regiment hadn't been able to stand the gaff; many had gone over the hill. Cooper couldn't bring himself to desert. The others, the ones who held on, needed him. They counted on him in a fight. He was a good man with a rifle; and he wasn't squeamish when it came to using the bayonet. After seeing enough combat, a man turns into a killer. Cooper had lost his fear of death and believed that the Yankee bullet which could kill him had not yet been molded. Edward Cooper had become two men— the old Cooper, who was a farmer, and the present one, the soldier. The farmer wanted to go home, but the soldier was stronger, so he stayed. Then, one day a letter came from Mary and it changed everything. The letter said:

My Dear Edward:

I have always been proud of you and since your connection with the army I have been prouder of you than ever before. I would not have you do anything wrong for the world, but before God, Edward, unless you come home we must die.

Last night, I was aroused by little Eddie crying. I called and said, "What's the matter, Eddie?" and he said, "Oh, momma. I'm so hungry!" And Lucy, Edward, your darling Lucy, she never complains, but she is growing thinner every day, and before God, Edward, unless you come home, we must all die.

Your Mary.

Now nothing could keep Cooper from going home, but even in his distress, the years of discipline told. He showed his captain the letter and asked for a furlough, but the request was turned down by the young officer.

Cooper returned to his tent, threw himself on his tattered blanket and stared at the canvas walls. The war wasn't anything to him now. He no longer cared whether the niggers were freed or the Yankees took over his farm. The Confederacy could go to Hell for all it mattered to him.

He had no life without Mary and the kids. For more than two years she had lived on the pittance he managed to send home from his army pay, never complaining. But she couldn't work the farm alone. The fields were falling fallow. The kids were starving.

That night, Edward Cooper deserted . . .

· 2 ·

Jefferson Davis never fully understood that his nation was no stronger than the will of the people. The rebellion had no hope of succeeding once their zeal waned. Mass loyalty was not a gift wrapped in pretty ribbons; it did not follow that because the President remained resolute the masses would automatically reflect his iron will. To Davis, loyalty was no matter for discussion. He was loyal; therefore the people must be, too. He believed they were. On a trip to the Western departments, he was met by cheering crowds everywhere. The people thronged to see him; he was showing by his presence that their Chief Executive had not abandoned them.

At Richmond's railroad station, on his return, Davis was given an enthusiastic welcome. The weather was crisp and bright that day, January 5, 1863. A band played gaily. The people bubbled with excitement and patriotic feeling. Perhaps, they felt, 1863 would be the year of destiny. Perhaps the President's western journey had smoothed the dissensions which raged among Generals Joe Johnston, Pemberton, and Bragg. Bad war news was mingled with good and there were some hopeful tidings. Sherman had been repulsed at Vicksburg; at sea, the raider *Alabama* under Captain Raphael Semmes was taking a heavy toll of Yankee shipping; and on New Year's Day General John Magruder had recaptured Galveston, Texas.

Davis was touched by the ovation. To him, it meant the people were strong and devoted to the cause. He did not understand that the crowd had come to greet him because the masses were frightened and unsure; to them, he embodied the strength and determination they no longer felt. Doubting themselves, the people wanted reassurance from him.

The President stood on the rear platform of his special train and looked out over the crowd that stretched for blocks. He was worn from the taxing journey over the rickety Confederate railroads. His health was precarious, and he would have been content to be excused after his appearance. But seeing him was not enough. "Speech! Speech!" the crowd roared.

Davis mustered the energy and in a strained voice addressed the eager onlookers. He gave them no rallying slogans, no word that everything would be all right and that his western trip had accomplished its purpose of bringing harmony among the squabbling Generals. Instead, for once, Davis felt obliged to make an excuse to his people. He said: "My friends, constant labor in the duties of office, borne down by care and anxiety which has left me with barely a moment of repose, I have had little opportunity for social intercourse . . . I can only give this as my excuse for my seldom appearing among you . . ."

He finished his brief speech without offering the crowd the encouragement it sought. Polite applause followed his remarks. The band played the President's favorite pieces, "The Mocking Bird" and "Dixie." A few voices took up the latter refrain, but the upsurge of enthusiasm was squelched. The people went home in poor spirits. Davis was driven to the Executive Mansion. Fatigue and illness overcame him at last, and he was confined to bed for almost a month . . .

Despite all the hardships, Richmond put on a bold face and buckled down to the tedium of carrying on the war. The pinch worsened. Even familiar commodities had disappeared now: one could get no envelopes—old ones were turned inside out and used over again; the back of wallpaper had to do as stationery. Prices were on the rise again: white wheat went to $4.50 a bushel; a barrel of flour cost $22; a pound of lard, $1, and butter was at $1.50; Irish potatoes were $5 per pound, sweet potatoes, $6; a pint of apple brandy brought $15.

The dismal list was endless; a cheap calico dress cost $30; one cake of soap, $1; turkeys could be had at prices ranging from $4-$11, depending on weight; coarse blue jeans, once 45¢ a pair, soared to $4; work shoes were $15 and riding boots, $30. Only the most opulent could afford even the most ordinary food and clothing.

Shortages were keenly felt in medical, pharmaceutical, and surgical supplies. Doctors and surgeons were forced to find substitutes for standard medicines and equipment. Even at $100 an ounce, quinine was almost unprocurable, so it was replaced by cottonseed, tea, and willow bark. Instead of opium, doctors used American hemlock. Hops and motherwort served for laudanum; blackberry root became a specific for dysentery; dogwood for malaria.

Ingenious and inventive minds dreamed up clever devices to overcome shortages of surgical supplies. Pliant tree bark took the place of tourniquets; penknives served as scalpels; and soft pine splinters were fashioned into bullet probes, while splints were made from fence rails.

While the majority suffered, for those in Richmond who had money, procuring the necessities was no problem and luxuries could easily be obtained. Wily blockade-runner captains brought in cargoes of wine, Parisian gowns, pins, needles, bonbons, and perfumes rather than war matériel. Guns and ammunition were necessarily sold to the government at fixed prices, but luxuries brought fantastic sums paid in gold instead of Confederate bonds or currency.

At a time in Richmond when "cats were staggering from hunger and mice starving to death" certain residents dined on the richest foods and finest wines. High-priced bordellos and elite gambling clubs were well stocked with liquors and Havana cigars. Every midnight their tables were laden with magnificent food.

Yet the average person in the capital was lucky to taste meat once a week. The people grew accustomed to daily rations of crumbly bread and thin soup. This meager diet was sometimes augmented by fresh vegetables from the small patches most townspeople cultivated in their backyards on tiny strips of land. Richmond's famed flower gardens were seen no more. They had been replaced by tomato plants and rows of sprouting beans. Even milk for babies was difficult to get and then it was usually watered down.

Actually it was not shortages, but poor management in the distribution of available foodstuffs, which caused the want. Farmers hoarded edibles because no efficient government agency existed to collect it. The nationalized railroads were badly run. Although government warehouses bulged with staples, the public markets were often bare. Pinch-faced children trudged to school in threadbare clothes; the shabby Richmond people grew thin, and anyone with fat cheeks and a paunch was looked on as a profiteer.

The Commissary General, Louis B. Northrop, was another of the President's close friends. The people clamored for his removal, but, as in the past, Davis refused to heed popular opinion. Along with Winder, Bragg, Pemberton, and many other presidential favorites, Northrop was the object of abuse and hatred. But Davis protected him, as he had protected Benjamin, and would hear nothing bad about his friend. In fact, the President took the attack on Northrop as a personal affront. As time passed he grew more and more stiff-necked about his Commissary General. As a result, Davis' rise in popularity did not endure . . .

· 3 ·

In March, 1862, George Randolph, an aristocratic Virginian, and a grandson of Thomas Jefferson, succeeded Judah P. Benjamin as Secretary of War. Randolph was an ardent Confederate patriot, an able and efficient man, yet Jefferson Davis managed to alienate even him and lose the services of a most valuable executive.

Randolph was popular and knew how to deal with people. He did much to heal the rift between Congress and the Army. However, he had one fault for a member of the President's cabinet—he refused to allow his office to deteriorate into that of a first-class clerk. Under Randolph, the War Department began functioning as a governmental unit, not a plaything of the President's whims.

Davis resented Randolph's independence. He was awed by the Secretary's illustrious lineage, and it irked him that this subordinate was considered his social superior.

Randolph's attempt to free the War Department from the President's hold finally cost him his office. Davis was no man to permit independent action by an underling. He wanted to be consulted on every move.

When Randolph, on his own authority, and without informing the President, ordered General T. H. Holmes to cross the Mississippi from Arkansas with his troops and take over the defense of Vicksburg, he went beyond his function as a cabinet member. Switching troops from one department to another without presidential sanction was not within the scope of Randolph's office.

Davis demanded that Randolph countermand the orders to Holmes and the chagrined Secretary complied. The matter should have been dropped there, but Davis felt he had been slighted by the Virginian and kept pressing Randolph. An acidulous exchange of correspondence took place between the men, and in November, 1862, Randolph resigned.

Bluff Stephen Mallory confided to his diary: "Randolph's resignation is a result of the President's habitual interference in the details of the War Department."

The passing of Randolph opened the way for another wealthy and prominent Virginian, James A. Seddon, who accepted the post.

Like Benjamin and a few others, Seddon learned the secret of getting on with Davis and stayed in office until the closing days of the war. He was pliant, giving in to the President on most matters—but he showed a capacity for firmness as well. Seddon had much influence over Davis, who both respected his intellectual attainments and envied his aristocratic background.

Men of good family impressed Davis. He was often intimidated by them, especially the Virginians—but eventually made them pay for humbling him. One of the few who escaped the President's wrath, even after publicly embarrassing him, was Robert E. Lee. Back in 1862, at the start of the Seven Days Battle, Davis and his numerous staff rode out to Mechanicsville where the fighting was going on. The President and his retinue crowded into Lee's headquarters tent when the General was very busy giving orders to front-line troops. The gentlemanly officer turned to Davis and gestured towards the group accompanying him.

"Who are all this army of people and what are they doing here? . . . This is no place for them," Lee said emphatically.

"Well, General, if I withdraw, perhaps they will follow," Davis said, flushing.

He walked out of the tent. After an embarrassed silence, his staff followed. Chagrined and mortified, Davis kept out of Lee's path for the rest of the day. After that minor incident, Davis felt uncomfortable in the presence of Lee for a long time, although the General never again showed him the slightest disrespect.

Lee was unique among Confederate generals. Easily the most outstanding talent in the Army, his scope was limited to only one theater of operations—the Department of Northern Virginia. Not until near the end of the war, when the situation was hopeless, did Davis appoint Lee General-in-Chief of the dwindling Confederate armies. Even then, Lee still retained active field command of the Army of Northern Virginia, in addition to his other duties, until Appomattox.

It was no accident that Lee and other important generals were not granted greater powers. Davis jealously guarded his constitutional role as commander-in-chief of the armed forces. He would not allow any general full autonomy. He insisted on retaining for himself the right to approve or reject proposed troop movements, campaigns and all tactical operations.

Davis devised the unwieldy Departmental system which divided the Confederacy into military areas and limited the scope of each departmental commander to his own sector. This rigid concept brought chaos to the Confederacy's Western armies. Instead of co-operating, the generals bickered. There was no one empowered to assume full responsibility, so the individual commanders passed the buck back and forth, and blamed each other for failures and losses, while the country crumbled to destruction.

A more flexible man than Jefferson Davis would have realized that the Western theater, a thousand miles from Richmond, required a single commander with authority to move troops anywhere he saw fit and conduct entire campaigns without awaiting instructions from the distant capital. But Davis, who was unable to intrust even routine paper work to his secretary, would not consign so much control to any general. Consequently, the Western armies suffered disasters that proved fatal to the Cause.

The President not only meddled in operations and basic strategy but also imperiled the morale of the western troops by his attitude toward his friend, Braxton Bragg. He would not remove Bragg from command long after that officer's inefficiency had cost him the confidence of both officers and men.

Davis still persisted in his inexplicable attachment to the inept General even after Bragg's disastrous defeat at Chattanooga. The army and the entire nation were shocked and mortified when Davis caused the following order to be issued:

WAR DEPARTMENT
Adjutant and Inspector General's Office,
Richmond, Virginia
February 24, 1864

GENERAL ORDER #23:

General Braxton Bragg is assigned to duty at the seat of the government, and, under direction of the President is charged with the conduct of military operations in the Armies of the Confederacy.

By order of the Secretary of War

S. Cooper

Adjutant and Inspector General

It almost seemed as though Davis were deliberately flouting the army and the public. In spite of Bragg's failure in the field, the President was actually promoting the man by making him Military Adviser, the very post Robert E. Lee himself had held in 1862.

Many people believed the President had brought Bragg to Richmond for the express purpose of founding a military dictatorship; they charged that Davis was surrounding himself with a "palace guard" of sycophants. These attacks distressed him greatly.

Among the Southerners who believed that Davis had abandoned democratic principles was Alexander Stephens. The gnomelike Vice-President may have resembled a man in the last stages of a malignant disease; his puny frame was more emaciated than ever, but the frail Georgian still burned with vigor and energy. His pen had not lost its sting. He expressed his feelings about Davis in a letter to Herschel V. Johnson. Stephens wrote:

> While I do not and never have regarded him as a great man or statesman on a large scale, or a man of any marked genius, yet I have regarded him as a man of good intentions, weak and vacillating, timid, petulant, peevish, obstinate but not firm. I am now beginning to doubt his good intentions. His whole policy on the organization and discipline of the army is perfectly consistent with the hypothesis that he is aiming at absolute power . . .

The rebellion within a rebellion gained momentum. Governor Joe Brown of Georgia opposed every order from Richmond so vehemently that he could almost be accused of fomenting revolution. Brown was a fanatical states' rightist. He also was a strict Sabbatarian. Despite the war he tried to keep mails, trains, and other essential services from functioning on Sunday.

To Brown, the central government in Richmond did not differ from the government in Washington. Both, he felt, were impinging on states' rights. In numerous ways, the Governor hampered the war effort. Despite feverish pleas for reinforcements from Richmond, he would not permit the Georgia State Guard to leave the state. Nor would he turn over to Richmond the stores of arms and ammunition cached in state arsenals.

A rebel at heart, Brown had seceded from the Union and, for all practical purposes, from the Confederacy as well. A hard-boiled politician who had never been defeated for public office, the white-bearded, gospel-spouting, homespun-clad Georgian was the hero of the poor—the workers and the dirt farmers. He rejected any support or favors from the wealthy slaveholders and planters. Brown said: "I was brought up among the working class. I rose from the mass of the people. They took me by the hand and sustained me because they believed I was true to them. I was one of them and they have never forsaken me in any instance when the popular voice could be heard."

Because he had the people solidly behind him, Brown turned out to be one of Davis' most powerful antagonists. The workers and "crackers" of Georgia listened to Joe Brown, and when he turned against the Richmond government, they did, too. With careful handling, Brown might have been won over to the President's side. The situation in Georgia was serious enough to warrant Davis' making a trip there for a face-to-face talk with the recalcitrant governor, but he scorned to do this. Davis possessed sufficient personal magnetism to have worked himself into Brown's good graces. Instead, the President treated Brown coldly and only succeeded in alienating him irrevocably.

An almost similar situation developed in North Carolina with Governor Zebulon Vance, who strongly objected to the draft and other central government ordinances, which he felt compromised states' rights. Vance had not been an original secessionist, and he fought hard to keep North Carolina in the Union, but his thinking changed suddenly and dramatically when Lincoln called for 75,000 volunteers shortly after the firing on Fort Sumter. This is how the Governor described his metamorphosis into a prosecessionist:

> I was addressing a large and excited antisecession crowd, large numbers of whom were armed, and literally had extended my arm upward in pleading for the Union of the fathers, when telegraphic news was announced of the firing on Fort Sumter and the President's call for 75,000 volunteers. When my hand came down from that impassioned

gesticulation, it fell slowly and sadly by the side of a secessionist. I immediately with altered voice and manner, called upon the assembled multitude to volunteer, not to fight against, but for South Carolina. I said if war must come, I preferred to be with my own people . . .

Vance was another man who might have been converted into a staunch ally of Davis. Instead, the President's attitude made him a bitter enemy. In parts of North Carolina, opposition to conscription reached insurrectionary proportions. Vance did nothing to suppress the dissidents. He was on their side. He hated conscription. To him it was tyranny—and Vance was against all tyranny—whether it originated in Washington or Richmond.

· 4 ·

Beset on all sides by criticism, active subversion and open disloyalty, Davis now witnessed an ugly example of discontent in Richmond itself.

On the morning of April 5, 1863, the usual tranquility of Capitol Hill was suddenly shattered. All at once, a mob gathered at the very gates of the Capitol. Nobody knew who had bid it come; nobody had even a hint of its coming. It was an ominously silent mob largely made up of women and children, with a sprinkling of men, some wearing bits and pieces of Confederate uniforms.

The faces in the crowd showed the ravages of hunger. The women were unlovely slatterns in worn and dirty clothing. The ragged children were, in many cases, without shoes. The startled onlookers who rushed to the windows of the Capitol noted many Negroes in the motley crowd. The demonstrators carried axes, crowbars, staves, bowie knives, and pistols. As the mob moved menacingly towards Capitol Square, a tremendous roar came from a thousand throats. "Bread! Bread! We want bread!" the marchers chanted.

They were led by a giant, disheveled, wild-eyed woman who brandished a pistol in one hand and a huge knife in the other. The throng boiled past the Capitol gates, down Ninth Street, marching in fierce cadence. Traffic was blocked. Hacks and private carriages careened away from the slowly moving mass. Homes were hastily shuttered. Terror spread through the city. The mob brushed aside a thin cordon of Winder's policemen. It surged down Ninth Street, flooding by the War Department, and turned into the shopping district on Main and Cary Streets. Glass shattered in shop windows. Yowling women leaped through the jagged holes to scoop up food, clothing, shoes, blankets, and furniture. A huge Negro woman trotted away balancing a settee on her head. Men lurched off lugging oddly assorted bits of clothing. The mob seemed to have forgotten its demand for bread. An orgy of unreasoning looting followed and violence broke out among the people.

Snarling men and women fought over useless pieces of crockery and worthless costume jewelry. One band crashed into a saloon. Kegs of lager beer were rolled into the street. Ax-wielders stove in the barrelheads, and the foamy brew spurted up in alcoholic fountains.

Slum dwellers from Butchertown crept out of their hovels and gleefully joined the looting and pillaging. Hunger had driven the mob to riot; now the lust of wanton destruction gripped them. Somebody cut loose a team of dray horses, and the frightened animals, neighing in terror, charged through the milling crowds. A gang of children opened a fire hydrant and danced in the spray.

The aged Mayor of Richmond, Joseph Mayo, called out the City Militia Battalion and the soldiers were rushed to the scene. Artillery batteries clattered through the city and field pieces were swung into position. Soon the mob was surrounded by armed men.

Mayo read the riot act to the demonstrators, who drowned him out with jeers and catcalls. Crude barricades were thrown across the streets. Rocks and paving stones were hurled at the soldiers. Women glared defiantly into the muzzles of the cannon and spat at the gunners. Mayo issued an ultimatum. He gave the mob five minutes to disperse before ordering the militia to open fire and charge in with bayonets.

As the tension mounted, President Davis rolled up in a carriage. He leaped out, mounted an overturned dray, and spoke to the mob. His exact words were not recorded, but he told the people that if they were hungry, he would share his last crust with them. But what they were doing was wrong; this was no way to settle grievances. He would see they received justice. If they believed in the Cause;

if they honored their dead, and thought of themselves as Southerners, they would return peaceably to their homes.

"We want food!" the rioters shouted.

"You shall have it!" Davis replied. "This afternoon, the government warehouses will distribute flour and rice to all!"

A ragged cheer went up. Sudden good humor replaced anger. The riot was over. That afternoon, thousands received free rations. The President still represented authority.

Davis acted wisely and courageously. But he still refused to believe that the riots had been caused by the incompetence of his friend, Northrop, in the Commissary Department. Consequently, Northrop was not removed, and the abuses continued.

Even the antiadministration press had been so frightened by the occurrence that they attributed the disorder to outsiders. According to the papers, the riot had not been the work of true Southerners. Yankee agitators and traitors had formed the mob. This was the line taken by the press, which allotted little space to the riot. One morning paper reported: "The disturbance was caused by a handful of prostitutes, professional thieves, Irish and Yankee hags, gallows birds from all lands but our own . . ."

In a few days, not even the physical marks of the outbreak remained. Storekeepers swept up the debris and replaced their shattered windows. By one means or another, the merchants managed to replenish their stocks. Richmond returned to wartime normalcy. There was, however, an aftermath to the riot. Loaded cannon were planted now at vantage points to sweep the streets with grapeshot. Artillery emplacements frowned on the approaches to Capitol Square. Military patrols toured the working-class districts and heavily armed police guarded the slums, for the authorities themselves realized that Yankee conspirators had not been the instigators. The mob had consisted of Richmond people driven to despair because they could not feed their children. It was not composed of alien thieves and whores.

After a week, the free distribution of government rice and flour was ended. And once again in the hovels of Butchertown, hungry children cried themselves to sleep. Thin soup, turnip greens boiled with a chunk of bacon, and stringy meat were the only food available in some working-class homes. Yet in more prosperous residences, people feasted on broiled quail and roast duckling. The war had touched everyone in Richmond, but not all had been equally affected. Richmond's poor and ill-fed had made their violent protest against injustice; now they were silent with the sullenness of the hopeless. . . .

· 5 ·

That grim year, 1863, the Southern armies won victories and suffered calamitous loses. Chancellorsville was canceled out by Gettysburg. And while the Federal rout at Chickamauga hurt the Yankees it did not exact payment for Vicksburg. Everywhere the battlefronts blazed. In the summer, Port Hudson, Louisiana, fell to the Union after the collapse of the Confederates at Vicksburg, and Lincoln could say, "The Father of Waters again goes unvexed to the sea." The Confederacy was now split in half.

1863 was the year of crisis—and before it was over the whole world knew the Confederacy could only postpone defeat. It could no longer dream of winning the war. Any hope of foreign aid was gone. It had died on the battlefield of Gettysburg—where Lee's failure wrecked the Cause. The British and French, who had been flirting with the Confederacy, now turned cold. Louis Napoleon, the French Emperor, was involved with his nefarious Mexican adventures.

Plump Queen Victoria's advisers no longer urged her to aid the South. The risks had become too great. The time to gamble had passed. Meanwhile, the Yankees themselves had found a strange and unlikely ally: the Czar of All the Russias. In 1863, that despot tacitly showed the world he stood on the side of the North. A strong Russian fleet visited New York. Russia still smarted under the defeat it had received from Britain and France in the Crimean War. Had those nations actively moved against the United States, Russia would have had a great opportunity to take revenge against them. The American Civil War could easily have been turned into a world conflict.

In England, Palmerston and Russell dared not risk such an eventuality. While sympathizing with the South, they owed fealty to Queen Victoria, not King Cotton. The Russian bear had sharp claws and strong teeth. It was better to abandon the South than to fight both Russia and the United States. The tides had begun running against the Confederacy. The glittering Cause was becoming tarnished . . .

Corteges and funerals were no longer a novelty in Richmond. The bright, eager youths who had been its boast and pride came back in cheap, splintery pine coffins. No one wept for them; all the tears had been shed. Men who had marched with long and confident strides shuffled through bleak streets. Laughter was hollow. Eyes were dimmed. The juices of life were drying up in Richmond and throughout the South.

The chivalry of the old days had long been forgotten. Desperate circumstances called for dark and evil measures. Any blow against the enemy was fair and any helper a suitable ally. Men whispered and plotted with Yankee traitors and Copperheads. The streets of New York were bloodied by frenzied draft rioters that July. There were raids, lynchings, bushwhackings, and murders. The war had destroyed more than human beings. It had crushed decency and morality as well.

The war made widows of young brides and orphans of babies who had never seen their fathers. Cold and hunger, suffering and pain, tall chimneys rising from the ashes of once-elegant homes, refugees and dispossessed persons—all these were the fruits of war.

The South was dying. The stink of death poisoned the air and smothered the fragrances of the flowers; once-verdant fields were blackened ruins. Too late now, Davis pleaded with planters to grow foodstuffs instead of tobacco and cotton.

Even the President felt doubt and dread at the signs of impending disaster. At such times of self-doubt, Davis turned to prayer. He attended St. Paul's Episcopal Church faithfully and devoutly. But he still remained convinced that none of the military failures were of his own making. The greatest setbacks, such as Vicksburg, he blamed on his generals. He believed that Joe Johnston's failure to reinforce Pemberton at Vicksburg, rather than his own interference with the field commanders, had led to the disaster.

Davis suffered keenly over the deaths of the brave men who died for the doomed Cause. He was upset about the news of "Stonewall" Jackson's fatal wound. To be sure, he had never been close to Jackson. However, his sudden and unexpected death, which blighted the victory of Chancellorsville, touched the President. Moreover, Davis

knew how deeply Lee was stricken and wrote a consoling letter to
his bereaved General:

> A great calamity has befallen us, and I sympathize with the sorrow
> you feel and the embarrassment you must experience. The announce-
> ment of the death of General Jackson followed. frequent assurances
> that he was doing well. And though the loss was one which would be
> deeply felt under any circumstances, the shock was increased by its
> suddenness. There is sincere mourning here and it will extend through-
> out the land as the intelligence is received.
>
> Your friend,
Jefferson Davis.

For a man of Davis' personality, this restrained letter was an emotional outburst.

The sky was darkening, but Davis did not relinquish his confidence in Lee and ultimate victory. On August 8, 1863, a month after
Gettysburg, Lee wrote the President suggesting ". . . the propriety
of selecting another commander for this army. I cannot even accomplish what I myself desire. How can I fulfill the expectations of
others?"

Lee's note was the equivalent of a resignation, but Davis refused
to accept it. He reiterated his faith in the beaten leader by writing
him: ". . . To ask me to substitute you by someone in my judgment
more fit to command, or who would possess more of the confidence
of the army, or of reflecting men in the country is to demand an impossibility . . ."

Davis was never given cause to regret his wholehearted support
of Lee, another of the handful of men with whom the President
found understanding and harmony.

Only once during their long association did Davis treat Lee with
the same autocratic harshness which had alienated so many others.
Towards the end of the war, a rumor arose that Lee had given orders to destroy all tobacco stored in Richmond to keep it from falling
into the hands of the enemy. The report spread alarm in the city.
Davis grew agitated. If Lee had given such an order and the fall of
the city was indeed imminent, he felt the General should have confided in the Chief Executive. Davis dispatched an urgent telegram
to Lee, who was in the field near Petersburg, requesting the General's presence in Richmond to discuss the situation.

Lee did not think it feasible to leave the Army at that time and wired back: "Send me the measures and I will send you my views."

While no disrespect had been intended, the tone of Lee's reply irked Davis. He sent a long, irate telegram to Lee which ended with this stinging rebuke: "Rest assured I will not ask your views in answer to measures. Your counsels are no longer wanted in this matter."

But instead of taking umbrage at the President's peevishness, Lee returned to Richmond, ironed out the difficulties, and mollified his testy superior.

· 6 ·

Gettysburg and Vicksburg had been terrible blows to the Confederacy and Richmond felt the full impact of these disasters. Gettysburg, especially, was a calamity for the capital. Lee had lost more than 30,000 men, almost one-third the total strength of the Army of Northern Virginia. This alone was severe enough; but even more painful for Richmond were the casualties suffered in General George Pickett's division, which had gone off to the battle with 4,500 men— all Virginians, many from Richmond or its environs. Only twenty-five percent of Pickett's men came back from their famous charge against the Union center.

During the hot July days, mourning crepe hung on many doors in Richmond. The wounded were brought back from Pennsylvania in box cars. The railroad station was crowded with rows and rows of litters; groaning, dying men filled every hospital bed; tents had to be pitched on the grounds of Chimborazo Hospital for the less grievously wounded. Although doctors and nurses worked around the clock, thousands of casualties had to wait days before receiving even the most primitive care. Hundreds died from want of medical attention.

Richmond had never endured such travail; but its ordeal was not yet over. Every day, columns of infantry marched through the city toward Petersburg or to the northern defenses of the capital. Artillery batteries, drawn by spavined, skinny nags, rumbled through the streets. The bands were muted. The romance was gone.

The thousands who had fallen at Vicksburg and Gettysburg were defiled by the nasty wrangling that followed the battles. Both John-

ston and Pemberton were singled out for special censure because of
Vicksburg. The papers called Johnston a weakling and a coward.
Pemberton was labelled all that and a traitor as well for having surrendered 37,000 men, nine generals, 90 guns, and 40,000 rifles and
pistols.

Lee did not escape journalistic blame. Just as Johnston was blis-
tered because he had not gambled on a reckless attack to relieve
Pemberton, Lee was condemned for losing the Pennsylvania campaign and for having launched that last, all-out assault on July 3.
The armchair military experts in the newspaper editorial rooms did
not understand that neither Joe Johnston nor Robert E. Lee could
have done more than they did. The failures did not lie with the
soldiers, or with the Generals either.

The fault lay with the leaders of the Confederacy who had underestimated the enemy. The Yankees had become good soldiers. Their
armies were hard and resilient. Great commanders had emerged:
Grant, Meade, Hancock, Thomas, Sedgwick, Sheridan, Sherman,
and many more. Even the once-scorned Yankee cavalry was now a
force to be reckoned with—Wilson, Custer, Devens, Buford, Grier-
son, Torbert, and others had shown themselves to be slashing, daring
horsemen, equal to the best the South could offer. The Rebels had
been forced to admit that their arrogant boast about one Southerner
whipping ten Yankees was an empty one.

Mr. Lincoln's armies were growing, not diminishing. Union arms
and equipment were improving, not deteriorating. Every Confederate soldier killed or disabled left a gap in the ranks; every Confederate rifle or cannon lost was well-nigh irreplaceable. By 1863,
even before the crucial battles of Gettysburg and Vicksburg, the
Confederacy was near exhaustion. Only courage, pride, and will
power kept its men fighting.

Equally as bad as the setbacks in the field was the economic pinch.
Inflation raced on unchecked. Prices doubled, tripled, and quadrupled, and the shortages grew. With the fall of Vicksburg, the
sugar supply disappeared in Richmond. Salt had long been a luxury
from another, happier day, ever since Union troops had captured the
salt works on the Kanawah River back in '62.

Life was difficult in Richmond; and the difficulties were multi-
plied by frequent alarms as Union troops or gunboats poked and
probed the defences. Weary clerks and government workers, formed

into battalions, were rushed to man last-ditch breastworks whenever cavalry raiders approached or some maneuver on the Rapidan-Rappahannock River line menaced the capital.

Even the loyalty and devotion of some government workers reached the breaking point in August, 1863. Postal clerks, unable to exist on their small, fixed salaries, resigned in a body. A few days later, they returned to work on the promise of better pay. Reports came in from North Carolina, Georgia, Mississippi, and Tennessee of large-scale desertions in the army. Unionists grew bolder. They started an effective whispering campaign advocating an end to the war. Even among the most stalwart Southerners, discouragement and a sense of futility spread like a disease-ridden fog, sickening all whom it touched.

Once well-to-do families were forced to let out rooms. Hundreds of refined ladies stood in line for hours trying to secure a single clerical position that was open in the Treasury Department. Yet profiteers managed to get mountains of luxuries hauled in by blockade runners. The railroads were apparently unable to move vital supplies needed for the army, so that tons of bacon and clothing and grain lay rotting in sidings, but they had remarkable success in bringing to Richmond the nonessentials arriving from England. Perfumes, silks, jewelry, and wines were still available in the capital for a price.

A hint of coming disaster was seen in the increasing numbers of wealthy people who fled the country to Europe. A considerable Confederate colony was springing up in Paris and London. John Daniel of the Richmond *Examiner* said of this group: "Let the rats go, the ship is not sinking."

The editor was wrong. The Confederacy was indeed foundering. Yet amid all the chaos and grief, a certain amount of normalcy remained. People discussed books newly arrived from England and some still being printed in the South. Literary-minded people were reading *Beulah,* by Augusta Evans, *The Moonstone* by Wilkie Collins, *Wild Western Scenes* by the Southerner, J. B. Jones, and *Les Misérables* by Victor Hugo. Months-old editions of *Godey's Lady's Book* were eagerly snatched up by fashion-starved women.

The New Richmond Theater was crowded nightly. Men wore shabby uniforms or threadbare civilian clothes. The ladies bravely tried to appear elegant in gowns made of damask draperies and satin curtains. Soldiers and civilians jammed the few restaurants which could still provide meals.

The most popular was the Oriental which featured a skimpy menu listing ham and eggs at $3.50; bread and butter, $1.50; a large mug of coffee, $3.00; a single boiled potato, $1. The sparsest meal cost almost $10 and for those who could afford it, the Oriental featured sherry wine at $35 per bottle; ale was $12 a quart; a pony of imported brandy cost $2 and a small drink of apple brandy, $2.

Despite the high prices and the general air of depression, nothing could completely dampen fun-loving Richmond. With the advent of fine weather, families held outings and picnics. Occasionally, a ham or chicken enlivened the festivities. People with relatives in the country fared somewhat better than their neighbors; baskets of eggs, tubs of butter, and bushels of potatoes were welcome gifts to city dwellers.

Richmond belles, although unmodishly dressed, still fluttered their eyelashes at handsome young officers. It was considered quite chic to hold "starvation soirees." At these, no refreshments were served, but the dancing and revelry went on until dawn.

Mrs. Davis resolutely clung to her practise of holding fortnightly levees at the Executive Mansion. The President seldom attended these functions. He remained locked in his small office studying official papers by flickering lamplight until his eyes smarted. Neuralgia seldom left him now, but he kept doggedly at his work. He shuffled papers and wrote complicated instructions; much of this was detail work that his secretaries could have handled as part of their routine.

Under the stress of adversity, Davis' appearance had altered. His face was drawn with care, and his posture, once ramrod-straight, had become stooped. Gray streaked his hair and the tuft of whiskers at his chin. He held midnight conferences with officers in from the field, the mud of the Rappahannock bogs still on their boots. The meetings were often pointless; he asked questions to which he already knew the answers: Were there shortages of rations and ammunition? Had the artillery carriages worn out? Did the cavalry need fresh horses?

The army needed everything. Jeb Stuart's troopers were now riding bony plugs. Bridles and reins, saddles and stirrups had been mended so often that little was left of the original leather.

Lee's artillerymen were making their own gun carriages by cutting timber and shaping green tree trunks to support the guns. If soldiers needed new shoes or even trousers, they had to capture them from the Yankees.

The 300,000 rifles carried by Southern soldiers in 1863 came from no central arsenals. In all, the South had acquired 400,000 rifles, in the following manner: 25,000 were on hand at the beginning of the war; 40,000 had been manufactured in Southern armories; 185,000 had been run through the blockade; and 150,000 were captured in the field. By 1863, 100,000 rifles had been lost in combat.

Richmond's great Tredegar Plant could not keep up production although General Josiah Gorgas, the Chief of Ordnance, performed miracles. However, even he could not make underfed mechanics work at full efficiency. Men simply fell ill from lack of proper nourishment. Blast furnaces that had been running day and night went out of kilter and there were no replacement parts. Coal and coke was short. The cannon castings that had been Tredegar's pride developed flaws, due to inferior metals.

Ammunition was faulty. After firing a few rounds, guns exploded. Everything was makeshift and jerry-built. The only first-rate asset left in the Confederacy was its soldiers. Somehow, the weary, stringy men were still able to march and fight. Few of them either knew or cared why they kept on fighting. The Cause had long since lost any meaning; the customs and the institutions and the way of life they had fought to preserve had now been abandoned, neglected or destroyed. No intelligent man still believed slavery could survive the war or that the South would ever return to the prewar *status quo.*

Yet because they were soldiers, the men continued fighting. War had become normal for them. The army was all many of them had left; homes, farms, and plantations were gone. The nation was ruined and so was its people. The Southerners had nothing to call their own except pride and courage. This they possessed in overwhelming quantities.

· 7 ·

In the early part of 1864, Yankee propaganda began to affect the slaves. Negroes who had long been faithful abandoned their masters. In Richmond, worried whites shuddered in apprehension; a slave uprising was said to be scheduled for the first week in January, 1864. While nothing came of these fearsome whispers, the signs were growing that the Negroes no longer intended submitting passively to bondage.

Negro resistance did not take a violent form. Outwardly the colored people seemed to be the same as ever—placid, gentle, and hardworking. Each morning thousands of singing Negroes marched out to work on Richmond's fortifications. Slaves labored willingly in the fields. Household servants did their chores smilingly. In the outlying districts, the Negroes hid valuables, mules, and horses when the Yankee cavalry raiders approached.

But the signs of discontent were discernible; a subtle difference in the Negro's attitude was gradually becoming apparent. He no longer stood with head bowed—humble and submissive, like a trusted pet dog. Even in the deepest South, the Negroes had heard that almost two hundred regiments of free colored men had been authorized by the Federal government.

Uniformed Negroes were marching into battle under the Union flag, like any white man. Free Negroes were being treated as human beings, not valuable chattels. The cadenced tread of Negro troops made the Southern earth tremble. It reached the ears of meek men and brought a new light into docile and servile eyes. Everywhere in the South, the Negroes went about their work believing that each day was bringing them closer to freedom.

The Confederate government reacted to Federal Negro troops with unreasonable vehemence. Orders were issued: Negroes and their white officers were not to be treated as soldiers—all prisoners from such units would be shot.

Lincoln answered this threat with firmness. Unless Negro soldiers and their officers were accorded the same treatment as white Federal troops, proper retaliation would be taken against Confederate prisoners of war. If Davis wished to assume the responsibility for unleashing war without quarter, the Federal government would not shrink from the challenge.

Davis withdrew his bitter order and announced that Federal Negro troops would be treated in the same manner as any other soldiers of the Northern army when captured. In fact the Confederate President was forced to relent even further in his attitude towards Negroes. Because of the critical manpower shortage in the Southern

Before an audience of governmental dignitaries and officials, President Lincoln hands Ulysses S. Grant his commission as lieutenant general in command of all the Union Armies. A few weeks later, in May, 1864, Grant's forces attacked the Confederates on all fronts.

army, a plan was formulated to incorporate Negroes into the service—not as combat troops, but as teamsters and labor battalions. Only white men were privileged to die for the Confederacy.

Early in the spring of 1864, an ugly incident, involving Negro troops, occurred at Fort Pillow, Tennessee. Soldiers under the hard-hitting Confederate, General Nathaniel Bedford Forrest, massacred the Federal garrison of Fort Pillow, when the Union soldiers made a last-ditch resistance there.

Forrest maintained that the stubborn refusal of the Federals to surrender brought on the slaughter. The fort had been manned by Negro soldiers—and Northern propagandists exploited this facet of the tragedy. The news of Fort Pillow had an effect among Southern Negroes as well. For the first time, reports of active insubordination by slaves drifted into Richmond. In fact, this spirit of unrest even appeared in Davis' own household. One night, the President's personal slave, Jim, and Mrs. Davis' maid, Betsey, ran away. It was alleged that Jim took with him a large sum in gold and Betsey was known to have had on her person $80 in gold and $2400 in Confederate currency.

Soon after that event, a fire broke out in the cellar of the Executive Mansion. Investigators blamed it on a Negro bribed by Yankee agents. Some did not accept this story. They believed it had not been the work of an individual, but was part of a Yankee plot to seize Richmond. Others in the capital believed it had been an attempt to kill the President and his family.

Troubles even deeper than danger to his own person bedeviled Jefferson Davis. A daring cavalry raid, led by Colonel Ulrich Dahlgren, to free Yankee prisoners on Belle Isle, had nearly succeeded. For eight hours Richmond was in a turmoil. Dahlgren's sortie failed and he was shot by Home Guards. Confederate authorities then declared that Dahlgren had carried orders on his person stating the purpose of his mission was not only to free the prisoners, but also to burn Richmond and execute all members of the Confederate government, using the escaped prisoners in this nefarious undertaking. The press screamed that every captured member of Dahlgren's command should be hanged.

As public frenzy was whipped up, Davis intervened and calmly pointed out that none of these crimes had been committed and that no proof existed of any intention to carry out the purported orders.

Even more weighty and sobering was his argument that many prominent Confederates were in Northern hands—among them General Lee's son—and these prisoners were liable to Yankee retaliation if the Dahlgren Raiders were summarily executed . . .

The great test was coming that spring. The untidy hero of Vicksburg, Ulysses S. Grant, had been transferred from the West, promoted to Lieutenant General, and given command of all Union armies. He was personally taking the field to direct the spring offensive in Virginia. The first week in May, 1864, Grant gave the order to march. At the same time, General William T. Sherman started his advance on Atlanta.

The battles in Virginia resulting from Grant's forward movement were the most ghastly and cruel of the war. Grant hammered at Lee day after day. The way through the Wilderness was marked by thousands of dead and wounded.

At Cold Harbor alone, Grant lost 5,000 men in minutes—and at Spottsylvania Court House, the carnage was equally great. Lee's Army of Northern Virginia stumbled from one danger point to another, blunting Grant's ponderous thrusts, protecting Richmond—but at a heavy price in men and equipment.

For once, Lee was facing an antagonist who was neither afraid to fight nor squeamish about casualties. Grant knew he could afford greater losses than Lee. He also knew that while politicians and civilians regarded Richmond as his primary objective, his real mission was to crush Lee's army. By forcing him to fight, Grant was slowly dooming Richmond and the whole Confederacy by his grinding tactics.

Grant swung south towards Petersburg and was forced to settle down to siege operations. Lee was pinned to Petersburg, and Grant was free to unleash Phil Sheridan and his eager cavalry to campaign in the Shenandoah Valley.

One last threat to Washington came in June, 1864 when Jubal Early's tough veterans broke out of the Valley and reached the limits of Washington. Grant rushed elements of the Sixth Corps to the capital and Early was driven back in an operation which Lincoln witnessed from the ramparts of Fort Stevens outside Washington.

Sheridan then went to work in the Valley, crushed Early in a series of battles, and ravaged that fertile area so completely that, in his reported words, "If a crow wished to travel through the Shen-

andoah Valley, he would have to carry his own rations." The Valley
—the back door to Washington—was closed forever to the Rebels as
an avenue of invasion against the Federal capital.

· 8 ·

In April, 1864, tragedy struck the Davis household. The six-year-
old favorite son of the President, Joseph Emory, fell to his death
while playing on the back porch. The bereaved father contained his
grief—but the loss of his boy affected him deeply. It was an added
burden for him in that terrible hour of Confederate ordeal. Sherman
was approaching Atlanta despite Joe Johnston's skillful defensive
maneuvers. The implacable Sherman was marching far behind
schedule—but the Federal Army moved relentlessly closer to its
goal every day.

Davis still clung to his belief that he himself was a great military
leader—and once, reading the news from Georgia, he cried out in a
fit of pique: "If I could take one wing and Lee the other, we could
still wrest a victory from these people."

In desperation, Davis replaced the cautious Johnston with fiery
"Sam" Hood, the dashing Texan. A worse choice could not have been
made. Hood broke his army to pieces against Sherman in reckless
assaults. Later, the remnants of his forces were annihilated by General George Thomas at Nashville, after Atlanta's fall.

Sherman marched from Atlanta to the sea. His "bummers" left a
swath of destruction across Georgia: a belt of ruined fields, charred
homes, wrecked railroads. They slashed a path of havoc as they
surged on to Savannah. Then Sherman turned northwards up the
coastal route; a thousand-mile trek through forest and swamps to
Columbia, South Carolina, and Greensboro, North Carolina. There
the toughened host linked up with other Union troops to complete
a march that no other army in history had ever equalled.

Even more devastating than Federal victories in the field was the
news that Lincoln had been re-elected in November, 1864. Davis
had counted strongly on the antiwar element in the North beating
Lincoln at the polls and electing his opponent, General George B.
McClellan.

A man of lesser stature would have been crushed by the shattering tasks Davis faced. The years of war took their toll on him; but, despite defeat and failure, he remained undaunted.

Then, with a reasonable administration in Washington, the Confederates could have made some compromise to end the war and negotiated a peace that ensured the existence of the Confederacy. This last hope was stifled with the return of Lincoln to office. Now the war would never be ended at the conference table—but on the battlefield. Lincoln would stop fighting only when the Confederate States of America no longer existed as a separate entity.

By now, the last forces left to the Confederacy were Lee's half-starved men, an army under Joe Johnston in North Carolina, and the unreliable troops of General Kirby Smith in the far-off Trans-Mississippi Department. By the end of 1864, Davis and his government no longer represented a nation. They spoke for just a small group of desperate men who held out because there was nothing else for them to do.

Desperation could not bring victory; it could only prolong the bloodshed. Lee was unable to withstand Grant's pressure at Petersburg; his thin lines had held out for months—all through the summer, fall, and terrible winter of 1864 and into the spring of 1865. Conditions were intolerable in all the armies Lee commanded—he had been appointed General-in-Chief in February, 1865—but the men of the Army of Northern Virginia suffered more than the other troops.

Some days the men received food only through the sacrifice of the townspeople of Petersburg, where everyone subsisted on corn bread. There was no garbage in the streets. Dogs and cats disappeared. Pigeons were caught and eaten. The population and the Army suffered incredible hardships—but still Lee clung to his positions.

However, on Sunday, April 2, 1865, a bright, sunny day, as Davis was attending services at St. Paul's, a breathless messenger dashed in, hurried to the Davis pew and whispered a few words to the President. Davis blanched, rose quickly, and left the church. Lee had moved out of Petersburg. Nothing now could stop the Yankees from taking Richmond.

The shocking news raced through the city. Frantic preparations were made to evacuate the capital. The commissaries threw their doors open to the public. Clawing people stormed into the buildings to seize whatever they could carry off. Banks opened for withdrawals. As the day waned, the frenzy grew. Panicky people ran about aimlessly. Carts piled with household belongings rocked across the

On April 9, 1865, Grant and Lee met in this modest farmhouse at Appomattox Courthouse, Virginia, to discuss the surrender of the Army of Northern Virginia.

The dreams and the hopes of the Confederacy were shattered when Lee surrendered. For Jefferson Davis, there remained only one alternative, to try to avoid capture. His flight ended in Irwinsville, Georgia, on May 10, 1865, when Federal cavalry troopers took him into custody.

bridges towards Danville. Carriages sped through the streets. Couriers and messengers galloped madly back and forth. Rumors spread that the Yankees were coming in at 3:00 A.M.

Uncontrolled gangs of looters broke open the stores on Main Street. At the railroad station a special train was prepared for President and Mrs. Davis, the members of his cabinet, and other officials. Sixty youthful midshipmen guarded the Confederate treasury, $500,-000 in gold, which was loaded aboard the train. In the center of the city, demolitions took place. The arsenals were blown up. Tons of ammunition went off, breaking windows for blocks around. Bands of vandals set homes and shops on fire, and from a distance it appeared that all of Richmond was ablaze:

The gutters ran ankle-deep with whiskey as marshals destroyed the government stores. Men and women—Negro and white—soldiers, and even children scooped up the liquor in cups, basins, ladles and bowls. Soon drunkenness took over and whiskey-soaked mobs howled in the smoke-darkened streets. The whole city seemed to have gone mad . . .

On that catastrophic Sunday, President Davis issued the necessary orders and then returned to the Executive Mansion, as though this were an ordinary Sunday. He showed no distress, but calmly supervised the packing of several suitcases, with the air of a man about to embark on a routine journey. He took with him coats, trousers, waistcoats, linen shirts, a silken tie, dressing robes, a roll of court plaster, a pair of gaiters, underclothing, extra shoelaces, a small dressing case, a razor strop, a comb and brush, two towels, two toothbrushes, eyeglasses, envelopes and notepaper, six boxes of cigars. He also packed a nine-shooter pistol, and a double-barreled revolver, two holstered pistols, a case of ammunition, and pictures of his wife, himself, and General Lee.

He dressed carefully in Confederate gray and then strode out of the Executive Mansion as if he were going on his usual Sunday afternoon stroll . . .

· 9 ·

President Davis refused to concede that the loss of Richmond meant the end of the Confederacy. He ordered the seat of the government moved to Danville, and on April 5, issued his last proclamation to the Confederate people from that temporary capital. The proclamation read:

> The General-in-Chief found it necessary to make such movements of his troops as to uncover the capital. It would be unwise to conceal the moral and material injury to our Cause resulting from the occupation of our capital by the enemy. It is equally unwise and unworthy of us to allow our own energies to falter and our efforts to become relaxed under reverses, however calamitous they may be . . .
>
> We have entered on a new phase of the struggle. Relieved from guarding particular points, our army will be free to move from point to point, to strike the enemy . . . Let us but will it and we are free .
>
> Let us, then, not despond my countrymen, but relying on God, meet the foe with fresh defiance and with unconquered and unconquerable hearts.
>
> Jefferson Davis

The position of Danville was precarious; it was in imminent danger of capture. Yankee cavalry was everywhere. The provisional capital's communications were cut off. No direct word came from Lee for almost a week and Davis had no knowledge of the army's fate. Both he and his cabinet clutched every hopeful rumor, until. on April 10, they learned the truth—Lee had surrendered at Appomattox, and Danville must be evacuated.

The President made his decision. He despatched Mrs. Davis and the children to North Carolina for a future reunion. Accompanied by his cabinet, a volunteer cavalry escort and the treasury gold, he would flee southwards to join Kirby Smith in the Southwest where he hoped to continue the fight for the lost Cause. Midnight had struck for the Confederacy. Southern independence was a vision that lived only in the hearts and memory of men . . .

· 10 ·

That dreadful night of April 2, Richmond died in flames and terror. At 3:00 A.M., eighty-year-old mayor Joseph Mayo and a few city councilmen set out in a hack to find the Union troops north of the James, and to surrender the city. Behind Mayo, the bridges were shrouded in flames. The wooden steamers and ironclads in the river were burned and scuttled. Buildings were gutted. Warehouses crashed in pillars of fire.

Broken-heartedly Mayo handed a note to a Federal picket:

Richmond, April 3, 1865

To the General Commanding the
United States Army in front of Richmond,

General:

The Army of the Confederate Government having abandoned the City of Richmond, I respectfully request that you will take possession of it with an organized force, to preserve order and protect women and children and property.

Respectfully,
Joseph Mayo, Mayor.

The plundering and looting continued all through the night; the screaming and the drunken orgy went on. The last Confederate troops marched out. A squadron of cavalry had to hack its way through a wild mob. Frightened people swamped the railroad station, trying to escape, but no more trains would roll from that depot. Ruin and desolation was everywhere.

Suddenly, a terrible cry went up: "The Yankees! The Yankees!" And now they came, husky Negro cavalrymen with naked sabers, galloping in fours. They waved their sabers and sang "John Brown's Body." Behind them came columns of weary infantry. Bands played them into the ravaged city. The Yankee soldiers cheered as they marched—and remembered the comrades who would never reach the goal . . .

At 11:00 A.M., Abraham Lincoln, holding his son, Tad, by the hand, and escorted by a dozen armed sailors, Admiral David Porter, some army officers, and his bodyguard, William Crook, came into Richmond after steaming up the James River on Porter's flagship, the *Malvern*.

It was Tad's twelfth birthday and this visit to the newly fallen enemy capital was his present. Porter's elaborate arrangements for the President's entry had gone awry. Instead of an adequate guard, only this handful remained as the group started out from Rockett's

On April 4, 1865, the day after Union forces occupied Richmond, President Lincoln, accompanied by his young son, Tad, visited the enemy capital. High spot came when he entered the Confederate White House to the cheers of Northern soldiers, ex-slaves, and pro-Unionist Richmond residents.

Retreating Rebel troops and rioting arsonists set fire to whole sections of Richmond in a wild night of plundering, looting, and incendiarism on April 3, 1865. This scene was sketched by a contemporary artist looking up Cary Street.

Landing to walk the two-mile route to the Confederate White House, where General Godfrey Weitzel, the Union commandant, had established his headquarters.

Lincoln and Tad trudged through the streets, surrounded by the alert sailors. Negroes flocked to the President. Some tried to kiss his hands; others prostrated themselves at his feet. They reached out to touch his clothing. They wept and laughed and called out their blessings to "Massa Linkum," the man who had delivered them from slavery.

Few white people appeared to watch the procession. One young lady stepped on a balcony with the Stars and Stripes wrapped around her shoulders like a cloak. Here and there, someone clapped or cheered. But for the most part, Richmond's people stayed behind locked doors or peered from curtained windows.

As the party neared the Confederate White House, a detachment of cavalry clattered up and deployed itself protectively. General Weitzel, sweating and nervous, stammered a greeting to the President. He had only just been informed of Lincoln's arrival.

The Chief Executive hesitated for a moment on the porch of the Davis home and then entered. He was shown Davis' office. Solemnly and wearily, he sat down at the desk of his enemy. Glancing around the room searchingly, he seemed to be trying to find some clue which would explain the man who had opposed him so stubbornly. The room revealed nothing. Lincoln ran his fingers over the polished surface of the desk. His eyes expressed not triumph, but sadness. Perhaps he thought of all that had transpired: the young men who were dead and maimed; the widowed women and the orphaned children; the property devastated; the wealth squandered. The war was almost ended now. There would be peace and prosperity for the torn nation. He stared out of the window at the garden. The trees were budding. It was springtime. The future loomed bright.

In ten days, he was dead . . .

Bibliography

ALTHOUGH I consulted many sources in preparing *Abraham Lincoln Versus Jefferson Davis,* I have included here only those works which I found most pertinent to my task. In addition to these volumes, I made wide use of Washington, Richmond, and New York newspapers and periodicals of the Civil War period. I have not listed them, nor such standard references as the *Officials Records of the Union and Confederate Armies, Battles and Leaders of the Civil War,* and the *Dictionary of American Biography.*

A complete bibliography on Lincoln and Davis would, in itself, constitute a mammoth volume. Therefore I have pared the list below to what I consider to be a minimal springboard from which the reader may launch his further studies of these men and their times.

Bill, Alfred Hoyt, *The Beleaguered City.* Alfred A. Knopf, New York, 1946.

Bradford, Gamaliel, *Confederate Portraits.* Houghton Mifflin Company, Boston, 1914.

Canby, Courtlandt, editor, *Lincoln and the Civil War.* Dell Books, New York, 1958.

Catton, Bruce, *Mr. Lincoln's Army.* Doubleday & Company, Garden City, N.Y., 1951.

Catton, Bruce, *Glory Road.* Doubleday & Company, Garden City, N.Y., 1952.

Catton, Bruce, *A Stillness at Appomattox.* Doubleday & Company, Garden City, N.Y., 1954.

Chesnut, Mary Boykin, *A Diary from Dixie.* D. Appleton and Company, New York, 1906.

Commager, Henry S., editor, *The Blue and the Gray* (two volumes). Bobbs-Merrill Company, Indianapolis, 1950.

Davis, Jefferson, *The Rise and Fall of the Confederate Government* (two volumes). D. Appleton and Company, New York, 1881.

Davis, Varina Howell, *Jefferson Davis, a Memoir* (two volumes). Belford Company, New York, 1890.

Dowdey, Clifford, *Experiment in Rebellion.* Doubleday & Company, Garden City, N.Y., 1946.

Dowdey, Clifford, *The Land They Fought For.* Doubleday & Company, Garden City, N.Y., 1955.

Eckenrode, Hamilton J., *Jefferson Davis: President of the South.* The Macmillan Company, New York, 1923.

Gordon, Armistead C., *Jefferson Davis*. Charles Scribner's Sons, New York, 1918.

Hanna, Alfred J., *Flight into Oblivion*. Johnson Publishing Company, Richmond, 1938.

Hendrick, Burton J., *Statesmen of the Lost Cause*. Little, Brown & Company, Boston, 1939.

Hendrick, Burton J., *Lincoln's War Cabinet*. Little, Brown & Company, Boston, 1946.

Jones, J. B., *A Rebel War Clerk's Diary* (two volumes). J. B. Lippincott Company, Philadelphia, 1866.

Leech, Margaret, *Reveille in Washington, 1860-1865*. Harper & Brothers, New York, 1941.

Long, E. B., editor, *Personal Memoirs of U. S. Grant*. The World Publishing Co., Cleveland, 1952.

McMaster, John B., *A History of the United States During Lincoln's Administration*. D. Appleton and Company, New York, 1927.

Moore, Albert B., *Conscription and Conflict in the Confederacy*. The Macmillan Company, New York, 1924.

Randall, J. G., *Lincoln, the President* (four volumes). Dodd, Mead & Company, New York, 1954-1955.

Sandburg, Carl, *Abraham Lincoln, the War Years* (four volumes). Harcourt, Brace and Company, New York, 1939.

Schaff, Morris, *Jefferson Davis*. J. W. Luce and Company, Boston, 1922.

Stern, Philip Van Doren, *An End to Valor*. Houghton Mifflin Company, Boston, 1958.

Swanberg, W. A., *First Blood: The Story of Fort Sumter*. Charles Scribner's Sons, New York, 1957.

Tate, Allen, *Jefferson Davis: His Rise and Fall*. Minton, Balch and Company, New York, 1929.

Thomas, Benjamin P., *Abraham Lincoln*. Alfred A. Knopf, New York, 1952.

Thomas, Benjamin P., *Lincoln's New Salem*. Alfred A. Knopf, New York, 1954.

Wiley, Bell I., *The Life of Johnny Reb*. Bobbs-Merrill Company, Indianapolis, 1943.

Wiley, Bell I., *The Life of Billy Yank*. Bobbs-Merrill Company, Indianapolis, 1951.

Wiley, Bell I., *The Road to Appomattox*. Memphis State College Press, Memphis, Tennessee, 1956.

Williams, T. Harry, *Lincoln and His Generals*. Alfred A. Knopf, New York, 1952.

Winston, Robert, *High Stakes and Hair Trigger: The Life of Jefferson Davis*. Henry Holt and Company, Inc., New York, 1930.

Index